Emily Dickinson and the Life of Language

Emily Dickinson and the Life of Language

A Study in Symbolic Poetics

E. Miller Budick

LOUISIANA STATE UNIVERSITY PRESS *Baton Rouge and London*

Copyright © 1985 by Louisiana State University Press
Manufactured in the United States of America
Designer: Patricia Douglas Crowder
Typeface: Linotron 202 Baskerville
Typesetter: G & S Typesetters, Inc.
Printer: Thomson-Shore
Binder: John Dekker & Sons

Published with the assistance of a grant from the National Endowment for the Humanities.

LIBRARY OF CONGRESS CATALOGING IN PUBLICATION DATA
Budick, E. Miller.
  Emily Dickinson and the life of language.

  Includes index.

  1. Dickinson, Emily, 1830–1886—Criticism and interpretation. 2. Symbolism in literature. 3. Philosophy in literature. I. Title.
PS1541.Z5B83   1985   811'.4   85-9609
ISBN 0-8071-1239-9

Portions of this book have appeared previously in journals, as follows: "Temporal Consciousness and the Perception of Eternity," *Essays in Literature*, X (Fall, 1983), 227–40, reprinted by permission of the editor; "The Assignable Portion: Emily Dickinson on the Dilemma of Symbolic Perception," *Dickinson Studies*, XXXVI (1979), 1–15, reprinted by permission of the editor; "When the Soul Selects: Emily Dickinson's Attack on New England Symbolism," *American Literature*, LI (1979), 349–63, copyright © 1979 by Duke University Press, reprinted by permission; "'I had not minded—Walls': The Method and Meaning of Emily Dickinson's Symbolism," *Concerning Poetry*, IX (Fall, 1976), and "Symbolizing Eternity: A Reading of Emily Dickinson's 'There Came a Day at Summer's Full,'" XVI (Spring, 1983); "The Dangers of the Living Word: Aspects of Dickinson's Epistemology, Cosmology, and Symbolism," *ESQ*, XXIX (1983), 208–24. Poem No. 1251 "Silence is all we dread" from *Emily Dickinson Face to Face* by Martha D. Bianchi, copyright 1932 by Martha Dickinson Bianchi, copyright © renewed 1960 by Alfred Leete Hampson, and Poem No. 988 "The Definition of Beauty" from *Life and Letters of Emily Dickinson* by Martha D. Bianchi, copyright 1924 by Martha Dickinson Bianchi, copyright renewed 1952 by Alfred Leete Hampson, both reprinted by permission of Houghton Mifflin Company; 428 lines from Poems No. 178, 243, 247, 263, 282, 306, 339, 378, 391, 398, 410, 430, 448, 516, 531, 546, 582, 673, 724, 741, 750, 797, 806, 822, 1071, 1252, 1295, 1333, 72, 281, 302, 370, 423, 451, 489, 575, 624, 721, and 1142 from *The Complete Poems of Emily Dickinson* edited by Thomas H. Johnson, copyright 1914, 1929, 1935, 1942 by Martha Dickinson Bianchi, copyright renewed © 1957, 1963 by Mary L. Hampson, by permission of Little, Brown and Co.; all other Emily Dickinson quotations reprinted by permission of the publishers and Trustees of Amherst College from *The Poems of Emily Dickinson*, edited by Thomas H. Johnson, Cambridge, Mass.: The Belknap Press of Harvard University Press, Copyright 1951, © 1955, 1979, 1983 by the President and Fellows of Harvard College.

To my parents

I found the words to every thought
I ever had—but One—
And that—defies me—
As a Hand did try to chalk the Sun

To Races—nurtured in the Dark—
How would your own—begin?
Can Blaze be shown in Cochineal—
Or Noon—in Mazarin?

—No. 581

Contents

Preface

WHEN Emily Dickinson decided to cut herself off from the social interactions of life in this world, she chose, in effect, perhaps even with full philosophical self-awareness, to concern herself, not with objects or people or events, but with words themselves—with the isolated processes of mental and verbal apprehension by which objects, people, and events are made known and acquire meaning. Withdrawing from traditional ways of seeing, she involved herself ever more intensely in a search for new modes of human perception. She separated her consciousness from almost all others and tried to understand the phenomenon that is consciousness itself. By stopping the clock of daily life she attempted to locate the meaning of time and timelessness. Most importantly, she "published" in her dresser drawers little volumes of carefully, if eccentrically, bound manuscript poems that endeavored to capture the living inner form of language itself. Dickinson's poetry is the record of her explorations and discoveries in the life of language.

The present study is about the symbolic vitality that Dickinson regarded as a universal feature of language. It concerns the life within language, the life of language, that Dickinson confronted and attempted to consolidate and control in her poems. Most especially, it describes the symbolic liabilities she believed to be inherent in all unimproved verbal expression, and that she endeavored to parlay into powerful poetic truths. In the following chapters I will argue that Dickinson's poetry constitutes a paradoxical condemnation and celebration of symbolic perception and symbolic language, that it articulates a complex but coherent argument against the conventional abuse of symbols, even while it makes constant use of symbols of a special kind. In Dickinson's hands poetry becomes a way of transforming what she considered the false and distortive assumptions of certain forms of symbolism into the logical, precise, and theologically reverent premises of a radically different symbolism. For Dickinson, this precise, revised symbolism constitutes the only possible medium for accurately representing cosmic reality. It is the only vehicle capable of transporting human consciousness beyond the spatial-temporal limitations of the physical world to the universe of divine reality.

In recent years discussions of Dickinson's use of language have tended to discard the traditional view of Dickinson as symbol-maker and to replace it with a more exclusively modern perception of the poet as a desperate wielder of words. Specifically, two fine books have appeared that (like the present study) focus on Dickinson's strange and baffling verbal pyrotechnics. But whereas Sharon Cameron's *Lyric Time: Dickinson and the Limits of Genre* (Johns Hopkins, 1979) and David Porter's *Dickinson: The Modern Idiom* (Harvard, 1981) have been interested primarily in the dynamics of the Dickinsonian word game, my own concern has been to discover the ideological, theological, and aesthetic premises that required (or correlated with) Dickinson's deployment of her own special poetics. This poetics is, I think, after all is said and done, abidingly symbolic, although in a uniquely Dickinsonian way. Thus, my work endeavors to carry on the tradition of such books as Charles R. Anderson's *Emily Dickinson's Poetry: Stairway of Surprise* (Holt, Rinehart, 1960) and Robert Weisbuch's *Emily Dickinson's Poetry* (Chicago, 1972), and it attempts to link this tradition to the growing excitement over the Dickinson manuscripts and the poetic processes therein revealed.

In its dissociation from society and the world, Dickinson's poetry is indeed a poetry about language. But the life of language, Dickinson shows, does not exist apart from the larger life of the universe and of God. In the end Dickinson discovers in her distance from the phenomenal world an aspect of life and language that itself provides the means for restoring the individual to nature and the divine. It is my hope to convey the dimensions of the interconnected life in which Dickinson's universe coheres and to describe how that life is captured and conveyed in her poetry.

As I have sat writing this book, the life that is not language has encouraged and permitted me to pursue the life that is. Rachel, Ayelet, and Yochanan have been like the children to whom a legendary Dickinson lowered baskets of cookies from her self-imposed seclusion. While, like that other Emily, I have escaped into the life of words, they have pursued the life of bees and butterflies; and their shouts of joy have kept me tethered firmly to the world that Dickinson too refused to reject. My husband Sandy has been a source of never-ceasing inspiration: he has edited both my life and my work, and breathed life into them.

I would like to thank Olin Library of Cornell University and the Houghton Library of Harvard University for their unstinting courtesy and helpfulness. Beverly Jarrett, Associate Director and Executive Editor, and Catherine Barton, Managing Editor, both of Louisiana State University Press, and Barbara B. Reitt have guided and encouraged me through the various stages of preparation; I am extremely grateful for their kind words and their expert advice.

All references to Dickinson's poems are to *The Poems of Emily Dickinson*, ed. Thomas H. Johnson (3 vols.; Cambridge, Mass., 1976). References to the letters are to *The Letters of Emily Dickinson*, ed. Thomas H. Johnson (3 vols.; Cambridge, Mass., 1958).

Emily Dickinson and the Life of Language

Chapter One

The Dangers of the Living Word

ONE of the most distinctive features of Emily Dickinson's poetic language is its wild animation and vital energy. Whether we choose to linger over each line or to read the poems at a clip, we cannot help but feel that in Dickinson's poetic worlds the very units of discourse—not the objects and events signified by words, but the words themselves—leap out at the reader like autonomous and freewheeling figures in a bold and vivid dance. In the following poem, for example, the metaphors and images of Dickinson's verse, capitalized and set off by dashes to declare their individuality and self-sufficiency, are in their own right the actors and sets that fill the stage of an intensely immediate drama.

> Blazing in Gold—and
> Quenching—in Purple!
> Leaping—like Leopards—in the sky—
> Then—at the feet of the old Horizon—
> Laying it's spotted face—to die!

Stooping as low as the kitchen window—
Touching the Roof—
And tinting the Barn—
Kissing it's Bonnet to the Meadow—
And the Juggler of Day—is gone! (No. 228)[1]

The cast of verbal characters is so wide-ranging, so diversified, that it includes not only substantive nouns and names of objects, like "Leopards," but abstractions, adjectives, participles, and verbs—"Blazing" and "Quenching," for example, or, in other poems, "Knowing" and "Fearing" (No. 1218), "Accustomed" (No. 149), "Fitting" (No. 1277), "Going Home" (No. 1376), and "Ascertain" (No. 157), which by virtue of the way they are exaggerated and segregated in the text become independent members of Dickinson's dramatic companies. In fact, so basic and self-sufficient is each individual word for Dickinson that she can compound graceful, seemingly artless catalogues of terms such as birds, hours, bumblebee, grief, hills, and eternity, which ought to seem, by any of the ordinary rules of logic or grammar, nonparallel and shockingly dissimilar in quality or quantity or kind. In Dickinson's poem, however, they become congenial members of the poem's tantalizing cast.

Some things that fly there be—
Birds—Hours—the Bumblebee—
Of these no Elegy.

Some things that stay there be—
Grief—Hills—Eternity—
Nor this behooveth me.

There are that resting, rise.
Can I expound the skies?
How still the Riddle lies! (No. 89)[2]

Many critics have commented on this special aliveness of the Dickinsonian word, on the verbal or "spectral" power of her verse, the "curi-

1. I have reproduced the variorum copy of this poem, located in packet 23 (H 127 a) of Dickinson's works. The manuscript copy in the Houghton is even more erratically punctuated and capitalized than Johnson's typescript suggests.
2. For an interesting discussion of this poem, see David T. Porter, *The Art of Emily Dickinson's Early Poetry* (Cambridge, Mass., 1966), 32.

ous energy in the words and a tone like no other most of us have ever heard." Dickinson, to quote one critic, seems to have "perceived abstractions and thought sensations."

> A word is dead
> When it is said,
> Some say.
> I say it just
> Begins to live
> That day. (No. 1212)

It is not surprising, therefore, that her first concern when she writes to Colonel Thomas Wentworth Higginson in 1862 is whether or not her "Verse" is "alive," or that she worries in her second letter whether by dressing her thoughts in words those thoughts do not become stilted and "numb" (LL 260 and 261). What critics have usually assumed or concluded about this Dickinsonian "passion for words" is that it expresses a "profound linguistic faith," a belief in the "saving power" of the word, and an unwavering confidence that language can "control nature and persons" and "say the unsayable." [3]

But if we pay careful attention to the specific kind of "power" that

---

3. On Dickinson's "spectral" power and the power to "say the unsayable," see Louise Bogan, "A Mystical Poet," in Archibald MacLeish, Louise Bogan, and Richard Wilbur (eds.), *Emily Dickinson, Three Views: Papers Delivered at Amherst College . . . October 23, 1959* (Amherst, Mass., 1960), 34; on her "curious energy," see Archibald MacLeish, "The Private World," in MacLeish, Bogan, and Wilbur (eds.), *Three Views*, 16–19; and on her "linguistic faith" and "saving power," see Elinor Wilner, "The Poetics of Emily Dickinson," *ELH*, XXXVIII (1971), 126–54; see also George Frisbie Whicher, *This Was a Poet: A Critical Biography of Emily Dickinson* (Ann Arbor, 1957), 227–49; Inder Nath Kher, *The Landscape of Absence: Emily Dickinson's Poetry* (New Haven, 1974), 32; Brita Lindberg-Seyersted, *The Voice of the Poet: Aspects of Style in the Poetry of Emily Dickinson* (Cambridge, Mass., 1968); David Porter, "Emily Dickinson: The Poetics of Doubt," *ESQ: A Journal of the American Renaissance*, LX (1970), 86–88; Rebecca Patterson, "The Cardinal Points Symbolism of Emily Dickinson (I)," *Midwest Quarterly*, XIV (1973), 206; Donald E. Thackrey, *Emily Dickinson's Approach to Poetry, University of Nebraska Studies* (Lincoln, 1954), 62; and Charles R. Anderson, *Emily Dickinson's Poetry: Stairway of Surprise* (New York, 1960), 30–46, 91ff., and 300–307. Even Col. Higginson comments on the "strange power" of Dickinson's poetry (L 330 a). Very recently Sharon Cameron, *Lyric Time: Dickinson and the Limits of Genre* (Baltimore, 1979), and David Porter, *Dickinson: The Modern Idiom* (Cambridge, Mass., 1981), have brought the matter of Dickinson's eccentric use of language into a contemporary context. See also Geoffrey H. Hartman's discussion of language in "Words and Wounds," in *Saving the Text: Literature / Derrida / Philosophy* (Baltimore, 1981), 118–57.

Dickinson's poetry displays, a troubling fact presents itself. "Blazing in Gold," for example, is certainly one of the poet's most enthusiastic cataloguings of the glorious events of nature. It offers, joyfully and exuberantly, a composite portrait of an exciting cosmic phenomenon. And yet it is a poem that trembles with a disturbing uncertainty. It quivers with hesitancy and doubt. Even before we begin to pore over the words and images for their deepest meanings, we sense that a vague but obstinate hint of uneasiness violates the poem's heady enthusiasm. The images seem frantic, almost embattled. There is, we may feel, more disruption in this poem than harmony. The very liveness of the language seems to threaten the cohesiveness of the poetic structure.

For all its ecstasy the poem harbors a subtle but definite intimation of unresolved human tension, a tension both emotional and sensual. For all the poem's integrity and wholeness, it implies disruption and disorder. This underlying chaos, which becomes more and more apparent as we begin to examine the poem carefully, first confronts us in the poetic texture. It is expressed obliquely but unmistakably in the poem's cracked and creviced surface, the words oddly capitalized and separated by eccentric dashes, the rhymes and rhythms slant and askew. Many critics have for one reason or another dismissed the irregularities of Dickinson's verse style, or, if not dismissed them, at least seriously underrated their function.[4] But the crazy-quilt surface of a poem like "Blazing in Gold" invites us to observe the universe from a new perspective. Subtly it coaxes us into recognizing how terribly frenzied, how frighteningly chaotic the otherwise serene, ebullient universe can seem.

The juggling act of day, for example, which represents both the natural appearance of day on the landscape and its poetic recreation in the poem, is not, Dickinson is warning, an unambiguous carnival of

---

4. For a different reading of this poem see Anderson, *Stairway of Surprise*, 135–38; cf. 122. For representative approaches to the typographic appearance of Dickinson's poems see Thomas H. Johnson, "Introduction," in *The Poems of Emily Dickinson*, 3 vols. (Cambridge, Mass., 1976), lxiii; R. W. Franklin, *The Editing of Emily Dickinson: A Reconsideration* (Madison, 1967), 120–21; Brita Lindberg-Seyersted, "Emily Dickinson's Punctuation," *Studia Neophilologica*, XXXVII (1965), 349–50; Wilner, "The Poetics of Emily Dickinson," 126 and 138; Roland Hagenbüchle, "Precision and Indeterminacy in the

vibrant sensations. It can also be seen as a clownish pantomime of universe and language in apparent disarray. Day blazes, quenches, leaps, and dies—all, perhaps, to no real purpose. It stoops, kisses, and then simply is "gone" in a veritable parody of meaningful action.

The details of the juggling act, therefore, which momentarily dazzle, can also terrify. The "Blazing in Gold," for example, and the "Quenching—in Purple," which have been thrown aloft by the adroit but dispassionate hand of the master juggler, are not just sensual events. They are principles of the natural order, two of the many balanced antitheses that are juggled simultaneously into momentary and unresolved suspension. Furthermore, not only do the opposed "Blazing" and "Quenching" represent a daily enactment of mutual annihilation, but each element incorporates its own principle of self-destruction. The blazing will eventually consume itself, if the quenching does not somehow succeed first; and the quenching is, by definition, not an additive substance but the absence of a substance, a power of cessation or deletion.

The poem's language reproduces a reality that flares and fizzles, excites and terrifies, at one and the same moment, a reality in which beauty and chaos, creation and destruction, exist side by side and in and through each other. Thus, the "Blazing" and "Quenching" that eventually cancel each other are balanced against each other on opposing lines; each self-annihilating force is isolated in its own stumbling fragment of speech. "Blazing in Gold—," the poem abruptly begins. The words are discrete and self-contained, set off not only from the "Quenching—in Purple" that is its direct negation, but also from the "and" that would connect it to any other natural event. "And," the poem continues, "Quenching—in Purple." The phrase is not only detached from the "Blazing" that is its opposite but is internally splintered between the "Quenching" that does not have sensuous existence

Poetry of Emily Dickinson," *ESQ: A Journal of the American Renaissance*, XX (1974), 54; and Robert Weisbuch, *Emily Dickinson's Poetry* (Chicago, 1972), 73. See also Porter, *Emily Dickinson's Early Poetry*, 140–45; Anderson, *Stairway of Surprise*, 300–307; John Crowe Ransom, "Emily Dickinson: A Poet Restored," in Richard B. Sewall (ed.), *Emily Dickinson: A Collection of Critical Essays* (Englewood Cliffs, N.J., 1963), 88–89; and Edith Stamm, "Poetry and Punctuation," *Saturday Review*, XLVI (March 30, 1963), 20–29.

and the "Purple" that does. Words that live can die; worse, they can even kill.

What the poem is trying to do, then, is not simply to describe day and sunset in the most graphic terms available, but to sketch out, as a working hypothesis, something not unlike the idealist configuration of reality in which dissolution follows emanation and a host of glittering phenomena occupy the ground between. (I will have more to say about the relevance of idealism later.) The poem, in this view, is not about harmonious interrelation, nor is it about unity and its reattainment since, from the vantage point of this state of the cosmos, unity exists only after phenomenal reality has disappeared to a realm beyond the powers of human knowledge and human language. But the poem is about the explosion into phenomenal being that defines the world as we know it. The poem's central strategy is to delineate a oneness that is really a seething competition of irreconcilable opposites, a "Blazing" and a "Quenching," that defy one another, or, to use another of the poem's special metaphors, a spotted leopard whose leap to the sky is both magnificent and menacing and who threatens cosmic serenity only to find himself the victim of his own threat and his own mortality. Reality, Dickinson implies, may be a juggling act that is indistinguishable from the juggler. It may be a hydra-like creature whose integrity is compounded of inharmonious, disjointed, and unrelated facets and phenomena and that is juggled into fragmentary existence by its own propensity to juggle.

This is not to deny the exquisite beauty portrayed in the poem. For Dickinson, however, beauty may be yoked to the very elements of cosmic disunity that seem to defy it. It may be fashioned of the components that seem to our partial, mortal vision to attempt its destruction. Beauty, therefore, may affect us not serenely, but turbulently. It may arouse in us fears more powerful than the sense of ecstasy for which we would like to believe nature has been created. Thus a pattern of cosmic disruption and accompanying human tension vibrates beneath the surface of "Blazing in Gold." Disruption and tension seem, paradoxically, both to contradict cosmic beauty and perfection and to represent their key constituents.

In "I'll tell you how the Sun rose—" Dickinson deals with precisely this painful paradox. In this poem, as in "Blazing in Gold," the poet luxuriates, unabashedly, in the beauty of sunrise and sunset. And yet here too a nervousness, a tremor of uncertainty—expressed in the poem's unsteady rhythm and faltering vocabulary, as well as in its stated meanings—seems to intrude and to diminish the poet's otherwise rapturous excitement about the gorgeousness of diurnal events.

> I'll tell you how the Sun rose—
> A Ribbon at a time—
> The Steeples swam in Amethyst—
> The news, like Squirrels, ran—
> The Hills untied their Bonnets—
> The Bobolinks—begun—
> Then I said softly to myself—
> "That must have been the Sun"!
> But how he set—I know not—
> There seemed a purple stile
> That little Yellow boys and girls
> Were climbing all the while—
> Till when they reached the other side,
> A Dominie in Gray—
> Put gently up the evening Bars—
> And led the flock away— (No. 318)

The poet's uneasiness can be traced to several causes. It derives in part from the conjectural quality of human knowledge: "That *must have been* the Sun," the speaker surmises; "There *seemed* a purple stile" (italics added). It is further produced by the fragmentary "Ribbon at a time" quality of nature's disclosure of itself, a process that defies a coherent, mellifluous rendering in verse (note the word "begun" in line 6) and that results in the profusion of disparate albeit magnificent actions that the poem faithfully reproduces. Finally, the poem's lack of firm, hopeful conviction seems to derive from the speaker's ultimate exclusion from the cosmic events she is breathlessly detailing. When, in the end of the poem, the unorganizable, helter-skelter fantasia of cosmic events, which is in itself troubling, does reach a conclusion, the cosmic finale does not reach out and extend its implications of om-

nipresent harmony to the poet. Day and the poem end in an absence
of images and meanings, in a void that can be as troubling to the individual as the commotion that precedes it. However gently and in-
offensively the "Dominie in Gray" puts up the "evening Bars," the individual discovers that she has been locked out of the rest and quiet
that have finally succeeded in quelling the racing chaos of the early
lines of the poem. What it means for humankind to be on the other
side of the "Bars" and for the "flock" of sense experiences and events
to be led away remains to be seen. But the silence that ends this poem
represents not reassurance but the loss of cheerful confidence that, at
the end of time at least, human beings will share in the restoration of
cosmic oneness.

Disruption and disturbance seem to be inescapable features of the
human experience of nature, and many of Dickinson's most exuberant
sketches of natural reality therefore vibrate with warnings of disunity
and impending disintegration similar to those described above. "She
sweeps with many-colored Brooms—," for instance, shares with "Blazing in Gold" and "I'll tell you how the Sun rose—" a lavish reveling in
natural beauty. And yet there is in this poem, too, something slightly
chilling about the wispy clutter of images that sweeps across the landscape, a haunting intimation of perplexing discontinuities that may
well end, the poet suggests, in dissolution.

> She sweeps with many-colored Brooms—
> And leaves the Shreds behind—
> Oh Housewife in the Evening West—
> Come back, and dust the Pond!
>
> You dropped a Purple Ravelling in—
> You dropped an Amber thread—
> And now you've littered all the East
> With Duds of Emerald!
>
> And still, she plies her spotted Brooms,
> And still the Aprons fly,
> Till Brooms fade softly into stars—
> And then I come away— (No. 219)[5]

---

5. For a different view see Anderson, *Stairway of Surprise*, 131ff.

The somber note with which the poem concludes is not simply an acknowledgment of death—"And then I come away"—but a suggestion of the vacuous center around which the cosmic phenomena swirl. The variant version of the third stanza reenforces the poem's more troubling implications.

> And still She plies Her spotted thrift
> And still the scene prevails
> Till Dusk obstructs the Diligence—
> Or Contemplation fails.

A similar alternation of clutter and hollowness is captured in another poem that plays with many of the same verbal principals.

> Like Brooms of Steel
> The Snow and Wind
> Had swept the Winter Street—
> The House was hooked
> The Sun sent out
> Faint Deputies of Heat—
> Where rode the Bird
> The Silence tied
> His ample-plodding Steed
> The Apple in the Cellar snug
> Was all the one that played. (No. 1252)

The insubstantial shreds, ravelings, and threads of the earlier poem are here converted into drifts of impounding snow and gusts of immobilizing wind. The brooms' soft fading is now explicitly identified with a deathly silence. Both poems, it is true, convey a sense of overwhelming pictorial beauty. But beauty may be the veneer behind which a turbulent reality prepares to explode.

Intimations of such disunities and discontinuities fill the Dickinson canon. For all the ecstasy of "I taste a liquor never brewed—," there is a disruption of rhythm and a slightly slurring excess that, though not refuting the poet's giddy love of nature, do suggest how easily innocent intoxication with the physical world can turn into genuine chaos-producing bloat.

> I taste a liquor never brewed—
> From Tankards scooped in Pearl—

> Not all the Frankfort Berries
> Yield such an Alcohol!
>
> Inebriate of Air—am I—
> And Debauchee of Dew—
> Reeling—thro endless summer days—
> From inns of Molten Blue—
>
> When "Landlords" turn the drunken Bee
> Out of the Foxglove's door—
> When Butterflies—renounce their "drams"—
> I shall but drink the more!
>
> Till Seraphs swing their snowy Hats—
> And Saints—to windows run—
> To see the little Tippler
> From Manzanilla come! (No. 214)

Similarly, in her well-known poem about a hummingbird there is a hint of frenzy that is intended not simply to replicate the motion of a bird but to warn us that both the bird and the poem are teetering at the edge of confusion and disarray.

> A Route of Evanescence
> With a revolving Wheel—
> A Resonance of Emerald—
> A Rush of Cochineal—
> And every Blossom on the Bush
> Adjusts it's tumbled Head—
> The mail from Tunis, probably,
> An easy Morning's Ride— (No. 1463)[6]

And, in the following poems, in which detailed natural beauty is also a primary factor, the sense of disorder and the hints of potential destruction, death, and dissolution, so tremulously repressed in other poems, begin to break through the surface in vivid images of carnage and strife:

> The name—of it—is "Autumn"—
> The hue—of it—is Blood—
> An Artery—upon the Hill—
> A Vein—along the Road—

---

6. Roland Hagenbüchle discusses this poem at length in "Precision and Indeterminacy."

> Great Globules—in the Alleys—
> And Oh, the Shower of Stain—
> When Winds—upset the Basin—
> And spill the Scarlet Rain—
>
> It sprinkles Bonnets—far below—
> It gathers ruddy Pools—
> Then—eddies like a Rose—away—
> Upon Vermillion Wheels— (No. 656)

and

> Whole Gulfs—of Red, and Fleets—of Red—
> And Crews—of solid Blood—
> Did place about the West—Tonight—
> As 'twere specific Ground—
>
> And They—appointed Creatures—
> In Authorized Arrays—
> Due—promptly—as a Drama—
> That bows—and disappears— (No. 658; cf. No. 1190)

The universe's lavish displays of lush colors, these poems suggest, are not as innocent as one might at first imagine, for the spectacular "Gulfs—of Red" are really a gaping abyss, and the colorful "Fleets—of Red" are a veritable army of enraged attackers, "Crews—of solid Blood." The poem's violent metaphors are not atypical of images in the Dickinson canon. Exhilarating beauty is often associated in her verse with images of warfare and death: the "Sudden Musket" in "The Dawn came slow" (No. 304), for example, or the "Armies" and "martial stirrings" of "The Sun kept stooping—" (No. 152). In "Whole Gulfs—of Red," Dickinson's choice of imagery and analogy, as well as her poetic form, serve to remind us that the blood that courses bounteously through the veins and arteries of the living universe, the color that defines shape and season and gives them meaning, may be the same blood, the same color, that spills out upon the landscape and stains it in death.

I do not want to press my case too hard too soon. All of the poems we have been surveying, even the poems about autumn, are, admittedly, among Dickinson's most extravagantly enthusiastic productions. At least, they must be said to be among her most purely sensuous and naturalistic verses. There is no denying the dazzling beauty of the "Duds of Emerald" or the shimmering grandeur of "Vermillion Wheels." What I am pointing to, therefore, is in these poems only a tentative undercurrent, a subtle but, I believe, fully purposeful hint of disruption, with a concomitant projection of imminent collapse. In my view, this slight quiver, this mild shortness of breath (other readers, with other interests, have noticed it as well), suggests that there lurks at the center of Dickinson's poetic vision a basic uncertainty, an anxiousness that she makes integral to her whole poetic enterprise.[7] In a letter written in 1876 Dickinson says that "Nature is a Haunted House—but Art—a House that tries to be haunted." Her poems continuously introduce us to the ghosts that flit fitfully through the kingdoms of nature and art and that may haunt even a poet's least somber verses.

These ghosts are associated, of course, with many of the problems and paradoxes that are commonly discussed in Dickinson criticism. In the first instance, the understated anxiety of her poems must be related to her constant, down-to-earth realism and to the sense of struggle and failure with which she everywhere modifies even her most ardent swings of hedonistic rapture in the world of nature and art. Dickinson writes to her sister-in-law Susan that life is "scramble and confusion" (L 178) and if Dickinson's poems also exhibit "scramble and confusion," these qualities or activities must, at least in part, be traceable to the way she perceives the activity of living. Furthermore, her cosmic suspiciousness is closely linked to the bald outlines of phenomenal reality as Dickinson sees them, to the blunt fact, for example, that days and people, for all their magnificent and brilliant displays in the universe, are not eternal and therefore must "fade," "come away," be stilled (No. 265), and, in short, "die." The universe, Dickinson fears, may be composed of an unfathomable mix of beauty and ugliness,

7. Richard B. Sewall, "Introduction," in Sewall (ed.), *Critical Essays*, 3, discusses Dickinson's hesitations. Cf. also John Cody, *After Great Pain: The Inner Life of Emily Dickinson* (Cambridge, Mass., 1971), 264ff.; and Porter, "The Poetics of Doubt," 88. For some of Dickinson's own related, statements about language see poems No. 1129 ("Shall I take thee"), No. 1212 ("A word is dead"), No. 1261 ("A Word dropped careless"), No. 1651 ("A Word made Flesh"), and No. 581 ("I found the words").

good and evil. The quantities and qualities of cosmic being she so straightforwardly portrays may, she confesses, exist in no apparent relation or proportion to one another. This condition of discontinuity is for Dickinson not merely a matter of human subjectivity. Even in terms of our most objective categorizations of reality, such objects, she believes, may be totally incommensurate with each other. They may compose one huge, coldly silent "riddle" or puzzle with no solution at all (No. 89 and No. 180).

But Dickinson's blinking, faltering, cinemagraphic view of the universe, her choppy, halting slide-show presentation of broken perceptions, does not originate solely in her deep conviction that the universe itself is severely fragmented. It also derives from her belief that the perpetual, wheeling contest between "Blazing" and "Quenching" is a continuous crisis of the poetic imagination itself.. Day is not the only juggler in the world of Dickinson's poems. The "Juggler of Day" *is*, also, the poem itself. The words and phrases the poet juggles into existence on the page, like the colors and shapes they evoke, also consist of discrete and unmergible fragments, sometimes breathtaking, sometimes stifling, which achieve no permanent synthesis, perhaps, even, no temporary harmony. Unity and peace occur only in the final moment of the poetic experience when, like day, the poet folds her carnival juggling act, disappears, and is "gone."

In other words, for Dickinson the perceived universe is definitely not an unqualified model of multidimensional harmony. Furthermore, the pervasive disparities between independent phenomena, which seem chaotic warfare, are not only products of the universe's juggling of itself into existence. They result also from the mind's sympathetic attempt to compose a coherent and yet accurate portrait of those events, to juggle words as day juggles lights and colors. Dickinson's interest is not simply in using words mimetically. Rather, she wants to convey the implicit connection between language and reality in which language, attempting to convey cosmic beauty, cannot but recapitulate and deepen its immanent discreteness, its apparent disorder. Chaos may, as David Porter points out, be a major component of Dickinson's poetic vision. But Dickinson does not, therefore, as Porter contends that she does, substitute the world of language for the disintegrating universe around her.[8] Language, Dickinson believes, contains within its own structure its own tendencies toward fracture. For this reason, it is as much the consequence of linguistics as of cosmography that Dickinson's poems quiver and quake, blaze and quench, start and stop, concluding as often as not in a series of dashes ("—") that do not resolve the chaos but simply end it, de facto.

Chaos, then, apparent or real, is not only the subject of many Dickinson poems. It is the underground current of almost all of her poetry, the very modus vivendi of her poetic technique. In fact, one of the most compelling reasons for not dismissing out of hand the strange dashes and capitalizations of her verse as either the mindless lapses of a dilettantish poetaster or the scrawlings of an editorially undisciplined pen is that the rapid, uneasy staccato of irregular capitalizations and the frenzied volley of obtrusive and disruptive dashes function so exquisitely well in conveying what I believe to be one major area of Dickinson's poetic concern: the relationship between a discontinuous, ostensibly chaotic universe and a species of language that is so eerily autonomous, so individualistic and alive, that in itself it is imperiously divisive. Disorder, therefore, is conveyed in Dickinson's poetry not only imagistically and thematically. It is represented linguistically and visually as well. It is captured in the dissociation and exaggeration of the poem's verbal units—the "Blazing in Gold—and—[the quite distinct] Quenching—in Purple"—and by the magisterial disintegration of the poem's major metaphoric constructs and analogies.

The following poem, for example, is about natural destruction: about leaves unhooking themselves from trees and dust throwing away the roads; about water wrecking skies and quartering trees. Therefore, it is not at all odd that a principle of destructiveness is actually enacted within the structure of the poem. But the words of this poem do not simply pantomime an unrelated drama. They do not content themselves with simply mirroring the isolation and fragmentation represented by the "Yellow Beak" and "livid Claw" of external nature.

8. Porter, *The Modern Idiom, passim.*

Instead, like the "one drop of Giant Rain" that is at the center of nature's storm, the poem effects upon itself a version of disintegration and dissolution so complete that the poem becomes the jumbled multiplicity of the elements it describes. Poetic cohesion, like cosmic cohesion, is almost totally unhinged.

> The Wind begun to rock the Grass
> With threatening Tunes and low—
> He threw a Menace at the Earth—
> A Menace at the Sky.
>
> The Leaves unhooked themselves from Trees—
> And started all abroad
> The Dust did scoop itself like Hands
> And threw away the Road.
>
> The Wagons quickened on the Streets
> The Thunder hurried slow—
> The Lightning showed a Yellow Beak
> And then a livid Claw.
>
> The Birds put up the Bars to Nests—
> The Cattle fled to Barns—
> There came one drop of Giant Rain
> And then as if the Hands
>
> That held the Dams had parted hold
> The Waters Wrecked the Sky,
> But overlooked my Father's House—
> Just quartering a Tree— (No. 824, second version)

(A significant alternate version of stanza one reads:

> The Wind begun to knead the Grass—
> As Women do a Dough—
> He flung a Hand full at the Plain—
> A Hand full at the Sky—)[9]

The poem records, and in recording sets into motion, a frightening cycle of confusion and chaos in which the presumably logical structures both of natural events and of human language fall apart. Ideas grotesquely metamorphose into things (a "Menace" becomes a con-

---

9. For an interesting reading of this poem see Aida A. Farrag, "J. 824: The Wind begun to rock the Grass," *Emily Dickinson Bulletin*, XXXI (1977), 65–69.

crete object that can be thrown). Animate and inanimate exchange places (wagons quicken while trees die). Identities merge and things turn into each other (the bird hides behind lightning-like bars while the bar-like lightning becomes a bird). Descriptions are self-contradictory ("The Thunder hurried slow"). Furthermore, in what is the most completely exploited and horrifying of the poem's linguistic consequences, the poem's central metaphor (of hands) undergoes a process of disintegration in which the metaphor is almost completely decomposed. The poem seems to be alive with a multitude of hands, explicit and implied, but the hands of the poem—of roads and trees, lightning and birds, wind and water—the hands that are supposed to uphold order, cosmic and poetic both, fail to do their job. For just as the "Hands / That held the Dams" allow the universe outside the poem to fall into disorder, so the poem's metaphoric hands shatter the poem into fragments, until our very concept of what a hand is or what it does or what it means within the context of real or imaginary experience is battered into confusion. Are hands unseen forces like the wind that rocks the grass or the divine essence that cups the rains in the heavens? Or are they leafy appendages or perhaps dusty ones? And do they control the body of which they are a part, or are they controlled by it? Are hands claws? And, if so, the claws of lightning or of birds? The poem becomes a kind of malevolent, self-contending octopus whose many arms, in wrestling with and attempting to destroy one another, lose their significance as arms and become, instead, one vast churning mass of destructive activity. Or to use another metaphor the poem introduces, the poem is like a fickle wind that changes abruptly from maternal breeze to bruising storm, at first cradling our auditory and aesthetic senses in a soothing, sing-song lullabye and then menacing those senses, punishing them in an assault of piercing and painful imagery. The poet, like the implied baker in the alternate version of the poem, pounds her potentially rising creation into crumbs. Words destroy each other.

In the same way, the confusion and fragmentation in the following poem are not just products of external nature. They result equally from the human thought process that attempts to comprehend nature.

Four Trees—upon a solitary Acre—
Without Design
Or Order, or Apparent Action—
Maintain—

The Sun—upon a Morning meets them—
The Wind—
No nearer Neighbor—have they—
But God—

The Acre gives them—Place—
They—Him—Attention of Passer by—
Of Shadow, or of Squirrel, haply—
Or Boy—

What Deed is Their's unto the General Nature—
What Plan
They severally—retard—or further—
Unknown— (No. 742)

All of the characters in this little drama—the trees, the sun, God Himself—are isolated or alone not just on the described landscape, but visually, typographically, within the poem as well. The "Four Trees" sit absolutely segregated upon the "solitary" domain of the poem's first line. So does God in line 8, divorced from His creation, introduced into the poem by a conjunctive "But" that dissociates even as it connects. No "Design" or "Order" or "Action," "Apparent" or otherwise, is made perceptible within any portion of the poem, either thematically or linguistically. In other words, the facts in the case are not just objectively stated or even metaphorically implied. Rather, the poem proceeds through a bombardment of optically and aurally disrupted words and images that, although they may seem, on one level at least, to imitate natural disunities, really, in an even more profound way, rival and surpass them. They create a heap of unraveled thoughts so tangled that even nature's apparent chaos cannot adequately be expressed. Therefore, the poem explicitly confesses that what is "Unknown" is not only "What Plan" nature may "further," but "What Plan" it may "retard." Words, it seems, cannot even embody the negation of meaning. Nor can they describe, through negative example, meanings positively or negatively conceived. Thus the poem circles

around meaning but never locates it. It raises hypotheses that it immediately abandons. It spasmodically starts and stops to no avail. Just as
literal sun and verbal sun are able to meet the trees only by the most
physically and syntactically involuted and interrupted pathway, so
each potential motion and meaning that the poem (like nature) raises
to view is thwarted or disturbed.

Every object is frozen into a severe paralysis within a plan that is
unknown because it has been scrambled beyond recognition in the
landscape and beyond comprehension in the poem. The lines "The
Acre gives them—Place— / They—Him—Attention of Passer by—
/ Of Shadow, or of Squirrel, haply— / Or Boy—" seem to be perversely aphasic. Syntax seems to dissolve along with meaning. Con-
nectives appear to fail with logic. And what seem to be the vestiges of
informing parallelisms or analogies in both natural and linguistic structures become dislocated elements in an unorganized listing of unrelated items.[10] A sentence, therefore, that ought to mean "The acres
give the trees a place to live, and the trees reciprocally give the acre
the attention of passers-by or give them shade or give them the attention of squirrels or *of* boys" becomes so garbled that no logically coherent meaning (or even negation of meaning—"What Plan / They
. . . retard") is asserted at all.

Dickinson's universe, it would seem, is a cosmos in tatters, in beautiful
tatters perhaps but nonetheless a world of isolated and antagonistic
"Beak," "Claw," and "Menace," defined by "Four Trees" stranded alone
on a "solitary Acre." This disarray does not reflect cosmic realities
only. It also represents the consequences of artistic activity. The hands
that let unity fall into disunity are human and poetic as well as divine
and cosmic. The strings of words that meander chaotically through
the recreated landscapes of these poems are the poet's, not God's. It
remains to ask why, in Dickinson's view, the mind can do no better than
to author a broken portrait of its thoughts and perceptions, why, precisely, language cannot resolve the disunities and disparities that char-

10. On the aphasic quality of Dickinson's verse, see Cameron, *Lyric Time*, 32–34 and
Porter, *The Modern Idiom, passim.*

acterize the external world. What, according to Dickinson, should we actually expect of human knowledge and art?

For Dickinson writing poetry is not just one of life's activities, it is a way of existence, life itself. "I dwell in Possibility— / A fairer House than Prose—" (No. 657), she writes. Poetry is not only a matter of potential triumphs and impending failures, but poetic exploration is synonymous with the form and content and process of living. Therefore, Dickinson's conceptions of language (of poetic language, in particular) and of phenomenal reality often serve as interchangeable counters in her continuing poetic discourse. For Dickinson there are intimate and important relationships among the structure of the cosmos, human perceptions of that cosmos, and the ways the poetic mind formulates its cosmological and epistemological discoveries.

Dickinson's poetry, then, is philosophical. The kinds and conditions of cosmic disparity her poetry records reflect (at an infinite distance perhaps) the rudiments of cosmic structure. But the mistaking of a part for a whole or a substance for a quality also suggests to her the essential nature of our perception of that structure. And it defines the features of language as the individual attempts to articulate his or her perception and knowlege. The various kinds of fragmentation revealed in the poems—the disparities that constitute the divine creation, our discontinuous, broken perceptions of that universe, and the autonomous, divisive aspects of language—are not, therefore, incidental cohabitors of the same poem. Nor do they represent three parallel, semidetached interests. Rather, they are fundamentally interconnected elements in a clearly developed, highly sophisticated description of cosmological, perceptual, and artistic interrelations. Disparateness and separateness form, for Dickinson, the bases of cosmic activity and poetic activity, both.

But cosmic disparity, perceptual confusion, and linguistic autonomy are not, and cannot be, neutral conditions for the individuals who inhabit a universe thus constituted. They are worrisome and problematical, painful in the extreme, especially for the artist. Thus, in Dickinson's view, it is not that the eye sees with triumphant accuracy what there is to see or that the artist perfectly records what there is to record. Instead, human perception, even when it is looking at a sunrise rather than at a rainstorm or at a garden rather than at a desolate wood, seems doomed never to escape the restrictions of the divisive rhythm, the disruptive punctuation mark, the misused word, or the isolating capital letter that represent the limitations of poetic expression. It is as if the human eye, capable of seeing only discrete, discontinuous frames of reality when it looks out at the world, can relay back to consciousness only still more isolated flashes and fragments of reality, which are then broken down even further into the tiny linguistic daguerreotypes of arrested poetic vision that we call poems. (It is useful to recall Poe's statement that "poetry *is* the practical result, expressed in language, of [the] Poetic Sentiment.")[11] To make matters worse, those verbal pictures of which we are so enamored are not just docile puppets frozen into unwavering attitudes of truthful representation. They are self-propelled little organisms with vibrations and nuances and a life's energy all their own. They are living creatures that are, according to Dickinson, alternately magnificent, alternately grotesque exaggerations of the ideas that first parented them.

Thus, the metonomy and synecdoche of her verse (the "Beak" and "Claw" and "Quenching," for example) that seem to some of her critics her most glorious affirmations of the power of words are not intended to assert, unambiguously and without ambivalence, the ability of language to describe. Rather, they represent the tendency of language to dismember and isolate further, more rigidly and more absolutely, the elements of a universe that is itself (for whatever reasons) characterized by its own disunity and disjuncture. As Kenneth Burke has aptly queried, in pursuing interests of his own, "Do we use words, or do they use us?" He continues in a passage that has a striking relevance to our understanding of Dickinson's own assumptions about language and thought: "An ideology is like a god coming down to earth, where it will inhabit a place pervaded by its presence."[12] In Dickinson's terms, words (highly suggestive, caption-creating) live and

11. Edgar Allan Poe, review of Drake's "The Culprit Fay," in James Harrison (ed.), *The Complete Works of Edgar Allan Poe* (16 vols.; New York, 1902), VIII, 284.
12. Kenneth Burke, *Language as Symbolic Action: Essays on Life, Literature and Method* (Berkeley, 1966), 6.

die, blaze and quench, all in the same linguistic instant. They are god-like creatures that autocratically dictate and dispose throughout their appointed realms.

The poet, therefore, confronts a grave dilemma. A truthful approach to cosmic realities seems, in the first instance, to demand a particularized, fractured presentation of cosmic phenomena. That is how those phenomena are both constituted and perceived. But that particularized, fractured presentation as it is rendered in language does not remain simply an accurate and therefore innocent portrait of reality. Because of the nature of our conscious minds, and specifically because of the nature of language, the work of art exceeds its picture-making authority. It creates its own universe of self-sufficient fragments that are not only far removed from the fragmentary substance and fragmented perception of the world in which we must live and choose and act, but that increasingly distract and divide us from a meaningful knowledge of the conditions of that world.

The particular crisis of philosophy and poetics in which Dickinson finds herself is in no way unique to her. Nor is her involvement in such fundamentally philosophical and aesthetic issues merely a fortuitous, independent development paralleling similar evolutions in other poets and philosophers. As a nineteenth-century American writer, Dickinson inherited a full and complex discourse on questions of cosmic perception; and as a creative genius she was led to quandaries and discoveries that, on the one hand, concluded a series of fertile, intellectual dialogues that preceded her, and, on the other, anticipated a set of similar results in a series of writers who followed her. Therefore, while Dickinson's solutions to the problems she raised may be very much her own, it is worthwhile, I think, to launch at least a short excursion into the philosophical terrain in which Dickinson may well have located herself and which, in any case, she was in fact exploring. My primary interest unquestionably remains Dickinson's poetics. But as I have been trying to suggest, her poetics may be largely inseparable from her philosophical insights. In fact, they seem to me to have been very intentionally structured by the poet within a philosophical framework that represented a careful choice from among the philosophical options available to her.

The clearly philosophical texture of Dickinson's poems makes it seem remarkable that so many of her readers have assumed that she neither had any interest in encountering philosophical issues nor had any meaningful knowledge of philosophy per se. Allen Tate, for example, goes so far as to say that Dickinson suffered from a species of "intellectual deficiency," that "she could not in the proper sense think at all"; Inder Nath Kher, who is certainly an eloquent defender of Dickinson's poetic sophistication, believes that "there is no place for a rational or philosophical system of ideas in Dickinson." [13] In the final analysis, of course, any claim that Dickinson was familiar with and systematically interested in the philosophy of her day will have to rest on the evidence of her verse; and, indeed, as I have already begun arguing and as I hope to show, many of Dickinson's poems so directly engage epistemological, perceptual, and cosmological questions that it is difficult to doubt that she was self-consciously exploring such questions in her poetry. But in the cause of credibility and for purposes of presenting a system of terminology to which Dickinson was likely exposed, it will be useful to pause for a moment to inquire into some of the possible sources of Dickinson's philosophical knowledge.

It is true that none of the books listed in Jack L. Capps' study of *Dickinson's Reading* are in any meaningful sense philosophical; and Dickinson's letters do not cite philosophical works that she might have been studying or at least hearing about. But access to the full and various sea of philosophical thought churning in Dickinson's world can be gained by turning to the periodical literature that Dickinson was known to be reading during the years of her greatest poetic activity.[14] Although I suspect that Dickinson's familiarity with the Western philosophical tradition was far greater than I am warranted to assert openly, a minimal index to the philosophical thought to which she was ex-

13. Allen Tate, "Emily Dickinson," in Sewall (ed.), *Critical Essays*, 23 and 22; and Kher, *Landscape of Absence*, 56. See also Thomas W. Ford, *Heaven Beguiles the Tired: Death in the Poetry of Emily Dickinson* (University, Ala., 1966), 14; Albert Gelpi, *Emily Dickinson: The Mind of the Poet* (New York, 1965), 60; Richard Wilbur, "Sumptuous Destitution," in MacLeish, Bogan, and Wilbur (eds.), *Three Views*, 41; Anderson, *Stairway of Surprise*, 79–95; and Hagenbüchle, "Precision and Indeterminacy," 39.

14. Jack L. Capps, *Emily Dickinson's Reading, 1836–1886* (Cambridge, Mass., 1966), 128–34.

posed may be compiled from contemporary numbers of the *Atlantic Monthly* and *Harper's New Monthly Magazine*, where numerous essays appeared on such topics as the mind's perception of reality, the existence of God, the origins of the universe, the relationship between image and idea, and the outlines of moral science.[15] Although I do not want to make specific "source" claims for specific ideas in Dickinson's poetry, one essay entitled "Gottfried Wilhelm von Leibnitz" that appeared in an 1858 number of the *Atlantic Monthly* seems to be particularly worth noting since it is extremely relevant to the philosophical patterns that I would like to indicate are part and parcel of Dickinson's poetic vision. In addition, the availability of this material may help to convince us that many of Dickinson's own conceptions incorporate a deep awareness of these and other broadly disseminated discussions of central problems in American and European philosophy. In strikingly vivid language the essay provides a thoughtful history of some of the principal features of philosophical thinking in the seventeenth and eighteenth centuries: Descartes' principle of dualism, Spinoza's objective idealism, Locke's sensualism, and Kant's subjective idealism, all of which, I would suggest, are significantly relevant to various issues raised by Dickinson in different poems. Even more important, however, the essay explains the realism that distinguished Leibnitz from his fellow philosophers. The author's discussion of Leibnitz's need to grant the existence of independent, individual fragments of being seems to me to offer unusually fruitful possibilities for defining the philosophical arguments that underlie Dickinson's work. Leibnitz, the essay states,

felt with Des Cartes, the incompatibility of thought with extension, considered as an immanent quality of substance, and he shared with Spinoza the

15. J. Eliot Cabot, "On the Relation of Art to Nature in Two Parts," *Atlantic Monthly*, XIII (1864), 183–97 and 313–29; review of *Substance and Shadow; or Morality and Religion in their Relation to Life: An Essay on the Physics of Creation by Henry James*, in *Atlantic Monthly*, XII (1863), 126–28; "The Ideal Tendency," *Atlantic Monthly*, II (1858), 769–78; review of *Philosophy as Absolute Science* by E. L. and A. L. Frothingham, *Atlantic Monthly*, VII (1863), 251–55; "A Chapter on Dreams," *Harper's New Monthly Magazine*, III (1851), 768–74; "Vagaries of the Imagination," *Harper's New Monthly Magazine*, IV (1851), 63–65; Editor's Table on "'Time and Space,'" *Harper's New Monthly Magazine*, IV (1851), 128–31; and "Apparitions and Visions," *Harper's New Monthly Magazine*, XI (1855), 376–84.

unific propensity which distinguishes the higher order of philosophic minds. [But] dualism was an offense to him. On the other hand, he differed from Spinoza in his vivid sense of individuality, of personality. The pantheistic idea of a single, sole being, of which all other beings are mere modalities, was also and equally an offence to him. . . . Leibnitz's universe is [accordingly] composed of Monads, that is, units, individual substances, or entities, having neither extension, parts, nor figure, and, of course, indivisible. These are "the veritable atoms of nature, the elements of things."

The author earlier clarifies the concept of the Leibnitzian monad by describing Leibnitz's nominalism. "The principle of individuation, he maintains, is the entire entity of the individual, not the mere limitation of the universal. . . . John and Thomas are individuals by virtue of their integral humanity, and not by fractional limitation, of humanity. Dobbin is an actual positive horse . . . not a negation, by limitation, of universal equiety. . . . In fine, there is and can be no horse but actual individual horses." Furthermore, "perception" in Leibnitz's view, "is always the act of a simple substance, never of a compound. And in simple substances there is nothing but perceptions and their changes."[16]

Most significant about this philosophical analysis, whether or not Dickinson read this particular essay and made use of it in writing her poetry, is, as I have already suggested, that it encourages us to probe Dickinson's verse for fully coherent, extensively affiliated philosophical insights and models. It suggests that Dickinson had available to her at least a modest wealth of philosophical materials, and there is no reason to assume a priori that she was simply immune to the lure of philosophical energies that excited so many of her nineteenth-century American contemporaries. In fact, it should be clear, even without the promptings of external considerations, that her poetry evidences a deep and sophisticated involvement with easily identified philosophical issues of great importance.

Whatever Dickinson's specific philosophical indebtedness may have been, it appears that for her, as for Leibnitz and Descartes, mind and matter are not interchangeable existents; and yet dualism is not for

16. "Gottfried Wilhelm Von Leibnitz," *Atlantic Monthly*, II (1858), 14–31.

Dickinson, as it was not for Leibnitz, a way of solving the problem of the "incompatibility of thought with extension." Like Spinoza and Leibnitz, Dickinson pursues a unific principle. But like Leibnitz and unlike Spinoza, she subscribes to a nominalist as opposed to a pantheistic view of the universe. In other words, the disunities and disparities that I have been pointing to in many of her poems suggest certain affinities with a theory of cosmic organization that is, on the one hand, skeptical (in Cartesian terms) and yet not dualistic, individualistic or monadic as opposed to unific in a pantheistic sense. Dickinson's poems seem to be insisting on discreteness on all levels. They seem to be declaring an inviolable incommensurability of cosmic parts.

This declaration of incommensurate constituents seems to begin with a kind of phenomenalist argument concerning perception. That argument, as clearly articulated in Hume or contained implicitly in Leibnitz, is that our perceptual faculties provide only discrete and discontinuous knowledge of the world, that all we human beings are entitled to know for certain are the bits and fragments of our cosmic encounters. This is nominalism at its phenomenalist rock bottom, although, as I shall suggest in a moment, phenomenalism and nominalism can become two of the warring antagonists in Dickinson's poems. A recent interpreter of Hume has usefully restated many of the phenomenalist questions that turn out to be most relevant to our study of Dickinson. Why, she inquires, do we suppose objects to have distinct existence apart from our perceptions of them? Why do we attribute continued existence to phenomena when we only see them intermittently and interruptedly? For Humeans the answer to both questions lies in the power of the human imagination. And that power is as deeply troubling to Dickinson as it is to Humeans: "We ascribe continuous existence to things where we have collections of impressions either virtually unchanging (as in the case with the group of impressions we call 'Mountains' or 'houses') or whose changes are regular (as are the seasonal changes . . .). [The Imagination] confuses similarity with identity, and thus the fiction arises that there is an identical object, the sun, when all we actually have is a number of very similar perceptions of light, heat, and so on." Thus imagination, in the

Humean view (and in the Dickinsonian view as well) is the "deceiver" that promotes a false security in an unreliable universe.[17]

One way to interpret Dickinson's faltering, hesitating collection of independent perceptual moments, therefore, might be as an attempt to restore and limit perception to its pristine, undistorted and undistorting, function. One could argue that this restored perception is the ultimate realism for Dickinson—to picture reality exactly as the eye beholds it, in discontinuous and disparate frames of sense information that cannot be synthesized into wholeness except by the dissimulations of the fictionalizing imagination. In poems like "Blazing in Gold," "I'll tell you how the Sun rose—," and "She sweeps with many-colored Brooms—" the poet, according to such an interpretation, contemplates what it is and how it is that the eye actually perceives when it looks at a particular set of sense impressions to which we have given a definition or name like *sunset* or *sunrise*. And she demonstrates how the processes and contents of perception are at odds with the wholeness and integrity that our descriptive terminologies imply.

If the elements of a Dickinson poem seem disjointed, then, one explanation might be that in Dickinson's view sense perception is thus constituted. And yet, as I have been insisting, the brokenness and unevenness of Dickinson's poems are not simply imitative of cosmic realities. They affect us as warnings, as hints of potential destructiveness and impending crisis. The language expresses hesitancy, doubt, not only about perception but even more importantly about the records of our perceptions and about their implications for human life in this universe. The question is why? What does Dickinson's cosmological and perceptual realism have to do with the nervousness that is also articulated in the poems? And what is the link between perceptual discontinuity and linguistic fragmentation?

There are several possible answers to these questions. The first might be that the poems express not only the equivalent of Humean phenomenalism but, as I have already suggested, a skepticism much

17. Mary Warnock, *Imagination* (London, 1976), 21–25.

like Descartes' as well. Certainly a poem like "I'll tell you how the Sun rose—" in part enunciates this particular kind of skeptical position. As I have already noted, the poet specifically wonders whether things really are as they seem. And it would not be difficult to locate moments of similar skepticism throughout the Dickinson canon—sometimes in a metaphysical context, sometimes in a theological one—cf., for example, "The Sun kept stooping—stooping—low!" (No. 152) or "I am alive—I guess—" (No. 470) or "To hear an Oriole sing" (No. 526).

But skepticism alone does not seem to me to explain the uncertainty and anxiety that haunt Dickinson's poems, for the effect of Dickinson's discrete verbal units is not to call into question the actuality of what the poet sees so much as to announce a level of authenticity about her perceptions that is above and beyond what even nonskeptics would insist upon. Dickinson's poetic images are, in a Leibnitzian sense, nominalist; they are monadic. The *Blazing* that the poem's language so self-consciously declares is emphatically a *Blazing*; the *Quenching* unequivocally a *Quenching*. In fact, it is the very self-sufficiency and independence of each of her poem's verbal units, the exaggeration of the perceptual moments, that seem to be intimately related to the poem's hesitations and fears.

Skepticism, therefore, does not in and of itself explain the crisis of verbalization expressed in the poems we have been examining. But skepticism does put us in mind of one possible corollary to skepticism that is, I believe, as profoundly involved in Dickinson's dilemma as it is in Leibnitz's; and it is probably no accident that issues of skepticism should arise in the very poems that assert a profoundly nonskeptical position. One way of solving the problem of skepticism, and of phenomenalism for that matter, is the system of dualisms that Descartes himself articulates and in which the separable, ultimately unknowable, and irreconcilable components of the phenomenal universe become simple containers for larger, more ideal or divine realities that stand behind them. In this sense, dualism is a version of idealism (and of pantheism) and though there is, needless to say, much to distinguish Plato, Descartes, and Spinoza from each other, yet idealism, dualism, and pantheism all share at least one fundamental tendency that is of paramount importance to Dickinson. All three systems seek to discover unity within the facts of cosmic disunity. All three attempt to assert harmony in the face of ostensible chaos. In other words, the disorder and disruption identified by a Leibnitz or a Hume can be dealt with, in this view, by converting such disunities into temporary aberrations of what is in fact an overwhelming, omnipresent cosmic oneness.

For the sake of expediency, the different systems that try to relate the one and the many in this way can be grouped under the heading of idealism, since so much of this extended chapter in the history of philosophy is in any case (as the philosophers themselves repeatedly note) merely a footnote to Plato.[18] Any one of a number of commentators (ancient or modern) could be called upon to educate us as to the implications of such an ideal system for literature and art. But here again we can apply, most efficiently, to another of Dickinson's contemporaries, this one writing in an 1864 issue of the *Atlantic Monthly*. I choose this essay not only because it is conceivable that Dickinson actually read it, but because the writer, J. Eliot Cabot, argues his case in language reminiscent of that used by Dickinson, and he points to one specific problem created by the ideal solution that greatly troubles our poet. Dickinson, as I shall show, rejects dualism; she argues against the usefulness of the ideal solution.

In his essay Cabot claims that the pictorial artist or writer, unlike the photographer, does not merely record the "fixed quantities" that the eye sees but strives to convey the "ideal form" toward which nature (and the rest of the universe) is tending. In other words, to surpass nature's fragmentation, the perceiver must project an "ideal" (God, for example, or Idea or Beauty) that subsumes nature and creates "harmony" out of nature's discordant voices. But idealism of this sort may cause its own incurable ills, as Cabot goes on to acknowledge: "the completion of the design [the 'idealizing' of nature] is also its limitation. It is final to the artist as well as to the theme, and cannot yield to further expansion. In Nature there is no such pretence of finality, and so her work, though never complete, is never convicted of defect.

18. See Joseph Chiari, *Symbolisme from Poe to Mallarmé: The Growth of a Myth* (London, 1956), 19.

Her circuits are never closed." [19] The form of Dickinson's poems, their precise rendering of the crises of perception and knowledge and their demonstration of the monstrous, dictatorial power of the word, suggests that for Dickinson the problems created by nature's discontinuities were definitely not to be resolved in a gloriously abundant, all-fusing idealism. Idealism, in the Dickinsonian view, limits, fixes, and reduces meaning. It implies defects where in fact there is really perfection.

I shall return to the subject of idealism in chapter three. For the moment, however, let me suggest that for Dickinson there is no ideal harmony in nature such as the idealists or dualists would insist upon. The "Blazing" and "Quenching" and "Beak" and "Claw" of her poems are not momentary distortions of a oneness that is ever striving to reconstitute itself. They are not intended to reflect an ultimate homogeneity and consistency. Thus, our fragmented perceptions of the fragmented universe are not to be understood as distortions of how the universe is composed or of how we ought to be seeing and interpreting it. Our images of chaos are authentic images not to be ignored. They are certainly not to be converted by the power-crazy poet into fraudulent and coercive images of order.

And yet, as Dickinson affirms over and over again in her poetry, a divine plan does exist. Disorder is more apparent than real. How, then, are we to understand cosmic disjunctures? How are we to record and describe and interpret them through art? Although for Dickinson the symbol is a most dangerous vehicle of human knowledge, one that must ruthlessly be defined and redefined, simultaneously empowered and controlled, if it is to convey anything meaningful about the universe in which we have our being, it is nonetheless the symbol that in large part provides the answers to the questions Dickinson is raising.

In commenting on Dickinson's use of language I have assiduously avoided the word *symbol*. I have done so in order to avoid running the risk, in the moment of setting out, of allowing so large and vague and

19. Cabot, "On the Relation of Art to Nature," 191. This essay mentions several artists who appear in Dickinson's verse, such as Titian and Giotto.

tempting a concept as symbolism to overwhelm the individuality of Dickinson's craft. It is now time, however, to introduce this dangerous word into the discussion—for two compelling reasons. First, Dickinson's peculiar deployment of verbal characters, whatever else it portends for her epistemological inquiry, is also self-consciously symbolic—symbolic, in other words, in a way that shows her awareness of symbolism as a philosophical issue. Her capitalized, dash-segregated words seem to declare themselves a kind of epitome of symbol usage. It is not surprising therefore that her poems have been subjected to extensive symbolic interpretation.[20]

Second, the cosmic discontinuity that I have begun to locate in Dickinson's poetry has been associated, historically at least, with the implications of symbolic thinking and representation. One familiar way to secure the universe against the fragmentation to which philosophical and scientific investigation has delivered it is to shift one's perception from phenomena to ideas, from the senses to the symbols that transcend phenomenon and sense both. As Joseph Chiari points out, the modern manifestations of symbolic tenets, viewed from the largest historical perspective, originate with Plato himself, and with the ongoing dialogue (carried on by Descartes, Hume, Locke, Berkeley, Kant, and others) about the nature of cosmic unity.[21]

My ultimate objective in this study is to describe the highly dissident nature of Dickinson's symbolism, to show how the poet rejects the symbolic attitudes and methodologies that are part and parcel of New England history, and perhaps also of most philosophical reflection from Plato onward, and how she substitutes her own challenging brand of symbolism for the garden variety cultivated so confidently in nineteenth-century America. There are surely many different Dickinsons in the 1,775 poems that she wrote, and these several Dickinsons

20. Among the critics who interpret Dickinson's work symbolically are Weisbuch, *Emily Dickinson's Poetry*; Kher, *Landscape of Absence*; Rebecca Patterson, "The Cardinal Points Symbolism of Emily Dickinson," *Midwest Quarterly*, XIV (1973), 293–317 and XV (1974), 31–48; Clark Griffith, *The Long Shadow: Emily Dickinson's Tragic Poetry* (Princeton, 1964); and Robert Gillespie, "A Circumference of Emily Dickinson," *New England Quarterly*, XLVI (1973), 254.

21. Chiari, *Symbolisme from Poe to Mallarmé*, 10–62.

speak to a wide variety of subjects in a large number of varied voices. Some of these Dickinsons may be conventional symbolists; some may be totally unconcerned with matters of symbolic consciousness. But the Dickinsonian voice with its corresponding subject that I would like to locate is the troubled, philosophical Dickinson, the Dickinson who tests and retests the premises of traditional symbolic philosophy, and who discovers, in her poetry, a symbolic system that is more meaningful, more theologically reverent than any that had been handed to her by the New England tradition.

It is not difficult, I think, to reconstitute an interest in Dickinson's animated verbal playlets as an investigation of her words and images for their symbolic valences. Dickinson's poetry is abundantly stocked with a teeming population of surcharged bees and butterflies, meaning-laden suns and flowers, that inevitably imply a level of philosophical and symbolic discourse we cannot afford to ignore. In fact, so widespread is Dickinson's use of a bold-faced mechanics of symbolizing that, as I have already noted, even verbs and adjectives, participles and participial phrases become personalized players in the dramatic world of her poetry. And her capital-letter, dash-riddled renderings of language seem to increase even further the symbolic weightiness of her individualized, nominalist words.

This extensiveness of symbolic technique, with its peculiarly typographic manifestations, suggests that for Dickinson the act of creating symbols is more than an inherited literary reflex, more even than a philosophical statement about elemental relationships in a multifaceted universe. For one of the subjects of Dickinson's poetry is the symbolizing imagination itself, the mind that posits a symbolic universe and peoples it with poetic creatures presumably reflective of divine or transcendental realities.

And yet, as a survey of commentaries on Dickinson's poems will show, her poetry resists clear-cut symbolic interpretation. Thus, even though Dickinson, like her fellow nineteenth-century American writers, would seem to see the world as symbolic, she also seems to be unable "to determine what nameless, unknowable quality it symbolizes": "what happens in Dickinson's poetry," says Clark Griffith, "is that the unity . . . Emerson and Whitman wrested from experience by not looking too closely, collapses under [her] genuinely tragic gaze."[22] The problem, therefore, to which Dickinson-the-symbol-inquisitor seems to be pointing is the same problem indicated by Dickinson the phenomenalist: the inability to either perceive or create order. What the mind produces, through its ordinary symbolic discourse, she will argue, is a poetic fragmentation that is even more frightening and bewildering than the chaotic and fragmented universe itself or than our chaotic and fragmented perception of it. Wilbur Urban explains the systematic and historical basis for just the set of symbolic assumptions that Dickinson continually challenges and tests and that she finally seeks to revise.

The essential character of all symbolism, in its primary form, is that images or ideas are taken from narrower and more intuitable relations and used as expressions for more ideal and universal relations which, because of their very pervasiveness and ideality, cannot be either directly intuited or expressed. The transcendental theory merely confirms and formulates this attitude. This theory is, of course, nothing more or less than the traditional or classical theory of symbolism from Plato on. Expressed in many ways, it has one underlying notion, namely, that the phenomenal world is an expression of a noumenal or intelligible world and, because of this relation, the phenomenal may be taken to represent or stand as a symbol for the noumenal.[23]

Traditional symbol usage, in other words, presupposes a cosmology and a philosophy in which the material creation and its replication in language constitute faithful mirrors of the divine or ideal reality from which they are supposed to have sprung. Conventional symbolism, furthermore, tries to solve the problems that we are grouping under the heading of idealism and dualism (Platonic, Cartesian, or otherwise) by adhering to the implicit tenet that symbols can restore the unity that emanation into being has destroyed. Thus, Erich Kahler explains that, although the symbol originates "in the split of existence, the confrontation and communication of an inner with an outer reality," it is designed to restore the unity that phenomenal reality has de-

22. Griffith, *The Long Shadow*, 268.
23. Wilbur Urban, *Language and Reality: The Philosophy of Language and the Principles of Symbolism* (London, 1951), 408.

stroyed. The symbol, in Burke's terminology, is "the building of a *terministic bridge* whereby one realm is transcended by being viewed in terms of a realm 'beyond' it."[24]

This is the traditional definition of the symbol—a bridging of two separate realms, the one material and the other spiritual. Or to provide a slightly different emphasis, the symbol might be conceived as a "synecdoche," what Charles Feidelson defines as an "attempt to find a point of departure outside the premises of dualism." The symbol, according to Feidelson, is a conflationary form "designed to capture the unity of a world artificially divided." Unlike logic, which is "atomistic," or dialectic, which "must respect the 'either-or' principle of logic," "the symbol," Feidelson explains, presents "opposing elements" in "absolute unity." It is, perhaps, like the act of fictionalization which for Humeans falsifies our perception of the sensual world. Feidelson argues that

logical language is built upon the principle of discreteness. Although in an ultimate sense logical statements may be purely symbolic, in practice they seem to entail a distinction between the speaker, his words, and what he talks about. Logical structure is typically atomistic. . . . In poetry we feel no compulsion to refer outside language itself. A poem delivers a version of the world; it *is* the world for the moment. And just as the language of the poem is a plastic symbolic medium in which subjective and objective elements are presented as an integral whole, so within the poem each word is potentially a standpoint, a symbolic crossroad, from which the whole poem may be viewed.

Although Feidelson claims that synecdochic symbolism as he defines it is a unique characteristic of American literature, it is easy to see how writers in other traditions frequently share the same synecdochic premises. Coleridge, for example (whom Feidelson discusses), defines the symbol as "a translucence of the special in the individual, or of the general in the special . . . the eternal through and in the temporal." And as Joseph Chiari has persuasively suggested, French Symbolism is also synecdochic, precisely because idealism and dualism, to which the

24. Erich Kahler, "The Nature of the Symbol," in Rollo May (ed.), *Symbolism in Religion and Literature* (New York, 1960), 53–54 (cf. Rollo May's discussion of this point in "The Significance of Symbols," in the same volume, 21–23); and Burke, *Language as Symbolic Action*, 186.

Symbolists were deeply committed, seem to necessitate this kind of solution.[25]

Whether the symbol is intended to bridge realms assumed to be separate but reflective of each other or whether it is made to project synecdochic unities that beg the question of dualism altogether, the symbol is traditionally seen as compacting and conflating elements that appear to the human perceiver to be disparate and even apparently irreconcilable, but that can, by an enlargement of one's perspective from the phenomenal realm to the spiritual one, be made to seem part and parcel of a more continuous, integrated whole. It is precisely this conflating and compacting that Dickinson objects to in her verse. It is the assumption that the particularized components of partial vision can be vaunted as an integrated symbol of vast interconnected meanings that, in Dickinson's opinion, frequently endows the symbol with its demonic, destructive power and that can cause it to reduce the actual largeness of cosmic complexity to a single, constricted unit.

For Dickinson the world of the poem, and specifically the language that creates that world, is as atomistic and divisive as any frame of reference located outside the poem. It creates its own elements of fracture and disunity. Furthermore, perception and knowledge, in Dickinson's view, come in spurts and not as encompassing syntheses. Dickinson's living language, therefore, does not try to deny the dualisms, bifurcations, and rifts of cosmic reality. It does not attempt either to legitimize them by having them transmit transcendent possibilities or to dissolve them by positing a point of departure outside them. Rather, Dickinson's language very literally, verbally, reproduces dichotomies and dualisms before her readers' startled eyes.

Dickinson's poems emphasize the inherent chaos of sense perception. They proclaim that what we call harmony is merely an illusion, an intellectual fabrication of what the universe is and how we see it. For her, neither bridges nor synecdoches can alter the facts of fragmentation. Nor should they attempt to. For Dickinson, in fact, such

25. Charles Feidelson, Jr., *Symbolism and American Literature* (Chicago, 1953), 64, 69, and 57; S. T. Coleridge, *The Statesman's Manual* in W. G. T. Shedd (ed.), *Complete Works of Samuel Taylor Coleridge* (7 vols.; New York, 1853), I, 437–38; and Chiari, *Symbolisme from Poe to Mallarmé*, 36 ff.

synecdoche or bridging can only recapitulate the basic condition of the universe, and it may do so with a forcefulness that is exceedingly disturbing.

Here I must pause to note that many of Dickinson's best critics have not failed to take note of the elusiveness, perhaps even skepticism and occasional negativism, of Dickinson's symbol usage. Inder Nath Kher, for example, explains that Dickinson's poetry must be understood as a "landscape of absence" in which images are "simultaneously concrete and intangible, present and absent." But for Kher, as for many other Dickinson scholars, this paradoxical *compositio* is itself symbolism that bridges and unifies: Dickinson's poetic technique, he concludes, is to "build interchangeable and interpenetrating symbolic structures on such perennial themes as life, love, despair, ecstasy, death, immortality, and self." In a similar vein, Robert Weisbuch, in one of the most illuminating studies of Dickinson yet written, takes note of the obscurity of Dickinson's symbolic referents by suggesting that the basic principle of her poetic procedure and, thus, the core of her aesthetic assumptions, is a kind of "sceneless" "analogy" that is a symbolism of the highest order: "Dickinson's typical poem enacts a hypothesis about the world by patterning a parallel, analogical world. . . . [Her] scenes [however] are not mimetic but illustratory, chosen, temporary, analogous. The poem is finally sceneless, and this scenelessness is the fully unique quality which identifies Dickinson's lyric technique." This "scenelessness," Weisbuch continues, "is one of Dickinson's weapons in her battle against 'hindering' subjects"; "symbolism," he goes on to explain, "is the other": "Dickinson's symbolism is not an exception to her intensely analogical poetic but a part of it; for a symbol, broadly defined, is simply an incomplete analogy in which the analogue is the only term and its subject(s) is left unstated." Weisbuch concludes with a position with which most critics would agree: "Like all the American romantics . . . Dickinson chooses to see symbolically, and to expand meanings to their furthest bounds,"[26] to use the symbol, in other words, as a bridge or translucent signifier.

26. Kher, *Landscape of Absence*, 2; and Weisbuch, *Emily Dickinson's Poetry*, 12–16, 40, and 7.

One difficulty with these kinds of symbolic interpretations of Dickinson's work, even when they are as skillfully managed as they are in the Kher and Weisbuch studies, is that they can imply a faith, presumably Dickinson's, as well as the critic's and our own, that through the use of a symbol the artist can identify, represent, and make meaningful and unified elements of a material-spiritual universe; that through the drama recorded by the symbolic story or poem, even if the poem is sceneless and its subject absent, the artist can make cogent statements about the configuration of the dual cosmos and of the human synthesis of cosmic realities. Yet Dickinson is not a subscriber to this faith. The universe that Dickinson's poems describe is characterized by gaps and not by bridges, by disruption and not by harmony. If it is true, as Weisbuch cogently argues, that Dickinson's poems are continuously pointing beyond material detail to the essentially transcendental "design" of the universe; if, indeed, it is the effect of the poems to cause the "inner" and "outer" components of experience to disappear and fade into the sceneless, analogical center of things,[27] then perhaps they do so not because Dickinson is trying to prove an underlying similarity or even coincidence between "inner" and "outer" but because she is endeavoring to visualize for us the total disparity that separates them. Dickinson may be forcing our attention away from parallelisms or analogies, however abstract and absent, and toward the awesome, gaping abyss at the center of phenomenal and noumenal reality both, the abyss that no symbol can bridge but that a multiplicity of false symbols can unwittingly widen.

The beauty and the terror exist side by side for Dickinson, and it may even be that the beauty exists because of the terror, because of the cosmic and perceptual discontinuities that seem terrible to the would-be synthesizer of cosmic oneness but that are, in fact, the demarcations that enable or cause beauty to exist. Here it is useful to remember that Descartes, who so adamantly insisted on the dualism of nature and the perceiving self, ultimately found his way back to God precisely because of the independence of the conscious mind and its distance from the objects of its contemplation. Coleridge, too, implic-

27. Weisbuch, *Emily Dickinson's Poetry*, 20 and 19.

itly acknowledges the importance of such discreteness when he speaks, in the same breath, of man's alienation from nature and God's withdrawal from the creation. Both are viewed as preconditions for creativity, whether human or divine. Similarly, in Dickinson's case, her poems may present a Humean view of the disparateness of sense reception not simply to identify a quality of cosmic organization and human perception but to declare the absolute necessity of discreteness and separateness as intrinsic elements of the divine purpose and process. God ordained that we see partially and intermittently. Dickinson believed it her job to fathom God's purpose and to cooperate in His process.

For this reason, it is very possible that Dickinson's poems display what Roland Hagenbüchle (invoking a different, more exclusively modern philosophical framework) describes as a "phenomenological reduction," a "metonymic" "'bracketing' of reality," a shift from "analogue" to "digital thinking." Dickinson, Hagenbüchle argues, does not use conventional "metaphors" that, "due to their relationship of equivalence, presuppose a stable world in which . . . the theme can still be incarnated." Instead, she employs "metonymically constructed metaphors, ambiguous signs, and multiple, often hypothetical, analogies." Because the poetry, Hagenbüchle concludes, is "symbolist" and not "symbolical," it rejects the synecdochic assumptions of conventional symbolism. Her words, he suggests, must therefore be called "transcends," linguistic elements that tend toward "mere reference or pure *deixis*."[28] They are, to adopt Feidelson's terminology, attempts to discover a point of reference outside the premises of dualism.

Hagenbüchle's study provides a nice corrective to the symbolic fallacies that can dog the heels of even the best Dickinson critics. It also accounts for many of the details that do not fit into a conventional symbolic model. But Hagenbüchle's discussions, it seems to me, lead to a further, related difficulty of much symbol usage. The "metonymic" "transcend," despite its alleged superiority over the traditional symbol, does not escape what is for Dickinson an additional, serious complication: the powerful reductiveness of human language that can

28. Hagenbüchle, "Precision and Indeterminacy," 34 and 35; cf. 51–52.

constrict the vital, aggressive fragments of our perception into dead and deadening words.

Hagenbüchle's interpretation of Dickinson brings us full circle, back to the perceptual and epistemological problems discussed earlier in this chapter. The reductiveness that to Hagenbüchle seems the triumph of Dickinson's poetry is necessarily double-edged. As an intimation of phenomenal reduction, verbal reduction is the ultimate poetic realism. It describes what it is and how it is that we see. But as a statement about cosmic relationships and meanings, reduction of the symbolic kind is something entirely different. The problem for the poet occurs at the moment when the designated reduction is mistaken for a wholly independent and autonomous meaning unto itself, a symbolic "transcend" as Hagenbüchle calls it. Dickinson is not a phenomenologist. She does not wish to examine the phenomenological world in and for itself alone, without positing any generalizations based on her own private experience. The reduction with which phenomenology concerns itself exists as the range and content of the only meanings accessible to human study. But Dickinson believes in a set of larger explanatory principles for the structure of the universe. Her verse is not exclusively descriptive but interpretative and metaphysical as well. And it is ardently theological.

In other words, if the concept of a bridge or interpenetrating reality of matter and spirit, substance and soul, represents for Dickinson one kind of radical misperception, phenomenological bracketing and reduction represent another. Dickinson does begin with phenomenalism (not phenomenology), with the reduction of the universe into phenomenal units. This is the point of departure in the epistemological exploration that is integral to her poetry. She does this, however, with the firm conviction that the fragmentary perception of reality will ultimately illuminate a divinely structured universe. Cosmic disunity, she believes, does have some function in a cohesive and integrated universe. For Dickinson, therefore, the bracketing is only one stage in a multistage or many-layered process. And it is that process that Dickinson's symbols endeavor to describe.

Martin Foss's discussion of the problems of symbolic reduction can help clarify why Dickinson is unable to accept the symbol either in

conventional symbolic terms, as a bridge or as a translucent synecdoche, or in phenomenological terms, as a bracketing of reality or as a
transcend. "Whenever symbolism is at work," Foss writes (and by *symbolism* Foss means the furthest reaches of the symbolist undertaking,
even as Hagenbüchle portrays them), "atomism is at hand as a device
of symbolism." This is the "paradox of symbolism," Foss shows, that
"the part is regarded as if it were the whole," and that, as a result, symbolism becomes single-termed and "static." It abandons what Foss calls
"the dynamic function of the propositional process," the continuously
generative relationship between subjects and predicates that alone
corresponds to the vital nature of reality and that, he believes, can
alone make that reality accessible to human consciousness. Most conventional symbolism, Foss goes on,

has found a refuge in a compromise which language and common sense have
sanctioned: The *subjectum* of the proposition, the unifying function has been
closed into one of the fixed terms, has been made the subject *in* the proposition. As such it has lost its carrying and forward-driving character and has
become a static, symbolically reduced entity, a predicative term, a part which
merely represents the whole. Every predicate can become a subject in a proposition, and this compromise between process and term has given birth to the
hybrid concept of the "universal."[29]

The manifestations of restriction and compression described by
Foss need not, we might note, lead us to despair. Kenneth Burke describes a process of "condensation" and "displacement" very similar to
that pictured by Foss. Yet such "substitution" for Burke actually "sets
the condition for 'transcendence,'" and Burke specifically links symbolic "substitution" with language: "There is a technical sense," he
writes, "in which the name for a thing can be said to 'transcend' the
thing named." Hagenbüchle believes that a species of such substitution is the very triumph of Dickinson's work. But Burke's and Hagenbüchle's assumption that substitution eventuates in transcendence depends on further assumptions about the subordinacy and efficacy of
language that Burke himself (not to mention Dickinson) is far from
accepting. We have already quoted Burke's suspicion that we do not
control words so much as they control us (Alfred North Whitehead

29. Martin Foss, *Symbol and Metaphor in Human Experience* (Princeton, 1949), 14–18.

makes a similar point). And in his essay "What Are Signs of What?" Burke raises the ultimate possibility (if only as a "tour de force") that words are not signs for things but rather quite the opposite, that things are signs of words, or at least become signs of words under the pressure of our all-pervading symbolic consciousness. In other words, in Burke's view, there may be innate structures of language that acquire the special contours of their meanings in the now named, now designated objects of the physical universe, much as poetic inspirations obtain perceptual form in poems. Furthermore, because of the potency of this internal language, because of this inherent desire of human beings from Adam on to name and symbolize the universe, words become the controlling force of the human world. They veritably banish the sensuous world, substitute for it, or at least define it in what may be the delimiting fixity of the separate word. In addition, as Burke also points out, the act of "substitution" that symbolism effects is inevitably "perfectionist" in a narrow and confining sense. Humankind's "entelechial principle," Burke explains, pushes the symbol into the terrain of absolute signification and meaning that eventually forces it to exceed its bridge-building authority.[30] In much the same way, Erich Kahler points out that, even though the symbol enters our consciousness as a processive quality, it quickly establishes itself as a separate entity, entire to itself and wholly self-contained.

Any made sign is a bridging act, an act of pointing to something or somebody. In the distinctive mating or warning *signal* of an animal species it appears in a somewhat stabilized form, but it has not parted with the living creature and settled down as a separate entity. The word, however, the articulate name of a person or a thing, is an objectified fixation of the act of "calling" him or "designating" it; it is a *frozen* act. It inaugurates what Alfred Krozibsky has called the time-binding capacity of the human being. It bridges not only spatial but also temporal spheres. This fixation, this consolidation and extension of the bridging act, this settling down of the meaning as a separate entity and established junction of diverse spheres of existence, marks the actual beginning of the symbol.

In the very power of the symbolizing act, in the very components of its transcending potential, are the elements of specification and substi-

30. Burke, *Language as Symbolic Action*, 8, 359–79, 16, and 20; and Alfred North Whitehead, *Symbolism: Its Meaning and Effect* (New York, 1959), 11.

tution that reduce the symbol to a mere shorthand notation for the fluid, multiphenomenal universe. As Foss remarks, "by transforming the infinite process into a finite object, symbolism has to substitute for the loss of universality." This substitution is inevitably accomplished, he continues, by "introducing the static concept of completeness or totality." The symbol, then, does not, as Coleridge had hoped, automatically substitute vitality for the deadness of the objective world. Instead, the danger is very great that the symbol will itself become a kind of deadness. The word, as Kahler puts it, is "frozen." It can reduce thoughts, Dickinson fears, to "numb"-ness.[31]

Although Dickinson's attitude toward symbols is not identical, of course, to that described in Burke's, Kahler's, Foss's, or anyone else's analysis, it is a species of such processive analysis, I believe, that underlies Dickinson's deployment of her own symbols. In Dickinson's dramatized world, as in the philosopher's schematized one, the created symbol threatens to assert its individuality and self-sufficiency at the expense of the equation or process, the "fluxional quality" as Emerson puts it, that is supposed to grant the symbol its meaning in the first place. As a self-ordained, self-contained bit of separable meaning, the symbol verges on becoming not an avenue of intercourse among different spheres of existence, not even an "asterisk" or "sign" pointing in a new direction, but rather a closed-off, dead fragment of a once larger, once vital meaning.[32] Dickinson's analogies may indeed be "sceneless" or "absent" or "multiple" in that there is no actual object or referent that the symbol is being made to represent. But as symbolic constructs or metonymies, Dickinson's words show us the tendency of language to create its own scenes, scenes of sunset and autumnal rain and winter chill, which become, within the poems, self-existing little realms suffering from precisely the same disintegrative, dualistic influences that afflict the real universe—the very universe from which they have so neatly, so cleverly, been severed by a human mind representative of all human minds.

31. Kahler, "The Nature of the Symbol," 54; Foss, *Symbol and Metaphor*, 18; and Coleridge, *Biographia Literaria*, ed. John Shawcross (2 vols.; Oxford, 1907), I, 202.

32. Ralph Waldo Emerson, "The Poet," in Brooks Atkinson (ed.), *Selected Writings of Ralph Waldo Emerson* (New York, 1950), 336; and Hagenbüchle, "Precision and Indeterminacy," 42 and 45.

Dickinson's own symbolism, then, is a demonstration of one possible response to the bridging and synecdochic assumptions of symbolic thinking and to the corresponding atomistic reductiveness of language as well. On the one hand the poems faithfully dramatize the potential liabilities of language, whether the linguistic unit in question is a mere symbol, entangled in all the distortions of symbolic fictionalization, or a so-called transcend that fully recognizes, in human terms, the "slant," "circumferential" quality of truth and knowledge.[33] And on the other hand, they demonstrate the "infinite process," as Foss calls it, whereby meaning is legitimately propounded. Many of her poems, in one sense, are diagrams of that process, portraits of cosmic separateness and of how it can be gloriously preserved and thereby apprehended. To appropriate Feidelson's set of terminologies, Dickinson is recurring to the principles of logic from which symbolism would seem to have spared us, and she is suggesting that it is only when the symbol can be made to expose the "either-or" quality of the world and of the symbol itself that it can be said to represent unity at all. "Either-or" is for Dickinson a version of Foss's "propositional process." It includes the fluxional alternatives that constitute, for Dickinson as much as for Emerson, the divine creation.

Dickinson's poetry reflects what I would call a symbolic realism. She insists that we see the world truly. She demands that we take into account not only actual phenomena or our perceptions of phenomena but the symbols on which our cosmic knowledge equally depends, even though symbolism, if mismanaged, can distort rather than clarify our understanding of the universe. I have spoken of Dickinson's perceptual and epistemological convictions. I have not yet described directly her own symbolic persuasions, nor will I be able to until after I have described the kind of symbolism Dickinson rejects. But it is already clear that for Dickinson, as for Cassirer, Burke, and others, man is "*animal symbolicum*," a "symbol-user." "We are symbols and inhabit symbols," writes Emerson, and Dickinson, I suggest, agrees.[34]

33. Hagenbüchle, "Precision and Indeterminacy," 39. For a discussion of circumference and slantness in Dickinson's work, see Anderson, *Stairway of Surprise*, 47–76.
34. Ernst Cassirer, *An Essay on Man* (New Haven, 1962), 26; Burke, *Language as Symbolic Action*, 3ff.; and Emerson, "The Poet," 328.

What remains for Dickinson to decipher, in her own poetic ways, is what kind of *animal symbolicum* we are, and what kinds of symbols we are meant to fashion. Thus it is not nearly enough to say that Dickinson's truth is "slant" or her vision circumferential. For Dickinson herself finds it necessary to tell us fully and precisely what she means by these terms. Dickinson's poems do not achieve meaning by a clever sleight of hand in which suffixes of "negation," "negated comparisons," and "syntactically ambivalent genitive appositions" (as Hagenbüchle suggests) are made adroitly to avoid the usual crises of symbolic form by immediately denying their own significance.[35] They acquire validity through a painful, always visible process of symbol revision in which one kind of symbol, fully embodied and fleshed out, is arrayed in all of its grotesque obesity and then is carefully, painstakingly forced to flay and carve itself of its excesses—until a true and reformed symbol can emerge. Again and again, Dickinson incorporates within her poems a vivid, even terrifying awareness of the complex nature of the symbolic mind and of its demonic potential for appropriating wholeness. Her poems parade before us words veritably gone mad, words that, as I shall attempt to show, masquerade as the absoluteness of cosmic law or the permanence of a natural principle and that therefore assume a dictatorial autonomy of their own; words that imitate their erring poetic creators and establish themselves as regents of an autonomous third realm, a realm that is neither human nor divine but that threatens to dislodge both man and God from the seats of their proper creative authority. And yet in the end Dickinson does finally subdue the word, does harness its energy for her own unique symbolic purposes. The very liveness of the word, which makes it so dangerous, can also be the source of its restorative power.

In the next four chapters I will examine the philosophical, religious, and historical bases of Dickinson's symbolic argument. I will attempt to sketch out the complex superstructure of the theological and intellectual commitment that compels Dickinson to identify and oppose the seductive appeal of much conventional symbolism. In the two closing chapters, however, when I advance the argument into

35. Hagenbüchle, "Precision and Indeterminacy," 39–40.

Dickinson's ultimate, symbolic terrain, I will try to show that, although one aspect of Dickinson's mind prompts her to flee symbols, another aspect allows her defiantly and courageously to invoke and utter symbols all the same. Symbolism of a radically modified kind is for Dickinson as much the inevitable modus operandi of the human intelligence as the unmodified variety is the great antagonist of that intelligence. From one point of view, therefore, Dickinson's poetry is a record of the ecstasy as well as the anguish of humankind's divine right and demonic compulsion to invent symbols. When Burke tells us that man is a "symbol-user," he means also that man is a "symbol misuser." [36] Dickinson takes into account both of these quintessential aspects of human character, and she believes that a specially defined mode of symbolism can and must be made a part of the intellective and artistic process that struggles to arrive at knowledge. I will recur to principles of symbolic thinking in chapter six. Specifically, I will reinvoke Burke's world of symbolic action and attempt to discover how Dickinson deals with a universe and a psyche that interact with one another only through our symbolic apprehension of the universe. But for the moment let me suggest that, by unraveling the restrictive assumptions of conventional symbolism in her poetry, Dickinson hopes to free the creative intellect for a journey that can, in the end, carry humankind toward a reliable, symbolic truth. Her symbols do arrive at a genuine signification of meaning, but only because they pirouette through an intricate acrobatic in which the symbol that is flung away in terror by one hand is retrieved, with chastened humility, by the other. The "Juggler of Day," it seems, does finally triumph in her act. But Dickinson will force us to follow every maneuver of her skillful hand. She will reveal to us every flex of every well-trained muscle as she spins into tense suspension the simultaneously beautiful and terrifying matter and symbols of the cosmic order.

---

36. Burke, *Language as Symbolic Action*, 16.

Chapter Two

The "Fraud That Cannot Cheat the Bee": The Dangers of Sacramental Symbolism

*A*LTHOUGH many of Dickinson's poems would seem to confirm a full complement of recognizable symbolic strategies and assumptions, much of her poetry incorporates a strain of argumentation that is distinctly antagonistic to conventional symbolism. Time and again her poems challenge the premises of doubleness and unity that determine a great deal of symbolic language and thought and that, in Dickinson's view, not only distort but ultimately reduce cosmic meaning. What I shall have to say about Dickinson's responses to conventional symbol usage will, I hope, help to describe the largest poetic dimensions of a large portion of the Dickinson canon. Yet my explorations of Dickinson's poems, even of those poems that seem to have a declared paradigmatic function, are by no means offered as an exhaustive description of her immensely varied verse. Dickinson is too great a poet not to have treated a multitude of different primary subjects, and not to have entertained the possibilities of many different poetic attitudes. Some of her poems may even directly refute positions taken in other poems. It is, perhaps, unforgivable to neglect the other Dickinsons who sparkle and rage, laugh and weep in so many magnificent poems and in so many interesting ways (I shall try to include a sampling of those other Dickinsons now and again), but my concern is with the philosophical poet, the symbolic Dickinson who not only uses a special symbolism in her poetry but who enriches and deepens her other selves by self-consciously engaging the omnipresent implications of symbolic theories and symbolic systems. This Dickinson, I believe, has not yet received her proper hearing in the annals of literary criticism. This too is an insistent, dramatic Dickinson, one whose philosophical denials and affirmations cry out to be understood as a shaping force in her poetic world. Thus, I would now like to resume the task of investigation by examining the symbolic assumptions that her poems, as a necessary first step, explicitly reject.

These assumptions cover widely divergent kinds of symbol usages, from the sacramental symbolism of church tradition, "rich in association and easily recognized," as C. M. Bowra puts it, and redolent with "august and splendid majesty," to the more private, mystical, and less easily categorized varieties, such as French Symbolism, which Bowra describes as an attempt "to convey a supernatural . . . beyond the senses."[1] What these and other general manifestations of symbolism have in common is the use of a bridging or synecdochic strategy to secure the universe of God or Beauty or Idea against what the symbolist imagines to be the ravages of dualism, skepticism, and scientism. In Dickinson's work, it is sacramental symbolism, resonating unquestioned with deep collective reassurances, that often emerges as the object of her probing, but not necessarily heretical, inquiry.

Dickinson understood that sacramental symbolism had a near incarnation in her immediate religious ancestry, the American Puritans, and more subtly in the Transcendentalists, who represented nineteenth-century America's democratic equivalent of a visible church. Therefore, Dickinson surveyed sacramental symbolism with special interest. She sought to expose the fallacies of a symbolic system in which the

1. C. M. Bowra, *The Heritage of Symbolism* (London, 1943), 7 and 5.

material and the spiritual world were conflated, heaven and earth proclaimed mirrors of each other, and (most dangerous in Dickinson's view) nature mistaken as a transcript for Christian and/or personal history. I will explore the intricacies of Puritan and Transcendentalist symbolism later, in chapter five. Let it suffice for the moment to suggest that many Puritan and Transcendentalist writers could easily seem to share a fundamentally medieval view of symbolic correspondences. Like the early church (from which both groups felt themselves so absolutely different) they seemed to see the world as the book of nature, finding (in the words of one critic) "connections between things based not upon cause and effect but upon similitude" only.[2]

Superficial similitude, for Dickinson, is the deceiver; fortuitous correspondences, the enemy. In Dickinson's view, ever-ready systems of sacramental identity harbor dangerous temptations that can ultimately damage Christian faith. Malcolm Ross's description of sacramental symbolism is extremely useful here, not only because it spells out underlying points of faith that, Dickinson believed, were frequently subjected to dangerous misinterpretation, but because Ross's analysis accurately renders many of the troubling habits of mind that distinguish that symbolic usage.

The fixed star at the centre of the Christian firmament of symbol is the dogma of Incarnation. In this dogma, respecting as it does both the divinity of the Word and the humanity of the flesh, is contained the whole principle of the Christian aesthetic. Some of the implications of the dogma, for art as well as for life, are certainly these: Though the flesh is frail, and though nature herself has suffered the wound of sin, the Incarnation redeems the flesh and the world, laying nature and the reasonable faculty open once more to the operation of the supernatural. In other words, the Incarnation makes possible, indeed demands, the sacramental vision of reality.

Furthermore,

the dogma of the Incarnation is sacramental not only in its implications for the artist's concern with nature, with things, with existence, but also in its implications for the artist's concern with history, with time, with event. . . . for

2. Melissa C. Wanamaker, *Discordia Concors: The Wit of Metaphysical Poetry* (Port Washington, 1975), 20.

the Christian, the death and Resurrection of Christ is decidedly not a cosmic myth. It is a historical event, but one which absorbs, sacramentally, the cosmic into the historical order.[3]

As I shall try to show in chapter three, there are aspects of sacramentalism that Dickinson accepts. Indeed, there are elements that she prefers to the more purely ideal symbolism that often seems, in the literary tradition, to be its alternative. But for Dickinson the redemption of nature suggests not a collapsing of the natural into the divine, not their connatural eternity, but their infinitely unequal coexistence, divided by an infinite chasm. For Dickinson, as for the Puritans, Incarnation was a less central mystery than Resurrection, than the restoration of deity to deity, pure and uncompound. For a poet with Dickinson's urge for precision and hard, individuated meanings, the vortex of conceptions described by Ross—the continuous interpenetration of nature and supernature, the total absorption of incommensurate orders of being (cosmic, historical, personal, divine) in an undifferentiable, ineffable superorder—represented, not a usable aesthetic principle, but a collapse of meaning, a deadening circularity. In sacramentalism of this hazy sort she saw the abrogation of human inquiry into the real configurations and meanings of the cosmos. This inquiry, combined with the attempt to understand and act by the divinely ordered relationship of distinct existents, constitutes for Dickinson a large part of a true *imitatio Dei*. At the heart of Dickinson's poetry, therefore, is the belief that an unbridgeable gap divides the kingdom of God from the world of humankind. And one of her most persistent subjects is the danger that ensues when that gap is ignored or when the divinely ordered cosmos is reduced in the would-be bridgings and abridgments of symbols.

Dickinson's opposition to the sacramental interpretation of nature has many bases. Like Emerson, Dickinson bears a "child's love" to nature. And yet the antisacramental resonance of her verse is more, I think, than a simple attempt to preserve the "something in a Summer's day" that transcends religious "exstasy" and "grace" (No. 122) and

3. Malcolm Mackenzie Ross, *Poetry and Dogma: The Transfiguration of Eucharistic Symbols in Seventeenth-Century English Poetry* (New York, 1969), 9 and 11.

that in Emerson's view and Dickinson's alike can make such interpretations of nature an insult to humankind's fostering mother (Emerson himself, of course, is a symbolist). Nor are her suspicions about symbolic strategies just a response to what Clark Griffith calls the "philosophical uncertainties" of nature. The fact that "the world struck her as a place of mystery, ambiguity, and obscure horrors" need not have led her to question a dualistic or synecdochic position at all. Griffith himself demonstrates this for us when he concludes that "Dickinson agrees that natural processes are indeed deliberate," and deliberately symbolic: nature's "symbolic gestures . . . suggest that Nature is actively antagonist toward the individual." Words, to adapt a key formula in Emerson's *Nature*, can still be signs of natural facts, even when those facts no longer express an Emersonian optimism.[4]

Similarly, Dickinson's objection to certain aspects of symbol usage is also not purely a response to the inevitable subjectivity of our interpretation of natural objects and events, although this, too, is a factor that she takes into account. " 'Heaven' has different Signs—to me—," she confesses in one poem.

> Sometimes, I think that Noon
> Is but a symbol of the Place—
> And when again, at Dawn,
>
> A mightly look runs round the World
> And settles in the Hills—
> An Awe if it should be like that
> Upon the Ignorance steals— (No. 575)

The poet's "Sometimes" here is not only multiple and changing. It is also private, limited, and, for matters of the spirit, theologically inadequate. As she comments in another poem,

> "Morning"—means "Milking"—to the Farmer—
> Dawn—to the Teneriffe—
> Dice—to the Maid—
> Morning means just Risk—to the Lover—
> Just revelation—to the Beloved— (No. 300)

4. Ralph Waldo Emerson, *Nature*, in Brooks Atkinson (ed.), *Selected Writings of Ralph Waldo Emerson* (New York, 1950), 33; and Clark Griffith, *The Long Shadow: Emily Dickinson's Tragic Poetry* (Princeton, 1964), 25–26.

All people, Dickinson realizes, interpret nature differently, according to the special circumstances of their perceptions. In her own case, the "Robins," "Buttercups," and "Daisies" of Amherst compel her to see "New Englandly" (No. 285). With good reason, and to very good effect, much has been made of Dickinson's decidedly provincial, New England vision.[5]

But Dickinson has far more serious reasons than these for rejecting a conventional, Christian interpretation of nature. The poems I want to examine are explicitly theological, and her repeated denials of synecdochic transference derive, I believe, from Dickinson's overriding conviction that, however similar the patterns of nature and of theology may seem to be, there is no necessary correlation linking earthly manifestations and divine intentions, material phenomena and spiritual meanings. Perhaps, to adapt Griffith's formulation, the problem is not that nature makes symbolic gestures that are hostile, but that nature does not make symbolic gestures at all—or at least not what we ordinarily define as symbolic gestures.[6] To interpret nature, therefore, as a version of heaven, or vice versa, or to see both nature and heaven as types of a third, even more highly abstract sphere might actually be to distort, perhaps even destroy, the validity of each. Dickinson simply does not believe that we can assume what many symbolic philosophers and Christian exegetes often insist that we must assume—that the phenomenal world is an "expression" of the noumenal, and that it can therefore "be taken to represent or stand as a symbol for it."[7] "Is Heaven a Place—a Sky—a Tree?" she asks in one poem, and she concludes, "Location's narrow way is for Ourselves— / Unto the Dead / There's no Geography—" (No. 489). Nature, Dickinson is suggesting, is not a transcript of divine realities. To perceive it as if it were, to infer "State" and "Endowal" and "Focus" from "Geography" (No. 489), is not only to misrepresent heaven but to jeopardize the entire terrain of faith. Faith is "larger than the Hills" and tran-

5. See, for example, George Frisbie Whicher, *This Was a Poet: A Critical Biography of Emily Dickinson* (Ann Arbor, 1957).
6. Cf. William Sherwood, *Circumference and Circumstance: Stages in the Mind and Art of Emily Dickinson* (New York, 1968), 27.
7. Wilbur Urban, *Language and Reality: The Philosophy of Language and the Principles of Symbolism* (London, 1951), 1.

scends them in time (No. 766). It cannot, therefore, be located in a
domain of natural evidences. When "sense" is "obscured," as it must
be in matters of belief, then, Dickinson stipulates, "I better see—
/ Through Faith—":

> my Hazel Eye
> Has periods of shutting—
> But, No lid has Memory— (No. 939)

This is not to deny that Dickinson is quite capable of using traditional symbols, traditionally sacramental symbols, in some of her
poems. Indeed, as I have already suggested, and as I shall treat further in the next chapter, Dickinson may actually have preferred some
of the strategies of sacramentalism, whatever its dangers, to the much
more hazardous presuppositions of idealism. Such poems as "Tie the
Strings of my Life, My Lord, / Then, I am ready to go!" (No. 279) and

> The Black Berry—wears a Thorn in his side—
> But no Man heard Him cry—
> He offers His Berry, just the same
> To Partridge—and to Boy— (No. 554)

might well have been penned by an Edward Taylor or a Donne or a
Vaughan. And these poems are not unique instances of Dickinson's
sacramentalism. They express an enthusiasm for natural-theological
relationships, an optimism in the first poem and an acceptance in the
second, that are by no means uncommon in the Dickinson canon.

But in a large number of those poems that seem initially to affirm
the basic equations of sacramentalism, the poet does not refrain either
from raising serious questions about her sacramentalist assumptions
or from severely qualifying them. Thus, in a poem like "So has a Daisy
vanished," the poet devotes seven lines to establishing a sacramental
relationship among the daisy, sunset, paradise, and resurrection, only
to conclude the poem with a question that is more than mildly un-
settling.

> So has a Daisy vanished
> From the fields today—
> So tiptoed many a slipper
> To Paradise away—

> Oozed so in crimson bubbles
> Day's departing tide—
> Blooming—tripping—flowing—
> Are ye then with God? (No. 28)

A similar pattern is traced for us in "Exultation is the going / Of an inland soul to sea"; in "What Inn is this?" the poet reverses her procedure and presents her sacramentalism as a series of questions that simultaneously describes and probes conventional sacramental relationships.

> Exultation is the going
> Of an inland soul to sea,
> Past the houses—past the headlands—
> Into deep Eternity—
>
> Bred as we, among the mountains,
> Can the sailor understand
> The divine intoxication
> Of the first league out from land? (No. 76)
>
> What Inn is this
> Where for the night
> Peculiar Traveller comes?
> Who is the Landlord?
> Where the maids?
> Behold, what curious rooms!
> No ruddy fires on the hearth—
> No brimming Tankards flow—
> Necromancer! Landlord!
> Who are these below? (No. 115)

"What Inn is this?" makes no secret of the difficulties that perplex the sacramental interpreter of the universe. Not only does the analogy developed between inns and heaven not yield any valuable information about heaven but, by the end of the poem, it has managed to cast into some considerable confusion the more ordinary and explicable inns "below." "So has a Daisy vanished" and "Exultation is the going" are even more complicated. The sacramental relationships they delineate seem unequivocal: "Exultation *is* the going / Of an inland soul to sea," the speaker insists; "So has a Daisy vanished . . . So tiptoed many a slipper / To Paradise away," she analogizes. But the sacramental identities established in these poems create more problems than they solve. The departures of natural phenomena like daisies and suns may, the poem assures us, put us in mind of death, but they do not finally prove to us whether or not God exists. In fact, they may actually raise serious doubts about the existence of God that might not have vexed us had the speaker not been pursuing sacramental formulae. Similarly, exultation, setting sail, and dying into resurrection may all seem aspects of an integrated cosmic experience, and each may seem capable of illuminating the others. But discovering the common denominator that relates one to the other may not be so simple. And even if such a common denominator could be located, it might contribute nothing at all to our understanding of things about which we do not yet have firm knowledge: Can the sailor, bred among the mountains, in any way understand the divine intoxication of the first league out from land? In these poems, as in others, Dickinson is suggesting that sacramental symbolism may not tell us anything more than we already know. And it may actually distract us with doubts that might otherwise not have arisen.

Sacramental symbolism, it would seem, depends upon a string of conditionals (*ifs* and *whens* abound in her sacramental poems) that are in and of themselves too tentative and frail to carry the burden of faith. The truth may simply be that faith alone is what ultimately assures us of heaven and that all other evidences, though convenient or apparently congenial, are therefore unnecessary. "When I count the seeds," Dickinson explains,

> That are sown beneath,
> To bloom so, bye and bye—
> When I con the people
> Lain so low,
> To be received as high—
> When I believe the garden
> Mortal shall not see—
> Pick by faith it's blossom
> And avoid it's Bee,
> I can spare this summer, unreluctantly. (No. 40)

The speaker's statement that she can "spare this summer, unreluc-
tantly" follows directly from her declaration of belief and faith. Count-
ing and cunning may be helpful. They are antecedents of earthly
renunciation. But without belief and faith they are veritably useless.
Similarly, in "As Watchers hang upon the East" (No. 121) the sacramental connections delineated in the poem are devoid of meaning *unless* the speaker believes, a priori, in the heaven that she is attempting
to describe in naturalistic terms: "Heaven" is "to us" as the many objects the poem records, only "if" it is "true." Furthermore, by ending
the poem with an ominous "if true" Dickinson is more than subtly
suggesting that the very process of seeking sacramental unities may
leave us with a painfully conditional and tentative faith.

In many of the poems, then, in which Dickinson seems to be celebrating nature's sacramental symbolism, she is in fact questioning and
qualifying our sacramentalist assumptions. And in some poems she is
actually intimating that the sacramental-symbolic view of nature may
damage faith rather than confirm or describe it. This, I think, is significantly the case with "These are the days when Birds come back—"
in which Dickinson explicitly treats what she here announces is the
"fraud" of sacramental symbolism, a fraud, she tells us in the poem,
that can "cheat" the perceiver into seeing the natural universe as a
symbol of Christian redemption and that can thereby distract the individual from true faith.

> These are the days when Birds come back—
> A very few—a Bird or two—
> To take a backward look.
>
> These are the days when skies resume
> The old—old sophistries of June—
> A blue and gold mistake.
>
> Oh fraud that cannot cheat the Bee—
> Almost thy plausibility
> Induces my belief.
>
> Till ranks of seeds their witness bear—
> And softly thro' the altered air
> Hurries a timid leaf.

> Oh Sacrament of summer days,
> Oh Last Communion in the Haze—
> Permit a child to join.
>
> Thy sacred emblems to partake—
> Thy consecrated bread to take
> And thine immortal wine! (No. 130)

Both the poem's narrative action and its cast of characters are, without a doubt, significantly suggestive of a symbolic world view: the "Bird" whose "backward look" "induces" the poet's "belief"; the "Bee" who will not be cheated; the "ranks of seeds" that bear "witness" to the coming of the "leaf"; and the "timid leaf" itself, which "hurries" "thro' the altered air"—these are the players that enact the poem's evocative drama. And as the poem draws to a close, we are told in what are presumably the forthright exclamations of the poet that nature is a volume of "sacred emblems," a "Sacrament" and a "Communion" unto itself. It is tempting, therefore, to interpret the poem, as many critics have done, as a record of the speaker's ecstatic realization that nature is the ultimate scripture and that birds, bees, seeds, and leaves are the archetypical enactors of Christian pageant. Even if we hedge somewhat on this position and conclude, as one group of readers has done, that what the poem symbolizes is natural and theological ambiguity, the poem, it would seem, is still the assertion of a clearly interpretable symbolic relationship between nature and Christianity.[8]

But it seems to me that the burden of Dickinson's poem is not to confirm the ordinary symbolic dimensions that it at first constructs, but to call them into serious question. For what Dickinson's symbols describe, what she emphasizes that they describe, is not the harmonious interrelation between nature and supernature or the multi-

8. For symbolic interpretations of Dickinson's nature poems, see Ruth Miller, *The Poetry of Emily Dickinson* (Middletown, Conn., 1968), 78ff.; Robert L. Berner, "Dickinson's 'These are the days when Birds come back,'" *Explicator*, XXX (1972), item 78; and Rev. Alfred Barrett, SJ, in Sister Mary James Power, SSND, *In the Name of the Bee: The Significance of Emily Dickinson* (New York, 1943), x–xi. See also Griffith, *The Long Shadow*, 25–26 and 84–93; Sherwood, *Circumference and Circumstance*, 31; and Inder Nath Kher, *The Landscape of Absence: Emily Dickinson's Poetry* (New Haven, 1974), 114–15.

dimensional ambiguity represented by both of them, but rather the "fraud" of a certain tendency of mind that would induce the perceiver to look for images of Christian resurrection within the natural world.[9] "These are the days when Birds come back," Dickinson's poetic persona begins. Birds, the speaker declares; not people or souls, but literal birds, and not even many of those. And, yet, even as the speaker of the poem is drawing implicit distinctions between birds and people, she finds herself compelled also to return and take her own "backward look," a look that Dickinson intends us to see is literal and reductive. The speaker, we realize, ignores a fact that she herself has articulated, that Indian summer is unquestionably a "blue and gold mistake." She indulges in a prayerful celebration of autumn's spring-like, Christianized significance: "Oh Sacrament of summer days," she cries, "Oh Last Communion in the Haze— / Permit a child to join." To confound matters more, the "old—old sophistries of June" of which the speaker is so enamored and which autumn seems to represent, are themselves, as the syntax suggests, a "blue and gold mistake." The specious, deceptive sophistries of June falsely promise birth from death and heavenly ("blue and gold") renewal. But the speaker herself believes the blinding sophistries, and she consequently glosses natural events as if they were indeed notes on a scriptural page.[10]

The "fraud" either of a physical Indian summer that augurs death even though it appears to avow life or of the doctrinal sophistries of a Christianized spring cannot, we are told, "cheat the bee." Nature's most primal creatures cannot be misled by the complexities of intellection and spiritual need; and because they do not see through false analogical conflations, they do not presume that autumn is spring or spring a sophistic emblem of Christian renewal. Like the unconscious "Stone" of another Dickinson poem, which "rambles in the Road alone" and cares nothing about "careers" and "Exigencies" (No. 1510), the Bee simply *bees*. He fulfills, like his stoney counterpart, the "absolute Decree" of self-existence, and he is not tempted, as is the poet, to

9. Cf. Charles R. Anderson, *Emily Dickinson's Poetry: Stairway of Surprise* (New York, 1960), 146.

10. A sophistry, of course, is a type of "specious," "falacious reasoning"; the "employment of arguments which are intentionally deceptive" (*OED*). Cf. Berner, "Dickinson's 'These are the days.'"

try and formulate a philosophy of symbolic interdependencies in
what for all practical purposes is a natural world.

But the archetypical, antique "sophistries of June," the "blue and
gold mistake," that issue with June and that are carried over in people's
minds to the actual twilight of autumn, almost do cheat the speaker of
the poem. "Almost thy plausibility," she confesses, "Induces my belief"—her belief not only in the autumn=spring analogy, but in the
nature=Christianity and death=birth equivalences as well. The per-
sonated lines of the poem create a momentum in which the symbolic
imagination, acting directly upon the natural world, begins to transform that world into a scriptural allegory, the fraud distorting the
speaker's perceptions until the entire physical creation is rendered
sacramentally symbolic, a "Sacrament of summer days." In the stanzas
of the poem that follow the transitional "Till," "belief" and the language of sacramental symbolism transfigure nature into an incarnation of biblical pageant. The "ranks of seeds" undergoing their regular autumnal dispersion become, for this symbolizing Christian, lists
of angels or legions of saints, bearing "witness" in the altar-like and
Christianly "altered" air, to the hurried coming of the "timid leaf"
that represents Christ or the Christian soul, perhaps even the poet
herself. Summer days become a "Sacrament," and autumn (the "Haze")
is converted into a "Last Communion." The entire creation is meta-
morphosed into the "sacred emblems" of the transubstantiation, the
"bread" and "wine" that, in a Christianized nature, would represent
the fruitions of both the earthly and the heavenly harvest, the body
and the soul of the universe and of the redeemer.

But the ecstatic revelation with which the poem concludes is not, I
think, meant to image an analogy between nature and spirit. Rather, it
suggests the fraudulence and deceptiveness of such an analogical perception. The negative connotations of the phrases "backward look"
and "old—old sophistries," the inferences throughout the poem of
"mistake," "fraud," and "cheat," and the highly questionable "plausibility" of the entire enterprise suggest that the transfiguration of
natural cycle into scriptural testimony is a distortion and a misperception of the physical world. "These are the days" of autumn, not June,
of the ends of things and not of new beginnings. And if one wants to

indulge one's sacramental, exegetical imagination, the ranks of seeds might just as well be interpreted as ranks of apostates bearing witness against Christ, who hurries softly and timidly to his crucifixion upon the altar of a false vision. Like her Puritan forebears, Dickinson is suspicious of interpretation, although, as I shall try to demonstrate, in interpreting much Puritan theology as sacramentalism, she will turn the Puritans' own logic against them. The sacrament and communion of her poem, therefore, are not events of an ongoing covenant of life, but rather the last rites of death. And the speaker of the poem, who is by her own admission a child, is, we feel, too young to suffer such rites. Yet she is compelled by the false analogy between life and death, June and Indian summer, to embrace death, to quest after it, and, therefore, to receive her "Last Communion in the Haze" of misperception and mistaken "belief." Because she allows the autumn to cheat her of the spring, she is consumed upon the altar of an altered and falsely spiritualized natural world. Dickinson partakes of the bread and wine of nature's autumn, not God's, and nature's autumn signifies expiration, not inception. She hurries like a "timid leaf" onward to a death whose finality is not ameliorated by Christian faith, for her Sacrament and her Communion occur only within the literal haze of an ambiguous, unredeemed and unredeeming, natural world.

Let me emphasize, before I go on, that the target of Dickinson's criticism in "These are the days" is not merely what some people might label simplistic allegory, a stilted fantasy that is meant to stand for more fully complicated, theologically rich truths or that can be seen as interpreting nature as if nature itself were simplistic and not richly complex. In "These are the days" Dickinson is dealing with the symbolic imagination itself, although she is also commenting on the problems of allegory and the relationship between allegory and symbol. "Allegory," explains Charles Feidelson, is "safe" because it depends "on a conventional order whose point of argument [is] easily defined" and that "imposes the pat moral and the simplified character." This is precisely the literary pattern that Warren and Wellek, in their discussion of symbolism, claim is often misunderstood by the naive reader to be "mere symbolism."

There is a kind of mind which speaks of "mere symbolism": either reducing religion and poetry to sensuous images ritualistically arranged or evacuating the present "signs" or "images" on behalf of the transcendental realities, moral or philosophical, which lie beyond them. Another kind of mind thinks of symbolism as calculated and willed, a deliberate mental translation of concepts into illustrative, pedagogic, sensuous terms.

Symbolism, claim Warren and Wellek, is a phenomenon far more complex, and they quote in defense of symbolism the passage from Coleridge that we have already cited: while allegory, Coleridge explains, is "a translating of abstract notions into a picture language, which is itself nothing but an abstraction from objects of the senses," a symbol "is characterized by a translucence of the special . . . in the individual or of the general . . . in the special . . . above all, by the translucence of the eternal through and in the temporal." Symbolism and allegory could not be further apart, according to Coleridge, and the special significance of symbolism derives from precisely the way in which it is presumed to keep allegorical reduction at bay.[11]

For Dickinson, however, allegory and symbolism (sacramental symbolism, that is) did not always represent two distinct alternatives, the one characterized by moral patness and simplicity, the other distinguished by a translucent complexity and validity. Rather, the supposed fact of the "translucence of the eternal through and in the temporal" too often effects a collapse in the symbolic representation that ipso facto reduces symbolism to allegory and locates meaning in the thus flattened, transparent plane of intended analogies and correspondences. In other words, the process of symbolic reductiveness can all too easily evolve, in Dickinson's view, into the lifelessness and woodenness that Coleridge would call allegory. As I shall discuss a few chapters hence, for Dickinson nature does have a symbolic aspect. It does enact meaningful, symbolically encoded dramas, and a poem like "These are the days" registers a wealth of complex symbolic meanings that must be examined. But in Dickinson's poems nature's meanings can only emerge when the tendency toward allegorical flattening

11. Charles Feidelson, Jr., *Symbolism and American Literature* (Chicago, 1953), 16; and René Wellek and Austin Warren, *Theory of Literature* (New York, 1956), 189.

and the temptations of translucence and synecdoche are resisted, when the motivating idea behind the dramatic action of the phenomenal world is seen to be pulling away from conflation and unity and toward disparity and discreteness.

Again and again Dickinson's poems revisit the siren lure of allegorical compacting, of symbolic conflation. The seasonal cycles and the cluster of natural occurrences, for example, that are traditionally seen as paralleling divine events, are, Dickinson warns, not only false but fraught with danger. In some of her poems the poet wishes that the parallels between nature and Christian theology were indeed true, as in the following poem in which she weeps for a plausibility that is painfully absent.

> Like Some Old fashioned Miracle
> When Summertime is done—
> Seems Summer's Recollection
> And the Affairs of June
> . . . .
> Her Bees have a fictitious Hum—
> Her Blossoms, like a Dream—
> Elate us—till we almost weep—
> So plausible—they seem— (No. 302)

In other poems Dickinson strikes a more humorous pose, in which the sacramental meanings are unstated and whimsical.

> From Cocoon forth a Butterfly
> As Lady from her Door
> Emerged—a Summer Afternoon—
> Repairing Everywhere—
> . . . .
> Till Sundown crept—a steady Tide—
> And Men that made the Hay—
> And Afternoon—and Butterfly—
> Extinguished—in the Sea— (No. 354)

We would like to think, Dickinson is suggesting, that nature sympathizes with humankind; that its likeness to "Some Old fashioned Miracle" and "infinite Tradition" (No. 302) has some purpose, that purpose being to embody the eternality of sensation that we imagine is immortality. But though nature's "Drums," Dickinson tells us, may seem to hail the "Queen of Calvary," they really are "unthinking" after all. Nature is oblivious to its transcendent communications, and thus, although we can force our imaginations to see in nature the unfolding of divine events, nature's nonchalance and inattention may reduce the most magnificent features of Christian promise to mundane trivialities (cf. "A Lady red—amid the Hill / Her annual secret keeps!"— No. 74). The illusion that nature participates in human affairs or the divine aspect of human affairs is only that—an illusion. As Dickinson puts it in poem No. 364, nature simply does not "care" about the tragedy of "Wo" that affects human life. The nature that can sear her own saplings unperturbed certainly cannot be bothered by purely human despair (cf. "Nature—sometimes sears a Sapling—" No. 314), and though Dickinson may even, on occasion, take comfort from this fact (cf. "If I should die," No. 54 and "Of Bronze—and Blaze—" No. 290), it does suggest to her that nature and the objects of faith constitute two separate, noninterpenetrating entities that must not be confused.

To see the natural world in sacramental-Christian terms, therefore, may be to cast some highly unpleasant aspersions upon Christianity itself. Like "These are the days," "A Bird came down the Walk" might seem to some readers a conventional symbolic account of Christian encounter within the world of nature, and the poem has been interpreted sacramentally by more than one critic. But the symbolic correspondences of the poem, which are imposed upon the physical universe by the poem's sacramental symbolizer, do not at all point to a convenient connection between natural events and divine realities, the "relation" of one thing to another as one critic has specifically claimed exists in this poem.[12] Rather, they signal to the reader the dangerous distortion of both natural and theological truths that can and often does occur when biological happenstance is promulgated as divine gospel.

---

12. Elinor Wilner, "The Poetics of Emily Dickinson," *ELH*, XXXVIII (1971), 146–48; cf. Anderson, *Stairway of Surprise*, 118–19.

A Bird came down the Walk—
He did not know I saw—
He bit an Angleworm in halves
And ate the fellow, raw,

And then he drank a Dew
From a convenient Grass—
And then hopped sidewise to the Wall
To let a Beetle pass—

He glanced with rapid eyes
That hurried all around—
They looked like frightened Beads, I thought—
He stirred his Velvet Head

Like one in danger, Cautious,
I offered him a Crumb
And he unrolled his feathers
And rowed him softer home—

Than Oars divide the Ocean,
Too silver for a seam—
Or Butterflies, off Banks of Noon
Leap, plashless as they swim. (No. 328)

The bird's attack upon a particle of nature can be read, easily enough, as a realistic if somewhat unsentimental account of some of the less cheery aspects of life in the natural world. But the protagonist's "thought" at the end of stanza three that the bird's eyes look like "frightened Beads," and her subsequent proffering of the crumb of Christian charity in stanza four, force us to search for some other, Christianly-informed meaning in the poem, a meaning, which it turns out, is not a confirmation but a critique of the Christian interpretation of events that the poem's persona is applying to the natural order. When we follow the poem's lead and apply the sacramental conventions of Christian symbolism to the events of the poem, a ghastly, reductive allegory unfolds. The bird, with his eyes like rosary beads and his "Velvet Head" like a priestly surplice, becomes, as birds often do in one kind of Christian symbolism, a type of Christian soul, perhaps even Christ himself. The bird's eating of the "Angleworm," therefore, and his drinking of the dew, become naturalistic versions of the communicant's communion experience (the bird even hops aside to let a beetle, i.e., beadle?, pass).[13] But worship in this natural sanctuary expresses anything but a Christian ecstasy in worship, either natural or divine. For the implications of the priestly bird's communion in the grass are "raw," carnal, and cannibalistic in the extreme. The body being devoured in this celebration is not a symbolic wafer but rather the literal body of a "fellow" creature; the body is not a savior's but a worm's, a serpent's if you will, and the Christian mass becomes a satanic celebration with damnation rather than salvation as its pivotal event.

It is important to remember that, if we consider the bird's behavior from a non-Christian perspective, it is, throughout the poem, totally natural and proper. The bird's actions become terrifying and grotesque, therefore, when the speaker forgets to maintain the necessary distinction between the unredeemed souls and therefore unredeemed activities of birds and the saved souls and consequently Christian behavior of saints. It is only when she begins in line 11 to *think* of the bird in terms of covenant theology that the nature symbolism begins to imply horrifying things about the experiences of grace and communion. Christian ritual, we begin to realize, belongs within a Christian framework and cannot be transferred to a natural one.

This crisis of symbolic misinterpretation draws to a climax in stanza four when the poem's persona begins to treat the bird as if he were indeed a member of the community of saints: "He stirred his Velvet Head / Like one in danger," the narrator tells us. "In danger" of what? we ask. The narrator seems to act as if the bird, because he is, from her point of view, heathenistically cannibalizing one of his fellow creatures, is literally in danger of losing his immortal soul. And so, "Cautious," she "offer[s] him a Crumb." In other words she tries, almost literally, to subscribe the bird in the lists of the elect by offering him the crumb of Christian charity and trying to induce him to eat the symbolic wafer instead of the literal body.

Of course, it is the mere physical presence of the narrator herself that, in a purely natural sense, puts the bird in any danger at all. But by converting the bird into a type of the Christian, the protagonist of

13. Wilner notes this pun, "The Poetics of Emily Dickinson," 148.

this poem seems to endanger the bird in another more serious way as well. By forcing upon the bird's world a Christian interpretation, she compels herself to damn the bird for the very mechanisms of his survival. Therefore, when the bird takes flight, it is not simply because he is a wild creature unaccustomed to human hands offering crumbs, but also, on another level of meaning, because he is being made by the poet to reject the meaningless and, for him, dangerously self-destructive symbolic framework that the narrator is attempting to impose upon his world.

In the final analysis it is not really the bird who is endangered by the narrator's Christian allegorizing of nature. The transition between stanzas three and four is purposefully vague, suggesting that it is the narrator who is really in danger: "Like one in danger, Cautious, / I offered him a Crumb," she says.[14] Of course the narrator is not literally threatened by the bird. Her symbolic interpretation of nature, however, endangers the whole of her religious faith. It puts into doubt the meaning and validity of the communion experience that she believes so basic to salvation and that she hopes her experience in nature will confirm. But communion, as it is seen acted out in the natural world, is more like cannibalism than transubstantiation; a literal devouring of a savior who is more like a worm or a satanic serpent than a deity because he seems to demand such cannibalism in the first place. As Dickinson's Puritan forefathers always understood, the very opposite of redemption is the unregenerate soul going through the form of Christian ceremony.

When the bird refuses the narrator's crumb and "rows him softer home" into the unmarred beauty of the literal skies, he is being made to refuse not only the bit of bread the narrator is offering him but the whole sacramental-symbolic enterprise with which she is investing her faith. From the speaker's perspective the bird's departure can only mean that she has been abandoned by her Christ (who is one of the several things that the bird can be said to represent) and by the whole

14. The lack of punctuation after stanza three has the effect of causing the phrase "Like one in danger" to apply equally to the speaker and to the bird. This effect is even more evident in the variant version of the poem, in which there is a dash-designated break after the line "He stirred his Velvet Head."

doctrine that prompts her to offer the crumb to begin with. The bird's refusal to accept the crumb of Christian symbolism and his disappearance into the softer, seamless home of the asymbolic earthly skies declares a gulf between the narrator and her faith that is absolute and eternal.

In Dickinson's view it is folly to imagine that humanly isolated symbols can substitute for the expansiveness of divine truth, whether those symbols are simply fanciful fictions easily dismissed or natural phenomena (like autumn) seemingly more worthy of symbolic interpretation. In "Make me a picture of the sun—," for example, Dickinson laughs away the make-believe that elsewhere has such dire consequences for her.

> Make me a picture of the sun—
> So I can hang it in my room—
> And make believe I'm getting warm
> When others call it "Day"!
>
> Draw me a Robin—on a stem—
> So I am hearing him, I'll dream,
> And when the Orchards stop their tune—
> Put my pretense—away—
>
> Say if it's really—warm at noon—
> Whether it's Buttercups—that "skim"—
> Or Butterflies—that "bloom"?
> Then—skip—the frost—upon the lea—
> And skip the Russet—on the tree—
> Let's play those—never come! (No. 188)

The poem is playful. It pretends the frost and russet will never come. But, of course, the "frost—upon the lea—" will eventually intrude, and the game, viewed from a slightly different angle, can have serious implications.

Similarly, in "The Gentian weaves her fringes—" (No. 18) Dickinson toys with the theme of autumn as an emblem of the coming resurrection, and she enjoys the analogies and parallelisms from which she recoils in "These are the days." But the poem is whimsical in a way that purposefully precludes our taking its promises as gospel. The cyclical continuities and apparent rebirths of the natural world, Dickinson wants us to understand, are incomplete and not supernal. Therefore, to commit the error of mistaking nature for a counterpart of the self or an incarnation of the divine may be to replace the redemptive promises of Christian faith with the flimsy departures and ubiquitous dissolutions of a natural world that is governed not by the complexly trinitarian God but by a far lesser trinity of minuscule insubstantialities: a bee, a butterfly, and a breeze, which however appealing in moments of whimsy are, Dickinson assures us in her more serious poems, destined to bestow only a "Communion in the Haze."

Because nature, in Dickinson's view, is frail and eminently perishable (however beautiful!), to mistake natural events for embodiments of divine realities is ultimately to diminish the facts of faith and to debilitate the very premises of belief. Nature and God, she argues, must not be confused.[15] But because earth is not heaven does not mean that earth must be disparaged and cast aside. Dickinson's deep emotional and intellectual attachment to nature, which she expresses again and again in her poems and letters, cannot be doubted. Nature, she believes, sustains us in our mortal existences. It surrounds us with beauty and joy.

Even more importantly, nature, in Dickinson's view, does have a unique and vital role to play in our mental apprehension of divine eternity. How nature plays this role, how God has defined its uses as an instrument in His divine pedagogy, remains to be seen in a later chapter. Nature, I will suggest, derives and draws strength from the very frailty that the sacramental symbolizer often ignores. For the moment, however, it is important to understand that when we deny nature its inherent naturalness (which includes its affecting perishability), we ironically deprive it of its rightful place in the process of confirming faith. When we strip nature of what Dickinson calls its "sorcery" of "Snow," when we convert it into an "Axiom" of one-to-one correspondences ("The Skies cant keep their secret!"— No. 191), we distort nature's true meaning, and in our misconceived violation of nature, we subvert these very same theological objectives that the proper perception of nature could help to achieve.

15. Cf. John Timmerman, "God and the Image of God in J. 609: A Brief Analysis," *Emily Dickinson Bulletin*, XXVIII (1975), 125.

Thus, although a poem like "I tend my flowers for thee" would seem to be the kind of ecstatic celebration we usually associate with one recognizable Dickinsonian mood, the poem is, I believe, a near relative of the poems we have just been examining in this chapter. Like "These are the days" and "A Bird came down the Walk," it records the consequences of the otherworldly perception of nature and of a symbolism that is facile and empty.

> I tend my flowers for thee—
> Bright Absentee!
> My Fuschzia's Coral Seams
> Rip—while the Sower—dreams—
>
> Geraniums—tint—and spot—
> Low Daisies—dot—
> My Cactus—splits her Beard
> To show her throat—
>
> Carnations—tip their spice—
> And Bees—pick up—
> A Hyacinth—I hid—
> Puts out a Ruffled Head—
> And odors fall
> From flasks—so small—
> You marvel how they held—
>
> Globe Roses—break their satin flake—
> Upon my Garden floor—
> Yet—thou—not there—
> I had as lief they bore
> No Crimson—more—
>
> Thy flower—be gay—
> Her Lord—away!
> It ill becometh me—
> I'll dwell in Calyx—Gray—
> How modestly—alway—
> Thy Daisy—
> Draped for thee! (No. 339)

In favoring the transcendental "Bright Absentee" God (or lover) over the flowers of the natural world, the ardent symbolizer of this poem allows her physical garden to crucify itself in a bloody "Crimson" death. The poem's halting rhythms, its short sentences and dashes, and the uncertain rhyme scheme (the breakdown of the *aa – bb* pattern of stanzas one and two in the later stanzas of the poem) reinforce the picture that Dickinson is painting of a world tearing and splitting and breaking apart: the coral seams rip; the geraniums tint and spot; the cactus splits her beard to show her vulnerable throat; the globe roses break their delicate flakes upon the ground. Significantly, all of this floral genocide occurs "while the Sower—dreams," while, in other words, the tender of this earthly garden reflects upon abstractions and ultimate realities that not only do not have any necessary connection to the natural world but that, when they are preferred to nature, become its enemies and subverters.

The gardener is so enraptured by an idea, that she can no longer perform her earthly duties. In converting her flowers into symbols of an idealized "thee" (whether "thee" is a lover or God Himself), she betrays their earthliness. Judas-like, she delivers them to their deaths. So totally does the gardener subscribe to the transcendental theory of nature that were it not for the concept of the "Bright Absentee" beyond nature, she would rather that the phenomenal universe perish altogether: "Yet—thou—not there— / I had as lief they bore / No Crimson—more," she says of her roses.

But the most devastating consequence of the dreamer's disregard for nature's physical well-being, of her desire to see nature as a mere emblem and shadow of a realm beyond nature, is that her symbolic interpretation of the flowers virtually destroys the gardener along with the garden. She herself realizes that "it ill becometh" her, who is also a "flower" in this symbolic display of the universe, to be any more gay or any more alive than the other flowers who are dashing out their lives on the landscape. Using an inverted version of the chrysalis image, the speaker, because of her synecdochic, symbolic assumptions, concludes that she must dwell in a calyx eternally gray. She must, in other words, exist in a perpetual condition of embryonic underdevelopment that promises not a green unfolding into life, as a calyx usually does, but a gray sterility tantamount to death itself. There is no consummation in this poem. The gardener-daisy is "Draped" "modestly—alway" in virginal, shroud-like unfulfillment, waiting for a "thee" who is eternally absent and unreachable.

"I tend my flowers for thee" suggests that to attempt to transcend what is mortal and earthly may be to embark upon a course that is not only destructive of nature but is spiritually suicidal as well. Clearly, Dickinson resists this impulse in some of her poems, as in the following tongue-in-cheek treatment of much the same problem represented in "I tend my flowers for thee."

> I had some things that I called mine—
> And God, that he called his,
> Till, recently a rival Claim
> Disturbed these amities.
>
> . . . .
> I'll institute an "Action"—
> I'll vindicate the law—
> Jove! Choose your counsel—
> I retain "Shaw"! (No. 116)

But in other poems she yields to the "rival Claim" and sees nature as an emanation of God's creating hand.

> Nobody knows this little Rose—
> It might a pilgrim be
> Did I not take it from the ways
> And lift it up to thee.
> Only a Bee will miss it—
> Only a Butterfly,
> Hastening from far journey—
> On it's breast to lie—
> Only a Bird will wonder—
> Only a Breeze will sigh—
> Ah Little Rose—how easy
> For such as thee to die! (No. 35)

It is not that humankind does not realize how wrong its tendency toward sacramental symbolism may be, or how devastating it can be to nature. Nobody, Dickinson admits, really "knows" or pretends to know what nature is or what it "might" mean in the cosmic scheme of things. But human beings nonetheless seem incapable of shaking loose from the grip of their analogizing imaginations. They must deny nature's intrinsic merit and thus launch their symbolizing attack. "It might a pilgrim be," the poet hypothesizes. The mere supposition that the rose "might" be a symbol, that like the other flowers it "might" point beyond nature to supernature, compels the narrator in this poem to develop a view of the rose that, like the gardener's attitude to the whole wealth of floral creation in the other poem, is deadly not only to the rose, which is literally plucked out of the real world and therefore killed, but to the narrator's cosmic faith as well. For when the speaker of the poem takes the rose out of its natural environment in order to offer it up to God, as her conflating idealist assumptions insist that she must, she inadvertently proves to herself that pilgrimage to God is nothing more special, nothing more redeeming than the meaningless death of an insignificant flower that is pulled out of its natural habitat by a cruel and imperious hand, whether man's hand or God's. The narrator's misguided symbolic view makes it "easy" for her to kill the rose, just as it is easy for the angels of another poem to destroy the flowers that clearly belong to a different realm and cannot survive in the angels' rarefied atmosphere.

> Angels, in the early morning
> May be seen the Dews among,
> Stooping—plucking—smiling—flying—
> Do the Buds to them belong?
>
> Angels, when the sun is hottest
> May be seen the sands among,
> Stooping—plucking—sighing—flying—
> Parched the flowers they bear along. (No. 94)

Precisely because it is so easy for the narrator and the angels to manage their depredations upon nature, faith is put into jeopardy. Just as the angels who drag their parched flowers out of the natural world, into the sphere beyond, are no longer "smiling" by the end of the poem (they are "sighing" instead), so the narrator who plucks the rose is also sighing, sighing, I would argue, not only for the rose, but for herself as well. "Ah Little Rose," she says, "how easy / For such as thee to die": God, she would like to imply, would not so easily dispense with a human being. But the positing of analogical relationships makes the narrator of the poem more like the rose than it is comfortable for her to be. She is also "such as thee," and the question that the poem is asking is what if the implications of existence for the creatures are also the implications of existence for humankind? Dickinson makes this query in "It did not surprise me—" (No. 39), where she tells the story of a departed "Birdling" and then asks,

> What and if it be
> One within my bosom
> Had departed me?
>
> This was but a story—
> What and if indeed
> There were just such coffin
> In the heart instead?

"If" the dying "birdling" is an image of the Christian soul, "if" the rose is an image of the Christian pilgrim, "if" the "story" is true, then can we respond passionlessly to a death that symbolizes our own deaths? Can we accept our own perishing in easy insignificance, or the perishing of the "One within my bosom," mourned only by an also perishing trinity of bee, butterfly, and breeze? It is "easy" for the individual to imagine himself or herself as a "rose," as Dickinson herself does on at least one occasion (poem No. 19). It is quite another matter to make the rose or birdling or flower capable of carrying the burden of Christian faith.

Dickinson's attitude toward the sacramental symbolizing of nature reflects her belief in the existence of a divide between heaven and earth so great that heaven simply cannot be described in what are the "Common" images of our earthly reality. The attempt to characterize heaven in ordinary symbolic language, Dickinson argues, can only result in a disappointment and loss that are both proximate and ultimate.

> It would never be Common—more—I said—
> Difference—had begun—
> Many a bitterness—had been—
> But that old sort—was done—
>
> Or—if it sometime—showed—as 'twill—
> Upon the Downiest—Morn—
> Such bliss—had I—for all the years—
> 'Twould give an Easier—pain—

I'd so much joy—I told it—Red—
Upon my simple Cheek—
I felt it publish—in my Eye—
'Twas needless—any speak—

I walked—as wings—my body bore—
The feet—I former used—
Unnescessary—now to me—
As boots—would be—to Birds—

I put my pleasure all abroad—
I dealt a word of Gold
To every Creature—that I met—
And Dowered—all the World—

When—suddenly—my Riches shrank—
A Goblin—drank my Dew—
My Palaces—dropped tenantless—
Myself—was beggared—too—

I clutched at sounds—
I groped at shapes—
I touched the tops of Films—
I felt the Wilderness roll back
Along my Golden lines—

The Sackcloth—hangs upon a nail—
The Frock I used to wear—
But where my moment of Brocade—
My—drop—of India? (No. 430)

The speaker of the poem knows that it is "needless" to "speak," that words are just as "Unnescessary" as her "former" "feet" or even as encumbering "As boots—would be—to Birds—." And yet she cannot refrain from speaking: "I dealt a word of Gold / To every Creature— that I met—." The effect is that she loses everything that her new immaterial condition promises to bestow upon her. Her riches shrink, her palaces drop "tenantless," and she is eternally, irredeemably "beggared."

To clutch at the "sounds" and the "shapes" of the material world, to search within the immaterial realm of the hereafter for literal counterparts to the "Brocade" and "India" with which the mortal imagination fashions its vision of heaven, is finally an impoverishing and not an enriching experience. The simple fact of faith is that heaven is form-less and therefore cannot be projected in the "shapes" of a former physical experience that must simply "drop" away at the climactic moment.

> I think just how my shape will rise—
> When I shall be *"forgiven"*—
> Till Hair—and Eyes—and timid Head—
> Are *out of sight*—in Heaven—
>
> I think just how my lips will weigh—
> With shapeless—quivering—prayer—
> That you—*so late*—"*Consider*" me—
> The "*Sparrow*" of your Care—
>
> I mind me that of Anguish—sent—
> *Some* drifts were moved away—
> Before my simple bosom—broke—
> And why not *this*—if *they?*
>
> And so I con that thing—"*forgiven*"—
> Until—delirious—borne—
> By my long bright—and *longer—trust*—
> I *drop* my Heart—*unshriven!* (No. 237)

Death will not undertake to reform the images by which we know life. It will discard them. Divine forgiveness is not God's attempt to remake the individual, but His effort to unmake him. The poet, therefore, must come to understand that she will ascend to heaven only when she allows her heart to plummet to earth "unshriven," unforgiven and therefore untransformed.

Thus, Dickinson is suggesting in these and other poems that at the center of the problem of symbolic consciousness is a confusion between what cannot be imaged (and is therefore divine) and what is material and earthly and therefore is in no way reflective of the kingdom of God. And this mistaking of the symbolic sign for the transcendent referent occurs because the human imagination cannot curb its analogizing hunger. It cannot discipline its reckless desire to see heaven as a logical, continuous extension of earth, and earth as a transcript of heaven. Therefore, when another Dickinson persona asks with apparent innocence, "What would I give to see his face?" and when she answers with only a moment's hesitation, "I'd give—I'd give my life—of course—," she realizes almost immediately that "*that* is not enough."

> Stop just a minute—let me think!
> I'd give my biggest Bobolink!
> That makes *two*—*Him*—and *Life*!
> You know who "*June*" is—
> I'd give *her*—
> Roses a day from Zenzibar—
> And Lily tubes—like Wells—
> Bees—by the furlong—
> Straits of Blue
> Navies of Butterflies—sailed thro'—
> And dappled Cowslip Dells—
>
> Then I have "shares" in Primrose "Banks"—
> Daffodil Dowries—spicy "Stocks"—
> Dominions—broad as Dew—
> Bags of Doubloons—adventurous Bees
> Brought me—from firmamental seas—
> And Purple—from Peru—
>
> *Now*—have I bought it—
> "Shylock"? Say!
> Sign me the Bond!
> "I vow to pay
> To Her—who pledges *this*—
> *One hour*—of her Sovreign's face"!
> *Extatic* Contract!
> *Niggard* Grace!
> My *Kingdom's worth* of Bliss! (No. 247)

The poem delights in the comedy of the situation, and yet the sense of loss and the accompanying criticism of God are serious. Because the narrator has chosen to image the universe in terms of an enormous corporate entity in which the individual imagination trades "Stocks" and "shares" according to some fantastic "Contract" between the human and the divine, she can comprehend the relationship between life and death, earth and heaven, in only the most crassly materialistic terms, and she can accept these terms only by trying to convert the whole enterprise into a joke. The joke, however, turns out to be at her own expense. Her loss, in dying, therefore, seems by the logic of verbal cost-accounting immeasurable, and the humor with which the poem begins sours by the end. "Grace" in purely quantitative terms has become only the most niggardly recompense of "her Sovereign's face," while God Himself has been reduced by the financial metaphor from beneficent deity to stingy "Shylock" or, even worse, to a mere bit of metallic coinage, a "sovereign" in a monetary rather than a plenipotent sense.

As Dickinson's Puritan ancestors had realized long before her, any attempt to bring God under the regulations of contract law was doomed to failure.[16] It was, furthermore, a sacrilege. But Dickinson took the Calvinist position one step further. Even trinitarianism seemed in Dickinson's radical critique of sacramental Christian symbolism a form of consummate symbolic reductiveness, as she suggests, again only half-jokingly, in the following poem:

> God is a distant—stately Lover—
> Woos, as He states us—by His Son—
> Verily, a Vicarious Courtship—
> "Miles", and "Priscilla", were such an One—
>
> But, lest the Soul—like fair "Priscilla"
> Choose the Envoy—and spurn the Groom—
> Vouches, with hyperbolic archness—
> "Miles", and "John Alden" were Synonyme— (No. 357)

Because of its desire to symbolize God, to find verbal counterparts to the divine order, symbol-wielding sacramentalism finds it necessary to conceptualize God in mortal terms, to demote Him (in Dickinson's view) to a man. God is thus demeaned. To save face and secure humankind's affections, He is forced to declare, "with hyperbolic archness," that He and Christ are "Synonyme." God is compelled to play word games, while, as a result, humankind is deprived of the legitimate comforts that a non-"distant," nonpunning deity could have provided. The problem for Dickinson is not simply, as it was for the Unitarians, that trinitarianism goes against human reason, but that the

16. See Perry Miller, "Introduction," in Perry Miller and Thomas H. Johnson (eds.), *The Puritans: A Sourcebook of Their Writings* (New York, 1938), 57–58.

fixed image of a three-personed God threatens to confine the expansiveness and incomprehensibility of divinity within a symbol that is limited, reductive, and uncomfortingly numerical.

The kinds of symbols that are employed by the narrators of these poems cannot, for Dickinson, be the instruments of precisely focused, deeply insightful perception. The dramas their symbols enact, the analogies they suggest, lead away from faith, not toward it. In an effort to dispense with one kind of dualism—a dualism that represents what is for Dickinson the necessary, theologically important distance between God and His creation—the sacramental symbols these poems display intimate unities and harmonies that destroy our relationship to nature and discredit God. They conflate the discrete parts of a divinely discriminated cosmos, and in the rubble that their collapse heaps up, in the confusion that they create between what is spiritual and what merely earthly, they create a barrier to genuine faith, a barrier that is reproduced for us, in all of its absolute rigidity, in the wry humor and in the halting brokenness of the poetic form.

In other words, in attempting to erase cosmic distinctions, sacramental symbolism may absolutize and concretize them. By trying to promote a reunion that Dickinson believes to be false, it may block the path to genuine resurrection and secure for human beings not their salvation in God but their permanent isolation and decay both in nature and in linguistic chaos. For such traditional symbolism implies an integrated reality in which matter and spirit together constitute the interpenetrating stuff of the universe and in which language can reproduce this cosmic homogeneity. Matter is the emanation of spirit; spirit is the source of the universe's wealth of physical display; and the word captures the relationship between the two.

Although Dickinson herself does not employ this kind of idealist vocabulary in her poems, it is this terminology that best conveys, in discursive terms, the outlines of her deeply philosophical, religious concerns. Behind the sacramental symbolism of the church exists idealist symbolism that is both independent of Christian thinking and (especially in the American tradition) intertwined with it. In Dickinson's view, sacramental symbolism, on the one hand, and idealist symbolism, on the other, represent humankind's most comprehensive efforts to

render reality unified and consistent in its own terms. They are therefore, she believes, also the most dangerous, most systematic threats to
faith ever fashioned by the human intellect. The symbols deployed in
the poems just examined can, finally, be used to embody what is for
Dickinson a true perception of cosmic reality. But they can be turned
to this good effect, they can be enlisted in a symbolic triumph, only
when they have been understood to negate, explicitly, the sacramental
and/or idealist assumptions on which much symbolism is built. My
next order of business is to try to define idealist symbolism, specifically Christian idealist symbolism, and to describe the outlines of
Dickinson's critique of the theological-philosophical assumptions in
which idealist tendencies may well involve us, and of the symbolism in
which those tendencies find their expression.

Chapter Three

Suffering an Exchange of World: Idealist Tendencies and the Loss of Faith

*D*ICKINSON'S effort to create a reformed symbolism is deeply rooted in her opposition not only to the sacramental concepts of the church but to the philosophical system that seems regularly to give birth to symbolism of the inadequate variety. A species of idealist thought, Dickinson believes, may be another primary enemy, for the tendencies toward idealist perception, if not properly controlled, can ensnare the human imagination in an almost inescapable web of faith-destructive judgments that express themselves as unifying or synecdochic symbols. Cleverly, duplicitously, idealist constructs can seem to bridge the gaps in cosmic reality that idealism itself first imagines to be harmful. Skillfully they can seduce humankind into a worship of the symbols of unity that, according to the idealists, are the agents of cosmic oneness but that are, according to Dickinson, the seditious, anti-Christian disrupters of the truly divine harmony (and of our perception of it), a harmony that consists in disparateness and not in conflation. For, in Dickinson's view, not only can the assumptions of idealism produce a species of symbolic language that goes against authentic divine unity, but it can set into motion an unending series of duplicate dualisms and falsely encoded emanations, all of which are as disruptive of our perception of real cosmic order, all as devastating to the relationship between man and faith, as the imagined first postlapsarian explosion into phenomenal being.

In *Poetry and Dogma* Malcolm Ross describes the problems inherent in the invasion of Christian theology by idealism. Dickinson's symbolism is not sacramental in Ross's terms. Nor are her attitudes toward the Incarnation identical to Ross's. Nonetheless, his discussion of sacramentalism and idealism is very useful in clarifying why the idealist alternative to a sacramental vision is no alternative at all for her. "Religious idealisms," Ross explains, "deny the validity of matter and . . . seek to reduce the world of things to the status of metaphor. Christianity has been invaded upon occasion by such alien idealisms," he acknowledges. "But the Christian artist," Ross claims, is "compelled, under the fixed star of the Incarnation, to believe in existence. . . . He is compelled to believe in the particularity, the uniqueness, the *value* of things. Therefore, the Christian artist may not, like the Platonist and all his hybrid brood, oppose a shadow world of things to a real world of value. Rather, for the Christian artist, all things have their own separately structured, intrinsic actuality and value, [they never cease] to be actual, specific, concrete."[1] Whether it is "the fixed star of the Incarnation" that forces the Christian's belief in "things" or something else (a phenomenalist or monadic philosophy, for example) remains a question. But for Dickinson the divinely sanctioned reality of the physical world is an indisputable tenet of Christian faith, one that, if denied, can have terrible repercussions for faith itself. Dickinson is indeed fascinated by idealist concepts. She is often enamored of the invisible universe. But just as she modifies her love of nature with a troubled recognition of the illusiveness and misperception that are part and parcel of its sacramental attractions, so she attaches her metaphysics to a critique of idealist perception that throws into vivid

1. Malcolm Mackenzie Ross, *Poetry and Dogma: The Transfiguration of Eucharistic Symbols in Seventeenth-Century English Poetry* (New York, 1969), 10–11.

relief the potentially destructive, anti-Christian underpinnings of an idealist interpretation of the universe.

"I had not minded—Walls—" seems to me a highly interesting poem particularly in this regard. I will discuss this poem in greater detail in chapter four, but I would like to exhibit it now as an introduction to Dickinson's highly complex insight into what it means for a universe to be conceived, physically or imaginatively, Christianly or secularly, in idealist terms.

> I had not minded—Walls—
> Were Universe—one Rock—
> And far I heard his silver Call
> The other side the Block—
>
> I'd tunnel—till my Groove
> Pushed sudden thro' to his—
> Then my face take her Recompense—
> The looking in his Eyes—
>
> But 'tis a single Hair—
> A filament—a law—
> A Cobweb—wove in Adamant—
> A Battlement—of Straw—
>
> A limit like the Vail
> Unto the Lady's face—
> But every Mesh—a Citadel—
> And Dragons—in the Crease— (No. 398)

This poem has, of course, been read very effectively as one of Dickinson's most poignant and painful love poems, a despairing recognition that there is a "law" (a "convention," perhaps, as Mark Van Doren has suggested, or "morality" or "something equally strong") that stands between individuals and prevents the consummation of their love. But the unnamed lover in Dickinson's poem, as Van Doren and others have pointed out, is also God, or if not God, at least a godlike entity or force.[2]

As the poem proceeds it begins to suggest the existence within the self or within the universe of some invisible, idealist-like structure or

2. "A Commentary on 'I Had Not Minded Walls,'" in Caesar R. Blake and Carlton F. Wells (eds.), *The Recognition of Emily Dickinson: Selected Criticism Since 1890* (Ann Arbor, 1968), 265 and 266.

law. It is not surprising that issues of love and of an ideal universe arise in the same poem. The law that Plato himself describes is a version of love and, as many poets (Dante and Donne, to name two) have demonstrated, human love may well be expressed in idealist as well as in sexual terms, even though neoplatonic concepts of love may well cause definite and painful frustration for human lovers. In fact, one of the reasons for Dickinson's casting her poem of cosmic inquiry as a love poem may well be her feeling that idealism becomes unreliable and unsound precisely when it is put to the emotional test.

Whether the poem, then, is read as a conventional love poem in the metaphysical tradition or as an explicit investigation of the structure of the "Universe," it contains a philosophical position that closely resembles the theory of cosmic emanation and hypostasis usually identified with idealism of the Plotinian variety. There are, of course, many versions of idealist philosophy, but Plotinus's system incorporates the salient features of most of the other important varieties and therefore serves well as a point of comparison with Dickinson's own idealism. The general similarities between the cosmological elements of the poem and the strategies of Plotinian idealism are straightforward and do not require lengthy demonstration. Dickinson's abstract, immaterial law can be taken as a version of the idea or monad from which all material reality, according to Plotinus, derives, while her three-staged descent from idea to matter—from the somewhat ethereal and flimsy cobweb to the more menacing but still straw-like battlement to the dragon-demarcated and citadel-spiked veil—can be seen as paralleling Plotinus's own three phases or hypostases, which proceed from the creation of the mind to that of the soul to what one critic has conveniently labeled the "farthest possible limit" (a "limit like the Vail" in Dickinson's language) that is the material universe itself.[3]

Both the Plotinian universe and the world of "I had not minded—Walls—" begin with law. But whereas the Plotinian law dictates reunion or "epistrophe" beyond the physical world, the Dickinsonian law culminates in an inflexible, unaccommodating "limit" that restricts love and destroys the hope of consummation. In the Plotinian system

3. M. H. Abrams, *Natural Supernaturalism: Tradition and Revolution in Romantic Literature* (New York, 1971), 147.

humankind does not remain eternally trapped in an adamantine web, the web of cosmic multiplicity and evil that lowers in the final lines of Dickinson's poem. Cosmic history, for Plotinus, is neither an unending linear progression through an eternally fragmented universe nor a journey to an unspecified conclusion even more hellish than fragmentation. Rather, the universe, in Plotinus's view, is an enormous, dynamic circle in which the cosmic inception and its inevitable demise meet at one and the same point, the point of primordial and perduring unity. As one commentator explains, "To [the] eternal 'procession' from the One, Plotinus opposes a counter-process of 'epistrophe,' or return to the source: 'To Real Being we go back, all that we have and are; to what we return as from what we came.'" Furthermore, as the same critic also points out, Plotinus's epistrophe is not simply a feature of collective cosmic motion at some final moment at the end of time. "Such a return" is also "achievable during this life," Plotinus promises, *if* the individual is willing to turn away "from the outer world" and contemplate his inner being, that cosmic "law," to use Dickinson's formula, from which he has emanated.[4]

Dickinson's and Plotinus's parting of the ways occurs just at this crucial juncture in the idealist's conception of the historical movement, when the great circle of being begins its ascent toward unity restored, whether on the cosmic or personal level. For in the model of the cosmic-personal drama presented in "I had not minded—Walls—" there is no acceding beyond the boundaries of the veil-obscured material universe, either for the universe as a whole or for the individual. In fact, in the first two stanzas of the poem Dickinson explicitly dismisses precisely those images of potential reunion, the tunnels and grooves and interconnecting blocks that, according to Plotinus and others, are distant reflections of the ideal, created just in order to provide the individual with an avenue of access for reattaining the ultimate recompense, the direct, eye-to-eye reunion with original being or with love.

4. *Ibid.*, 148. It is curious how often philosophers use "walls" as an image of their philosophical systems. Mary Warnock, *Imagination* (London, 1976), 75 and 103, points out several instances.

Certainly Platonic and neoplatonic concepts of love and their corresponding cosmologies, as expressed in many idealist systems, held certain real attractions for Dickinson. As a recent essay on Dickinson points out, such poems as "Love—is anterior to Life—" (No. 917), "Unable are the Loved to die" (No. 809), and "The Test of Love—is Death" (No. 573) reveal the basic configurations of a much desired idealist universe.[5] But Dickinson tempers this inclination for the abstract and the immaterial with a stern recognition of the costs involved. She is wholly capable of seeing glamor and beauty in the disappearing universe, as she demonstrates, for example, in the following celebration of evening:

> I've known a Heaven, like a Tent—
> To wrap it's shining Yards—
> Pluck up it's stakes, and disappear—
> Without the sound of Boards
> Or Rip of Nail—Or Carpenter—
> But just the miles of Stare—
> That signalize a Show's Retreat—
> In North America—
>
> No Trace—no Figment of the Thing
> That dazzled, Yesterday,
> No Ring—no Marvel—
> Men, and Feats—
> Dissolved as utterly—
> As Bird's far Navigation
> Discloses just a Hue—
> A plash of Oars, a Gaiety—
> Then swallowed up, of View. (No. 243)

But she recognizes that the capacity for idealist perception, if viewed from a slightly different angle, carries with it frightening consequences that cannot be waved away by the universe's apparently "shining Yards" and "Marvel" and dazzling beauty. The most serious implications of idealism have less to do with human love than with love for God. For if idealism complicates human relationships, it veritably destroys theological ones. Thus Dickinson writes in another poem,

5. M. M. Khan, "Conceptions of Love and Immortality in Emily Dickinson's Poetry," *Emily Dickinson Bulletin*, XXXVI (1979), 16–25.

> It knew no lapse, nor Diminution—
> But large—serene—
> Burned on—until through Dissolution—
> It failed from Men—
>
> I could not deem these Planetary forces
> Annulled—
> But suffered an Exchange of Territory—
> Or World— (No. 560, cf. L 280)

The cosmic finale is not portrayed here as a "lapse" or "Diminution" that can be perceived as a "Hue" and "Gaiety" or that can be seen as revealing to us the gradients of perception that lead from earth to heaven. Instead, it is a total "Dissolution" that is tantamount, in the language of the poem, to a cosmic failure.

Furthermore, it involves no apocalyptic recall to God. The sun's failing and the universe's dissolving are simply functions of mechanistic realities. The old "Planetary forces" of the purely mechanical model of the universe demanded by idealist assumptions are not "Annulled" in the final moment of epistrophe. Rather, they are reborn, in infinite extension, as new, duplicate universes. The facts of the phenomenal world do not give way to a wholly new reality, a law of grace, which is not simply a repetition of earthly events, not even analogous to earth. Instead, they suffer "an Exchange of Territory— / Or World—." Pieces of the puzzle change places and the game goes painfully on.

Locked in at the center of this mindlessly wheeling, endlessly cycling universe is the sacrificial lamb, humankind. The human race, if viewed through the lens of Dickinson's idealist interpretation, may become the prisoner caught between emanation and failed epistrophe, the pathetic victim of a pattern of events that leaves no room for sympathy or love or redemption.

> Banish Air from Air—
> Divide Light if you dare—
> They'll meet
> While Cubes in a Drop
> Or Pellets of Shape
> Fit.
> Films cannot annul
> Odors return whole

> Force Flame
> And with a Blonde push
> Over your impotence
> Flits Steam. (No. 854)

No matter how hard he or she tries, the individual cannot carve out a safe space between the crowding, suffocating densities of "Air" and "Light" that define phenomenal reality in each of the succeeding emanations of the cosmic plan. And if humankind should try to "Force" the "Flame," if it should try, in other words, to extinguish the solar center that defines physical reality, it will simply discover that "Air" and "Light" have again returned, only more hellishly, as "Steam." Humankind is the "Term," the imprisonment "between" "Eternity" and "Immortality," as Dickinson so conveniently puts it in another poem (No. 721). In an ideal universe of this kind, humankind is impotent.

Although Dickinson claims in a letter to Higginson (L 622) that she is not very familiar with Poe's work, a glance at a passage from his *Eureka* is here in order, for whether the similarities between Dickinson's philosophical intuitions and Poe's are accidental or causal, they serve well in pointing up the complexities of the Dickinsonian position.

There was an epoch in the Night of Time, when a still-existent Being existed—one of an absolutely infinite number of similar Beings that people the absolutely infinite domains of the absolutely infinite space. It was not and is not in the power of this Being—any more than it is in your own—to extend, by actual increase, the joy of his Existence; but just as it *is* in your power to expand or to concentrate your pleasures . . . so did and does a similar capability appertain to this Divine Being, who thus passes his Eternity in perpetual variation of Concentrated Self and almost Infinite Self-Diffusion. What you call The Universe is but his present expansive existence. He now feels his life through an infinity of imperfect pleasures—the partial and pain-intertangled pleasures of those inconceivably numerous things which you designate his creatures, but which are really but infinite individuations of Himself. . . . These creatures are all too, more or less conscious intelligences; conscious, first, of a proper identity; conscious, secondly and by faint indeterminate glimpses, of an identity with the Divine Being of whom we speak—of an identity with God. Of the two classes of consciousness, fancy that the former will grow weaker, the latter stronger, during the long succession of ages which must elapse before these myriads of individual Intelligences become

blended . . . into One. Think that the sense of individual identity will be grad-
ually merged in the general consciousness—that Man . . . ceasing impercep-
tibly to feel himself Man, will at length attain that awfully triumphant epoch
when he shall recognize his existence as that of Jehovah.[6]

As several critics have shown, Poe's cosmology is in many ways idealist,
specifically Plotinian. The universe emanates from a divine being that
now exists solely in the created matter of his universe. Eventually, the
universal fragmentation will coalesce. Oneness will be restored. But
what Poe focuses on that Plotinus and other Platonists by and large
ignore are the emotional and psychological implications for the individual who is expanding into and out of existence at the will of his
primordial creator, the individual who is feeling the "partial and pain-
intertangled" joy of separate identity on the one hand and "identity
with God" on the other.

Although many details distinguish Poe's idealist glosses from Dickinson's, the stark, almost Poesque horror recorded in many of Dickinson's
idealist poems suggests that for Dickinson, as for Poe, human involvement in the otherwise ahuman principles of cosmic organization push
us toward a realization that the implications of idealist history can
often seem terrifyingly gothic.[7] This view recurs again and again in
Dickinson's verse. Like Poe, Dickinson does not absolutely deny the essential premises of a Platonic or neoplatonic theory. As she explains in
one straightforward and unemotional statement of neoplatonic philosophy, "The Outer—from the Inner / Derives it's Magnitude— / . . .
The Inner—paints the Outer—" (No. 451). The "House" of the phenomenal world, she admits, points back to the "Augur" and the "Car-
penter" that built it:

> The Props assist the House
> Until the House is built
> And then the Props withdraw

6. *Eureka*, in *The Complete Works of Edgar Allan Poe* (16 vols.; Boston, 1902), XII,
313–15. Dickinson writes in one of her letters, "I endeavored to shrink away into pri-
meval nothingness—but sat there large as life" (L 99).

7. See Edward Davidson, *Poe: A Critical Study* (Cambridge, Mass., 1957); Allen Tate,
"The Angelic Imagination," in Eric W. Carlson (ed.), *The Recognition of Edgar Allan Poe*
(Ann Arbor, 1970), 236–54; and my own essay, "Poe's Gothic Idea: The Cosmic Geni-
ture of Horror," *Essays in Literature*, III (1976), 73–85.

> And adequate, erect,
> The House support itself (No. 1142)

But the implications of such idealist tendencies, if not controlled and overruled by Christian belief, may not promote human happiness and may even be ghastly in the extreme, as Dickinson suggests in the following poem:

> A Spider sewed at Night
> Without a Light
> Upon an Arc of White.
>
> If Ruff it was of Dame
> Or Shroud of Gnome
> Himself himself inform.
>
> Of Immortality
> His Strategy
> Was Physiognomy. (No. 1138)[8]

In an idealist view of the universe, it may be that only a "Spider"-like deity can know whether the phenomenal web of creation is a harmless decorative "Ruff" or a suffocating "Shroud." Worse, he may have no desire to let humankind in on the secret. As he is portrayed in the poem, he is concerned solely with his own egomaniacal goals: to "Himself himself inform." In other words, the inseminator of the idealist cosmos seems to construct the whole "House" of the universe out of nothing just so that it can collapse again into nothingness restored and can reveal to its helpless tenants the gargantuan "Soul" that built it.

In these poems Dickinson is disallowing the false optimism by which conventional idealists and conventional moralists glibly heal the rifts and dualisms of the universe. Idealism inclines toward positing a dual universe, fragmented and chaotic. Then it chooses either to ignore that dualism, to pretend that it does not exist, or, even worse, to celebrate it, to press it into the service of the ideal One of which matter, if the idealists are to be consistent, can be only the barest, most disjointed reminder, a lurid, nightmarish glimpse of what is now hor-

8. For different interpretations of the poem, see Charles R. Anderson, *Emily Dickinson's Poetry: Stairway of Surprise* (New York, 1960), 125–28 and JoAnne De Lavan Williams, "Spiders in the Attic: Suggestions of Synthesis in the Poetry of Emily Dickinson," *Emily Dickinson Bulletin*, XXIX (1976), 26.

ribly lost and not of what will one day, gloriously, be regained. Moralists, in a similar way, celebrate the nonphysical passion of love to the excruciating torture of actual lovers.

Idealist theory, in other words, balances precariously on a diabolical paradox. Perfection and unity, evil and chaos, it claims, exist in and through each other. The fractured material creation represents a falling away from the ideal and yet is the ideal incarnate.[9] Dickinson is unwilling to accept this kind of solution. She will not worship a condition of earthly fragmentation that, by definition, has to be painful and punishing, especially when it affects our most fundamental, physical relationships. The idealist perception of the world or of love, Dickinson concludes, may not lead humankind back to oneness at all. It may instead set humanity adrift in a chaos of misperception and ignorance that is tantamount to spiritual, intellectual, and emotional blindness, a blindness that may be more absolute than any associated with nonidealist perception, a "limit" like a "Vail." It may press us inevitably onward to the kind of symbolic or allegorical reading of nature and of self that can "cheat" Christians of true faith and bar them from heaven, or that can prevent the sexual-spiritual union of two lovers who sadly define themselves and their world in idealist, neoplatonic terms.

The idealizing gloss on the configuration of cosmic events that characterizes one large group of New England writers unfortunately has many troubling consequences for the aspiring idealizer, and the purpose of Dickinson's idealist-related poems is, in part, I think, to detail for us some of the dangerous liabilities of idealist thought, especially the ways in which idealist theorizing had been mismanaged and abused in American symbolism. A neoplatonic rendering of cosmic history, for example, may not only disenable genuine human relationships, as it is seen to do in "I had not minded—Walls—," but it may preclude the moment of resurrection on which reunion with God depends. This is what Dickinson seems to be suggesting in "It knew no lapse." In fact, the tendency toward an idealist interpretation of the universe

9. See Arthur Oncken Lovejoy, "The Dialectic of Bruno and Spinoza," *University of California Publications in Philosophy,* I (1904), 156–57.

may actually result in denying the existence of a benevolent and personally intervening deity altogether, as "A Spider sewed at Night" and "The Props assist the House" seem to suggest. And even if idealist patterning can be made to serve the doctrines of Christian faith and be seen to affirm reunion and rebirth, these features of Christian promise may suddenly be forced to assume nuances and implications that make God and heaven either undesirable or inappropriate as objects of human aspiration.

What bothers Dickinson far more than the fact that there is paradox or ambiguity or downright confusion in the idealist universe—that for some reason or other the "One" of primordial being is "rapt / Forever from the Eye" (No. 282) or that "The Star's whole Secret—in the Lake— / Eyes were not meant to know" (No. 451)—is that this universe takes such pleasure in throwing out the tempting web-like, house-like, wheel-like illusions that ensnare man. It revels in teasing him to take note of possible cosmic meanings and then in thwarting his efforts to achieve that knowledge.

> How noteless Men, and Pleiads, stand,
> Until a sudden sky
> Reveals the fact that One is rapt
> Forever from the Eye—
>
> Members of the Invisible,
> Existing, while we stare,
> In Leagueless Opportunity,
> O'ertakeless, as the Air—
>
> Why didn't we detain Them?
> The Heavens with a smile,
> Sweep by our disappointed Heads,
> Without a syllable— (No. 282)

In other words, Dickinson does not doubt that a divine plan exists.

> The Love a Life can show Below
> Is but a filament, I know,
> Of that diviner thing
> That faints upon the face of Noon—
> And smites the Tinder in the Sun—
> And hinders Gabriel's Wing—

And the "diviner thing" that "Life . . . Below" can embody is magnificent beyond analogy. But the method whereby the "diviner thing" proceeds to make itself known is, when considered through the abstracting lenses of idealism, as painful as it is pleasurable, and its painfulness must be taken seriously.

> 'Tis this—in Music—hints and sways—
> And far abroad on Summer days—
> Distils uncertain pain—
> 'Tis this enamors in the East—
> And tints the Transit in the West
> With harrowing Iodine—
>
> 'Tis this—invites—appalls—endows—
> Flits—glimmers—proves—dissolves—
> Returns—suggests—convicts—enchants—
> Then—flings in Paradise— (No. 673)

The string of descriptive verbs that conclude the poem do not, I think, simply amplify the ecstasy by comparing it to pain. Undoubtedly Dickinson is dealing with a complex phenomenon about which she feels highly ambivalent. Nonetheless, her words suggest elements of genuine suffering that culminate in the somewhat clumsily expressed, uncertain grace that ends the poem: "Then—flings in Paradise—." This flat, jarring conclusion to the poem expresses little confidence in a process that is throughout characterized by "harrowing" possibilities. One cannot deny the poem's ecstasy, and I do not wish to do so. But one can also not deny the collective effect of such terms as "faints," "smites," "hinders," "pain," and so on, especially when they find their culmination in a painfully abrupt word like "flings." Something is hampering the speaker's full relish of the divine moment, and that something, I suggest, is not just a natural reluctance to being teased but a suspicion that an emotionally unreliable universe, or at least an inconstant one, may not be innocently loving. It may be downright sardonic.

In other words, Dickinson is suggesting that to see the universe through the contours of idealist history may indeed enable us to envision a divine plan working itself out on the material landscape. It may even enable us to derive a certain comfort from the analogies and promises which that plan provides. But an idealist interpretation of cosmic events may also force us to conclude that the cosmic plan is the work of a sadistic deity whose sole purpose is to build and destroy a universe in order to "Himself himself inform," or who "invites" our interest, "enchants" us, only to fling or discard us in the end in a very much reduced version of "Paradise." Dickinson acknowledges in another poem that indeed "This World is not Conclusion" (No. 501). But the "Species" that she suspects "stands beyond" does not comfort mankind, and the enchanting burlesque of the cosmos may be a joke that human beings cannot afford to enjoy. Like the "diviner thing" that "invites—appalls—endows— / Flits—glimmers—proves—dissolves— / Returns—suggests—convicts—enchants—" and "Then— flings in Paradise—," the "Species . . . beyond" in "This World is not Conclusion" "beckons" and then "baffles," "slips—and laughs, and rallies—" all in a charming but ultimately humiliating tease. And "To gain it, Men have borne / Contempt of Generations / And Crucifixion." "The nearest Dream," Dickinson claims in another poem, "recedes—unrealized—"

> The Heaven we chase,
> Like the June Bee—before the School Boy,
> Invites the Race—
> Stoops—to an easy Clover—
> Dips—evades—teases—deploys—
> Then—to the Royal Clouds
> Lifts his light Pinnace—
> Heedless of the Boy—
> Staring—bewildered—at the mocking sky— (No. 319)

At very least, heaven is heedless of humankind. And often it is intentionally mocking.

In poems like "The Love a Life can show Below," "This World is not Conclusion," and "The nearest Dream," Dickinson portrays her narrators as primarily willing and able to enjoy the universe on its own terms, even if the cosmic condition is as painful as it is gratifying, and even if her tone and use of language in these poems suggest that deeper hurts are being concealed behind a somewhat forced ebullience. But Dickinson acknowledges, even in these poems, that from a slightly different perspective, idealist assumptions can lead to a view of God in which the deity is seen to act as an overbearing monster or a heartless tyrant.

This is indeed the hypothetical view of the deity that emerges in a good number of Dickinson's poems. It is an interpretation of God that, she suggests, can be a direct consequence of humankind's idealist assumptions. Thus, for example, "I know that He exists" begins with the same unquestioning affirmation of some of the major premises of an idealist-defined, Christian neoplatonic universe: God "exists," "Somewhere," in transcendental "Silence." This world, therefore, is but a "gross" veil simultaneously concealing and revealing His "rare" being, and death is epistrophe or apocalypse, reunion with God. But instead of rejoicing in this happy coincidence of scriptural authority and neoplatonic patterns, the poem concludes with an awful shudder that effectively denies all of the comfortable assumptions of Christian idealism on which the poem is built.

> I know that He exists.
> Somewhere—in Silence—
> He has hid his rare life
> From our gross eyes.
>
> 'Tis an instant's play.
> 'Tis a fond Ambush—
> Just to make Bliss
> Earn her own surprise!
>
> But—should the play
> Prove piercing earnest—
> Should the glee—glaze—
> In Death's—stiff—stare—
>
> Would not the fun
> Look too expensive!
> Would not the jest—
> Have crawled too far! (No. 338)[10]

The problem is, quite simply, that the "fond Ambush," the teasing "instant's play" of the phenomenal world, whereby God presumably pre-

10. For a very fine discussion of this poem, not concerned with its idealist elements, see Clark Griffith, *The Long Shadow: Emily Dickinson's Tragic Poetry* (Princeton, 1964), 73–76.

pares His worshipers for their ultimate reunion in the next, is no mere game, no innocent foreplay anticipating sexual and spiritual consummation. For "Death's—stiff—stare" is not procreative. It is destructive. God, in this poem, is not a passionate lover who brings to fruitful climax the romance between the human and the divine. And death, therefore, comes to be seen as a perverse instrument for perpetrating the ghastly "jest" of implied neoplatonic meanings. Death becomes a grotesque, funereal worm (a Poesque image) that has "crawled too far." "Life," by implication, is "Murder by degrees," in which the deity "mashes" mankind "to death." It is a "teaze" that is a consummate torture.

> The Whole of it came not at once—
> 'Twas Murder by degrees—
> A Thrust—and then for Life a chance—
> The Bliss to cauterize—
>
> The Cat reprieves the Mouse
> She eases from her teeth
> Just long enough for Hope to teaze—
> Then mashes it to death—
>
> 'Tis Life's award—to die—
> Contenteder if once—
> Than dying half—then rallying
> For consciouser Eclipse— (No. 762)

God, Dickinson writes to Higginson, may just be an "Eclipse" (L 261), a "Pause of Space" (L 418), and if He is, her poem suggests, then His sole purpose in the universe may be the neoplatonic game of affirming His own existence by creating for His creatures a "Plated [also Plaited] Life—diversified / With Gold and Silver Pain" that ends in chaos and "Annihilation," "Eclipse" made "consciouser" and regained.

> A Plated Life—diversified
> With Gold and Silver Pain
> To prove the presence of the Ore
> In Particles—'tis when
>
> A Value struggle—it exist—
> A Power—will proclaim
> Although Annihilation pile
> Whole Chaoses on Him— (No. 806)

This is the "Perturbless Plan," the inhuman "Creation," which in no way takes account of the human victims of God's presumed neo-platonic self-revelations.

> It's easy to invent a Life—
> God does it—every Day—
> Creation—but the Gambol
> Of His Authority—
>
> It's easy to efface it—
> The thrifty Deity
> Could scarce afford Eternity
> To Spontaneity—
>
> The Perished Patterns murmur—
> But His Perturbless Plan
> Proceed—inserting Here—a Sun—
> There—leaving out a Man— (No. 724; cf. No. 1624)

Dickinson is not, in these poems, simply venting an irrational, antitheological rage. Rather, she is suggesting how an idealist and especially a Christian neoplatonist interpretation of cosmic organization can, in the end, force us to deny God and abandon faith. This should not come as a complete surprise. Critics have long noted the hostility to God that is often expressed in Dickinson's poetry. I would like to suggest here that Dickinson's apparently heretical rampage against the deity does not represent the heart of her deepest-felt convictions. Rather, it reflects her understanding of the possible consequences of a neoplatonic interpretation of the creation. As Erich Kahler has pointed out, scientism and symbolic consciousness have the effect of impersonalizing God.[11] Because of their own philosophical logic, Dickinson shows us, the proponents of the idealist view of God may have to conclude that God is not only detached from human affairs, but that he is a tyrant bent on human destruction.

In the prephilosophical days before the advent of Christian idealism, there had been a way of escaping the implications of poems like these. The faithful Christian would, at the appropriate moment in time, simply be recalled into the arms of a loving and beneficent deity, and both

11. See Erich Kahler, "The Nature of the Symbol," in Rollo May (ed.), *Symbolism in Religion and Literature* (New York, 1960), 55–56.

man and God, their human and human-like qualities fully preserved, would dwell in the kingdom of heaven forever.

> "Houses"—so the Wise Men tell me—
> "Mansions"! Mansions must be warm!
> Mansions cannot let the tears in,
> Mansions must exclude the storm!

But the problem is that mankind no longer knows deity in the same personal way.

> "Many Mansions", by "his Father",
> *I* dont know him; snugly built!
> Could the Children find the way there—
> Some, would even trudge tonight! (No. 127)

The processes of philosophical idealization remove God from the realm of humanly felt, humanly cognizable emotions. Death is debased from reunion to obliteration, heaven from paradise renewed to "everlasting" "Blank" (No. 761). (It can have other, equally disastrous consequences, as I shall show in the next chapter.) Thus, the return to original being, which is at the center of the Christian and idealist-neoplatonist plots both, becomes, for Dickinson, a most "reluctant" "journey," punctuated by doubt and fear. It is a passage through a grim "Forest of the Dead" to a prison-house heaven in which the soul is sentenced to an irreversible "Term" of hellish "Eternity," without reprieve. God no longer seems father or lover but a menacing warden instead, who mans "every Gate" and allows of no "Hope" and no "Retreat."

> Our journey had advanced—
> Our feet were almost come
> To that odd Fork in Being's Road—
> Eternity—by Term—
>
> Our pace took sudden awe—
> Our feet—reluctant—led—
> Before—were Cities—but Between—
> The Forest of the Dead—
>
> Retreat—was out of Hope—
> Behind—a Sealed Route—

> Eternity's White Flag—Before—
> And God—at every Gate— (No. 615)

The pattern of idealist thought creates a correlative pattern of cosmic experience that, in its turn, leaves the soul alone and desolate, suspended between the two (supposedly) analogous halves of the divine universe.

> Departed—to the Judgment—
> A Mightly Afternoon—
> Great Clouds—like Ushers—leaning—
> Creation—looking on—
>
> The Flesh Surrendered—Cancelled—
> The Bodiless—begun—
> Two Worlds—like Audiences—disperse—
> And leave the Soul—alone— (No. 524)

The soul, in this poem, does not traverse the distance between "Two Worlds," but rather the "Two Worlds" disappear into their inevitable nothingness, leaving the soul alone.

It remains for us to see what redemption finally means to Dickinson, where she locates immortality and eternity, and how she understands the relationship between God and the creation. All these, we shall learn, will emerge as flawlessly from the logic of her critiques of inadequate symbolism and unbridled idealism as does her vision of uncertainty and fear. But it begins to be clear already, I think, that for Dickinson the configurations of idealist theorizing unwittingly demonstrate that no smooth and easy reconciliations can heal the gap between the human and the divine. No nonstop flight will speed us on our ultimate journey to unity restored. Even more important, our acceptance of the false premises of idealist thought may transform the author of the universe into the mindless center of a seething hotbed of wheels and cycles and annihilating eclipses. Worse, it may convert Him into an obsessed madman who satisfies his egomaniacal lust through the destruction of his creatures. The creator of this kind of universe could not be the God of true Christian faith. Nor could it resemble Him in any way.

Thus, Dickinson's accounts of how idealist conceptions affect our understanding of cosmic events go beyond an uncomplicated emotional realism. They transcend the knowledge that, on the one hand, the rhetoric of idealism cannot so easily smooth away the dualisms that idealist dispositions themselves posit, and that, on the other, such dispositions are guilty of creating rifts between God and humankind that are more oppressive, more unmanageable than any the natural-Christian universe might have provided on its own. Her purpose in the poems I have just been discussing is to show us how ideal theorizing affects our existence in the world; how, specifically, it can determine our attitudes toward God and toward Christian faith. Inherent in the idealists' efforts to collapse the universe into one interrelated homogenous reality, Dickinson suggests, is an impersonalization of cosmic events that results, ironically, in a distancing of God from humankind and of humankind from nature that is unlike any that Christianity could ever imagine. If the tendency toward such idealist perception is not resisted, all of the figures in the cosmic drama, even God Himself, can seem helpless participants in an ongoing process that is self-generating, self-propelling, and mindlessly mechanistic. A universe that prior to the appearance of human idealizing might have been a highly personalized, gracefully articulating relation of discrete cosmic parts—a universe that Dickinson describes in "I had not minded—Walls—" as a cohesive, homey universe of rock, governed by a God who is also a lover and who promises a definite "recompense" and reconciliation—can inadvertently be converted into the bits and pieces of a world in shambles, a world that is bodiless and soulless both. If sacramental symbolism errs in its disregard for cosmic discontinuities, idealist symbolizing, especially as it occurs within a Christian framework, extends the error by abolishing the literal personality of God and by questioning the substantial reality of His creation.

But the assumptions of idealist thought can have another equally serious result, one that also makes the wayward tendencies of sacramental symbolism seem minor in comparison. Idealist configurations can influence the individual to invent a symbolic language that is expected to capture and convey the unity in which the proponent of idealism believes. Idealism and symbolism, as the critics point out, are inevitably related. But, as I have already argued, in Dickinson's view, language does not promote unity. Indeed, it seems to recapitulate the alleged neoplatonic fall into fragmented being, and to reproduce it in a form that is even more fractured than the universe it wishes to describe. In an effort to envision the universe as one continuous whole, the idealist imagination tends to consolidate and conflate the elements of reality into symbol-units. It (inadvertently perhaps) manages to reduce God's multifaceted variety into a race of hybrid monsters that not only do not reflect divine reality as it is actually constituted, but that threaten to breed immoderately, until they have totally overrun the kingdom of God with their hellish verbal vitality.

In the next chapter I shall look at how the mind may perpetuate, through its symbolic offspring, the problems that an infatuation with idealist theorizing can set into motion. I shall begin with "I had not minded—Walls—," for this poem both presents, with full critical suggestiveness, the problems of using idealist conceits as a way of describing reality, and also indicates, within its own structure, how the idealist perception of the universe may lead to a species of symbolic language that can be as destructive and fragmenting as the idealist formulae themselves. One of the most serious dangers of the idealist tendencies of perception, in Dickinson's view, is that they may lead to new and equally corrupting emanations and hypostases, ad infinitum, every time the mind gropes inward to discover and reunite itself with what it imagines is its own self-contained remnant of primordial being, every time it seeks to articulate in language what it believes to be the symbol of cosmic truth. Language, words, and symbols, if not properly controlled, can, in Dickinson's view, become the rubble strewn upon the landscape of the human imagination by humanity's uncontrollable urge to imitate the Platonic God, to play idealist god-in-miniature. Such symbol usage, Dickinson tells us, is the mortal, and mortally fatal, expression of the desire to escape the implications of divine dualism by discovering a center of unity either within an ideal universe or within the conceptualizing creative self. It represents the desire to conflate the many separate constituents of multivarious cosmic order within a mental precept that, in the end, substitutes a divine force or an idea or even the self for the personal God who is usually imagined to be the organizing center of the universe. The consequences of this idealist symbolizing are even more devastating to our perception of cosmic cohesion, even more destructive of our relationship to divine purpose, than are the consequences of our tendencies to indulge in idealist musings generally. It is the causal connection between idealist pretenses and a false symbolic language that Dickinson sets out for us in "I had not minded—Walls—" and that is my next concern.

Chapter Four

A Hair, A Filament, A Law: The Process of Symbolic Reduction

*T*HE mind's inherent attraction to sacramental symbolism on the one hand and idealist symbolism on the other tempts it toward the pattern of perceptual distortions that conflate and reduce and hence destroy faith and denigrate value. As I tried to show in chapter one, unific and synecdochic symbolism, either of the sacramental or idealist variety, is fraught with dangers and, as I also tried to suggest, these dangers are created and compounded by language even as they are generated by the organization of reality, or by our organized perceptions of the elements of that reality. The poet, therefore, is as much a juggler as is the day, and symbolic reductiveness is very much a consequence of the poet's unenlightened linguistic games. In the poems I will now examine, Dickinson deals directly with the process whereby symbolic thought issues in a species of symbolic language that reduces and distorts cosmic truth. In trying to articulate a concept or idea that is beyond the representational powers of language, the mind, Dickinson shows us, may be forced by its own misguided logic to resort to a code it knows to be restrictive and destructive but that seems to be its only means for representing cosmic unity. The idealist tendencies analyzed in the poems discussed in chapter three may well, Dickinson demonstrates, issue in symbolic reduction, and the language in which that idealism formulates itself may be that reduction incarnate.

This, it seems to me, is a principal concern in one of Dickinson's most intensely philosophical-literary poems, a love poem in which the irreconcilable separation of the lovers comes to represent the ultimate destruction of cosmic unity. By any criteria, "I had not minded—Walls—" is a strange and baffling poem. Its effect is not only emotional—the message of the poem being one of cosmic disorder and personal despair—but it is virtually physical as well. Its rhymes discomfit; the bizarre and irregular capitalizations startle; and the chaotic welter of dash-designated disruptions alternately snare and assault the reader's senses. "I had not minded," the narrator begins calmly enough, when suddenly "—Walls—," prominently capitalized and emphatically set off, thrust themselves upon the speaker's consciousness and literally block the progress of her thought. The speaker and her reader are set wandering through a frustrating, barrier-filled maze of aspiration and disappointment that becomes increasingly more restrictive as the poem proceeds. Although I have already quoted this poem in chapter three, I would like to repeat it here, since so much of its forcefulness depends upon the intricacies of its language.

> I had not minded—Walls—
> Were Universe—one Rock—
> And far I heard his silver Call
> The other side the Block—
>
> I'd tunnel—till my Groove
> Pushed sudden thro' to his—
> Then my face take her Recompense—
> The looking in his Eyes—
>
> But 'tis a single Hair—
> A filament—a law—
> A Cobweb—wove in Adamant—
> A Battlement—of Straw—

> A limit like the Vail
> Unto the Lady's face—
> But every Mesh—a Citadel—
> And Dragons—in the Crease— (No. 398)

Why the narrator would prefer that the universe were one rock rather
than a single hair is intriguing in a familiar literary way; and, indeed,
as I have already noted, the poem has been explicated along several
conventional lines by some of Dickinson's most astute critics.[1] But when
the capitalized "Walls" and "Block" are thrown up in the narrator's and
the reader's face, and when the capitalized cosmic "Hair" begins its
awful proliferation into a horrific "Cobweb"—"wove in Adamant"—a
"Vail" in which "every Mesh" is a "Citadel" and there are "Dragons—
in the Crease," then normal critical investigation must, I think, give
way to the deciphering of a hauntingly gothic cryptograph such as Poe
himself might have devised.

"I had not minded—Walls—," whatever its immediate subject, seems
to me an attempt to explore the dangerous potentialities of a particular variety of symbolic language. It tries to describe the relationship
between these humanly created symbols and what the narrator of the
poem perceives as the impetus both of the universe and of the self
toward dualism and division. The narrator proposes two antithetical
descriptions for primordial cosmic unity and its postlapsarian dispersion into multiplicity. Both of these descriptions may be called
Plotinian in plot, and neither, we must note at the outset, is ultimately
regarded as a satisfactory sketch of the actual configurations of cosmic
reality. In stanzas one and two the narrator describes the universe as a
materially substantive, verbally cognizable entity. The universe, she
tells us, is "one Rock," a wholeness of density and extension in which
familiar, visually realizable walls, grooves, and tunnels all conspire to
create intercourse and communication (the reattainment of oneness),

1. See, for example, Mark Van Doren, "A Commentary on 'I Had Not Minded
Walls'" (already discussed in chap. three), in Caesar R. Blake and Carlton F. Wells (eds.),
The Recognition of Emily Dickinson: Selected Criticism Since 1890 (Ann Arbor, 1968),
264–68; Robert Weisbuch, *Emily Dickinson's Poetry* (Chicago, 1972), 158–59; Robert
Merideth, "Dickinson's 'I had not minded—Walls—,'" *Explicator*, XXIII (1965), item 25;
and William Sherwood, *Circumference and Circumstance: Stages in the Mind and Art of Emily
Dickinson* (New York, 1968), 88–89.

and in which the universe itself, we are assured, promises humankind a definite "Recompense" on "the other side" of a concrete, perceivable "Block." But the universe, the same narrator goes on to tell us, is, unfortunately, not a "Rock." It is, instead, an unfathomable and painfully abstract "law," whether that law is a law of self, cosmos, or God. It is, in other words, an indescribable, unimaginable idea that cannot be conceptualized or visualized at all. Its physical manifestations in the material world, therefore, are only an ironic and bewilderingly chaotic reflection of its essential nature—the cobweb, battlement, or veil, which carries the thread of the original impulsion of idea into being but which, at the same time, distorts and horribly materializes that idea. It is almost as if Dickinson had Emerson's "The Transcendentalist" in mind when she wrote the poem. In that essay Emerson distinguishes between a materialistic view of the universe and an ideal one, and he explains, in language similar to that used in the poem, that

as thinkers, mankind have ever divided into two sects, Materialists and Idealists; the first class founding on experience, the second on consciousness. . . . The materialist, secure in the certainty of sensation, mocks at fine-spun theories, at star-gazers and dreams; and believes that his life is solid, that he at least takes nothing for granted but knows where he stands, and what he does. Yet how easy it is to show him that he also is a phantom walking and working amid phantoms, and that he need only ask a question or two beyond his daily questions to find his solid universe growing dim and impalpable before his sense. The sturdy capitalist, no matter how deep and square on blocks of Quincy granite he lays the foundations of his banking-house or Exchange, must set it, at last, not on a cube corresponding to the angles of his structure, but on a mass of unknown materials and solidity, red-hot or white-hot perhaps at the core, which rounds off to an almost perfect sphericity, and lies floating in soft air, and goes spinning away, dragging bank and banker with it at a rate of thousands of miles the hour, he knows not whither—a bit of bullet, now glimmering, now darkling through a small cubic space on the edge of an unimaginable pit of emptiness.[2]

Once the materialist has been converted to an idealist perspective, he can never return to his former materialism. Once he has questioned the substance of his life, he can never more dwell in "certainty" and

2. Ralph Waldo Emerson, "The Transcendentalist," in Brooks Atkinson (ed.), *The Selected Writings of Ralph Waldo Emerson* (New York, 1950), 88.

must become an inhabitant of his own "darkling," "glimmering" consciousness. Herein is the problem that particularly interests Dickinson.

In "I had not minded—Walls—," both of the speaker's initial sets of
cosmic assumptions are portrayed symbolically. Both accordingly display that intensity of individuation and particularization which, as I
argued in chapter one, characterizes Dickinson's view of the essence of
language and of perception. And thus, individual component parts of
the cosmic design and their names—in this case, both the "Call,"
"Block," "Groove," "Recompense," and "Eyes" of the universe of rock,
and the "Cobweb," "Battlement," and "Vail" of the universe of law—
resist (like the "Four Trees" and "Toe" and "Claw" of other Dickinson
poems) the subordination to the whole that would signal an interpenetrating, unified cosmic design. But the significances of the two
cosmic symbolizations are really quite different from each other, and
together they tell us something about the problems of consciousness,
of symbolic language, in our attempts to articulate our cosmic perceptions. Both of her speaker's described universes appear in the poem to
be postlapsarian and therefore chaotic and fractured. In the universe-
of-rock section, for example, the upper-case letters that begin the
words "Call," "Block," "Groove," "Recompense," and "Eyes," and the
rhythms of the verse-lines in which these words are singled out and
emphasized, suggest that there is something independent about each
of these elements, that they are in some ways mere, unrelated terms in
a catalogue of mutually exclusive and perhaps even antagonistic objects. But the shattering of cosmic unity into a multiplicity of disparate
fragments and the correlative disintegration of language into symbolic chaos are rendered at their highest pitch in the universe-of-law
stanzas of the poem. In the second half of the poem not only do the
"Cobweb—," "Battlement—," and "Vail" stand in isolation of and opposition to one another, and to the "law" they represent, but the "Cobweb" appears to be separate even from the "Adamant" out of which it
is woven, as is the "Battlement" from its "Straw"; and the "Vail" is portrayed not as a flowing gossamer but as an oppressive cross-hatching
of "Mesh" and "Citadel," "Dragons" and "Crease." In other words, although both the universe of rock and the universe of law represent
dispersion and a falling away from perfection, the poem's two hypo-

thetical cosmoses are not fragmented in the same way or to the same degree.

The kind of cosmic disharmony represented by each cosmos is, I would argue, directly related to the narrator's desire to see unity and to the role, in each cosmic construct, of symbols and of symbolic perception. The universe of rock, although it, too, depicts cosmic disintegration, allows for the possibility of an aesthetic harmony and a religious faith that can ameliorate the more extreme implications of materiality and disorder. This possibility does not seem to exist in the universe of law. Therefore, the speaker hypothesizes that, were the universe "one Rock," all things—the original cosmic idea, the creation, humankind, love—would be material and therefore easily and appropriately representable in the concrete images of a Wall, a "Block," a "Groove," and so on. These capitalized terms would, to be sure, represent dispersion, the departure from wholeness and perfection that characterizes the fallen universe. They would certainly image for us the self-assertive obstructions and isolated restrictions of the postlapsarian physical world of objects and words. They would be barriers to the consummation of love. But the "Walls" and "Block," precisely because of their material largeness, would also represent a potential movement toward restored wholeness. In the material-symbolic universe of rock, all elements would conspire toward the reattainment of unity, the apocalyptic reunion (sexual or otherwise) described in the second stanza of the poem. Furthermore, even in its imperfect, temporal configuration, a universe of rock would exhibit a principle of friendly cohesion and homey bigness. Such a universe, the speaker happily indicates, might be implicitly likened to a house or neighborhood whose walls or blocks protect its residents or guide their passage to the other side. "Groove[s]" would "tunnel" through surface disharmonies; there would be a compatibility of cosmic parts that would be expressly sexual in nature (see lines 5 and 6); and the universe, as a whole, would assure its inhabitants a consummation and a rebirth that would be perceptual, spiritual, and erotic: "Then my face take her Recompense— / The looking in his Eyes." The mere corroboration of the fact that an "other side" to the creation exists, that there would be some place to "push through" to, would be, from the speaker's point of view, an immeasurable source of joy. It would indicate to her that her interpretative imagination and her earthly senses (her ears, for example, which hear "his silver Call / The other side the Block") had some purpose; that she would be able to operate legitimately and successfully upon the physical data of the material creation, and that she could expect to be rewarded, first, by an authentic portrait of cosmic realities and, second, by the eventual fulfillment of the creation's theological, philosophical, and sexual premises.

Were the universe "one Rock," the narrator theorizes, then she would not have "minded" the universe's "Walls." But the "—Walls—" that startle the speaker's vision in line 1 are not the temporary and manageable barriers of home or neighborhood. They are not passages of access and exit as well as agents of restriction. Rather, they are cruelly assertive obstructions that position themselves absolutely and, the speaker hints, eternally, between humankind's perceptions of this world and its theoretical conception of another, between the self and the other, whether the other is lover, God, or cosmic oneness. However comforting the universe-of-rock thesis may be, the universe, the narrator realizes, is not a "Rock," "But 'tis a single Hair— / A filament—a law." Like Emerson's *Nature*, the poem seems to record the necessary but dangerous awakening into an idealist consciousness of reality. The universe is not matter. It is an almost unidimensional wisp of self-containment and self-sufficiency, a concept or an idea that is not material, and that therefore cannot perhaps be represented verbally or imagistically. The universe-of-law proposition raises the crucial question not only about idealist perception but about all attempts to perceive and communicate the nature of spiritual and emotional realities. How, the poet is asking, can we talk about something that is clearly not material and that therefore seems to belie verbal expression? How can the human mind, which is material and neither ideal nor divine, perceive and represent the most important realities? The halting, disrupted progression of words in the "single Hair— / A filament—a law" definition of the universe represents the speaker's attempt to articulate the unutterable. It is also her initiation into some of the problems of symbolic language. " 'Tis a single Hair," she begins confidently enough, but no sooner has she proposed the symbol of the "Hair," capital *H*, than she recognizes the imperfectness of the symbol. "A filament," she offers instead, her mind whittling away at the Hair's slender but offensive materiality. But even the symbolic filament does not satisfy her: "a law," she concludes; the universe is an immaterial, theoretical, law inaccessible to symbol making.

The Hair-filament-law sequence reproduces for us the speaker's struggle to discover an absolutely pure term for an essentially abstract concept. To call the universe a rock, she insists, however reassuring such a materially solid and analogically promising assumption might be, is to misrepresent the essential structure and nature of the universe. The universe, the speaker thus declares, is unequivocally a "law." But the effect of the speaker's rigorous consolidation of cosmic unity is not to bring the creation under her control. Her idealizing process instead causes her to lose her idea to a symbol that is not only inadequate but dangerously reductive. Without any philosophical warning or linguistic transition, the universe of unimaginable, indescribable law suddenly begins its awful proliferation into the kinds of symbols the poet wishes to reject; into the "Cobweb—wove in Adamant— / A Battlement—of Straw— / A limit like [a] Vail. . . ." Ironically, the mind's effort to make matter disappear, or, to put it in other words, the speaker's assumption that the cosmos itself denies the validity of physical reality, results in an emanation and a materialization of the hair or filament or law that is even more absolute and baffling than any of the consequences (the walls or block, for example) of an inherently materialistic universe of rock. The uncompromising dematerialization of the idea, it would seem, is like a nuclear fusion in which a carefully achieved compression explodes again into material being, tracing exactly the pattern of cosmic creation described by Plotinus, Poe, and other idealists. But the material symbols of the second half of the poem do not comfort in the least. They blind the speaker and imprison her in a nonredemptive nonvision of "Adamant" and "Vail." No "other side" to the universe of law emerges. The bifurcation between the abstract, ideal law and the material realities of the cobweb-battlement-veil become for her absolute and incomprehensible.

Both of the speaker's initial hypotheses—that the universe is a rock and that it is a law—err in trying to establish a principle of continuous unity and homogeneous wholeness. And because the mind of man is an integral part of reality that exists in a relationship of reflexivity and mutual determination with the objects of consciousness, each such hypothesis becomes directly responsible for the destruction of genuine cosmic integrity. The universe is not simply a rock: the very fact that *He* (or he) exists, that there is an "other side," militates against the universe-of-rock hypothesis. But neither is it purely a law, for if it is, then physical reality is a barrier or wall even more obstinate than rock, and humankind is trapped in a snarled multiplicity of unstrung filaments and frayed laws that not only distort the universe's (or the self's) essential idea but that violate its immaterial nature as well.

For Dickinson, the problem of idealism is more serious than the problem of materialism because, just as Emerson claims, once the idealist position has been entertained, we can never return to a false materialism. The idealist itch for abstraction, professed in the opening lines of stanza three, contributes directly to the destruction of the universe's spiritual-physical wholeness. The implications of idealism, according to Dickinson, if carried to their logical conclusion, necessarily issue in a chaos of false symbols. In denying the validity of concrete perception—which is, as I shall argue, a crucial element in humankind's interpretation of the universe and which is also an accurate accounting of the solidly material creation—the thoroughgoing idealism of Dickinson's speaker destroys for her the possibility of properly understanding order and purpose in the universe. She can no longer see the actual relationship between matter and spirit, creation and God.

There is no transition between the lines " 'tis a single Hair— / A filament—a law—" and the symbols of the cobweb, battlement, and veil because in Dickinson's view there is no continuum between matter and idea that is subject to pure comprehension or verbalization. The explosion into gross materiality that characterizes the emanation from idea to form in the speaker's mind represents for Dickinson natural consequences of a deficiency (a divinely ordained deficiency, I shall suggest) on the part of human optics to perceive the fine points of progression from idea to matter or from law to cobweb. Man's "tunnel" sight—his lack of peripheral, abstract vision—forces him to employ material "grooves"—symbols, if you will—by which to reach a meaningful conception of transcendent reality. But the symbols will have to be of a special sort—"grooves" and not springboards—if they are to do their job. They will have to reveal the universe to the individual's sight, not withdraw it from his perception (in a word like "law") or obliterate it in a wealth of noncommunicating, material debris. For this reason, "I had not minded—Walls—" is a poem about different ways of seeing and it formulates its theme in vision-related images— the "Eyes" in stanza two and the "Vail" in stanza four. If the universe were a rock, man's physical, object-oriented vision would have been able to perceive and interpret cosmic meaning correctly. But because the universe is not a rock or because it is more than a rock or a rock plus something else, man leaps to the conclusion that the universe is an idea, a law. And his inability to envision the nullity or ideal that he insists is the only authentic metaphor for the cosmos results ironically in an avalanche of merely physical images that blind the perceiver to anything but the earthly density of the material world. The ultimate figure for the cobweb and battlement is the "Vail," which, hung too close to the eye, obscures human vision. This veil forces the eye to focus upon the immediate and therefore disproportionately large elements of its own meshwork, which thereby become prominently exaggerated—the "Citadels" and "Dragons" of the concluding stanza. The veil divides man and his redeemer whether that redeemer be an anthropomorphic deity or an anthropomorphically detailed cosmology, or simply a lover.

Like the black veil worn by Hawthorne's minister, the narrator's veil casts the world in its own dark, oppressive image. The linguistic structure of Dickinson's poem, therefore, achieves an exacting verisimilitude of cosmic disharmony and chaos. It begins with the speaker's attempt to formulate a simple, declarative sentence: "I had not minded." Suddenly the "—Walls—" leap out at her and demand her complete attention. The effect of this concrete object on the speaker's voice is overwhelming. The simple pluperfect indicative tense, which the narrator's opening statement might have assumed, is immediately transmuted into the subjunctive. The description of the universe that follows in stanzas one and two and that is meant, I think, to convey primarily a positive, optimistic view of the universe, already begins to exhibit the elements of tension more fully realized in stanzas three and four. The absolute rhyming of the capitalized words "Rock" and "Block," for example, causes the word "Rock" to seem harsher, more fixed and restrictive, than the sense of the lines suggests that it is meant to be. Similarly, the "Block," which is an image of analogical promise and neighborly containment, asserts itself cruelly and abruptly in opposition to the orphic and biblical "silver Call." The capitalizations of the words "Call," "Groove," "Recompense," and "Eyes," furthermore, suggest (as we have noted) a disjointed particularity about the elements of the poet's vision that runs counter to the expressed hopes for sexual and spiritual reunion. In stanzas one and two, in other words, the narrator is already troubled by the use of symbolic language, and her attempt to describe the composite wholeness of the universe of rock is marred by her self-conscious and awkward use of symbols.

Nonetheless, when compared with the painfully clipped language of stanzas three and four, the lines of stanzas one and two virtually sing and flow. The rhythms of "And far I heard his silver Call / The other side the Block" are (if the secondary implications of the word "Block" are momentarily ignored) decidedly musical; the liquid rhyming of "his" and "Eyes" is haunting and erotic. This lyricism, however, comes to a swift halt in stanza three. The autonomous symbols of the poem's concluding catalogue are strung together not by verbs or commas but by frantic and emphatic dashes. There is, in fact, only one verb in these lines—the painfully contracted " 'tis" that begins stanza three. Dickinson's language—the form of the poem itself—becomes a kind of veil, darkening and obscuring her quondam creation.

Through her use of capitalizations, dashes, and a special kind of rhyme, Dickinson verbally builds the walls of her universe. In writing the poem, she concretely creates the barriers that thwart and baffle her narrator and herself. For even if cosmic fragmentation and the irreparable gap between the ideal and the material are essential features of the actual cosmos, man's twofold, symbolizing and transcendentalizing imagination is, for Dickinson, the individual's own means for perpetuating and eternalizing the chaos. In mimetically, symbolically reproducing the discord and disintegration of the fallen universe of law, Dickinson's poem not only describes what the universe looks like, but it suggests the ways in which words, i.e., the symbolic constructs of the imagination, abet and increase disorder.

As we shall see further in chapter six, Dickinson does not reject out-of-hand the necessity for the symbolic "grooves" of human perception. The walls that the poet builds are necessary walls. But she does insist that we firmly acknowledge *both* the universe-of-rock *and* the universe-of-law principles of cosmic organization, and that we not make one the mere manifestation of the other. The reconstructed symbolism of Dickinson's own theory of language triumphantly resists the symbolic conflation that in "I had not minded—Walls—" results, finally, in the destruction of cosmic wholeness.

As Dickinson stipulates so precisely in another poem,

> To fill a Gap
> Insert the Thing that caused it—
> Block it up
> With Other—and 'twill yawn the more—
> You cannot solder an Abyss
> With Air. (No. 546)

Therefore, when the narrator of "I had not minded—Walls—," gripped by her fixation on neoplatonic patterns and habituated to symbolic renderings, tries to "solder an Abyss / With Air," she discovers that, truth to tell, the "Abyss" does "yawn" all the "more" for her efforts. In trying to formulate an idea that is by definition immaterial and therefore beyond verbalization, in words that are by the same definition material and encumbering, she succeeds only in destroying the very meaning of the idea she wishes to preserve. According to the logic of the poem, the mind seems to be caught in an impossible lurch in which it can either choose to remain silent and therefore not violate the integrity of a universe of law that is inaccessible to symbols or it can make the valiant effort to reach for the appropriate symbol only to find that the nullity it is endeavoring to image cannot remain intact, that it must, because of the pressures of language and of human optics, immediately explode into a welter of phenomenal substance that is even more oppressive, more fragmentary, than the physical universe itself. Dickinson has her own means for releasing the mind from this paralyzing choice. But for the moment what is important to note is the kind of symbolism that Dickinson considers reductive and distorting.

In the context of Dickinson's concern for the symbolic reductiveness of language itself two of her most discussed, most frequently reprinted poems, "I died for Beauty" and "This was a Poet," become intensely interesting. One hesitates to comment on such familiar and cherished poems, especially to attempt to alter our readings of them. But whatever else these poems are about, they (and others I shall look at) become in the Dickinson canon models of language's inherent tendency to fragment and concretize what the speaker of the poem seems to intend to abstract and unify. To appropriate contemporary terminology, they display the gap between signifier and signified, stressing the potency of the signifier to become an autonomous power divested of the legitimizing or normalizing authority of a signified. In "Words and Wounds" Geoffrey Hartman recalls Derrida's comments on the dislocated autonomy of written language: "The written text cannot be questioned like a speaker, it *orphans* words by depriving them of a voice that is alive and present. 'The specificity of writing,' Derrida alleges, 'is related to the absence of the father.' This absence is said to undermine the univocity of discourse by introducing words that are, at once, as weak as orphans who must be adopted and as strong as an unfathered, self-authorized voice." This double condition of patriarchy and orphanhood seems to me to characterize much of Dickinson's language. It is especially apparent in a poem like "I died for Beauty," where the principal subject of the poem is language itself, in particular the word's symbolizing function. In "I died for Beauty" Dickinson self-consciously displays what Hartman calls the power of language to wound, to open the gaps that language at first would seem to heal.[3]

3. Geoffrey H. Hartman, *Saving the Text: Literature / Derrida / Philosophy* (Baltimore, 1981), 119.

> I died for Beauty—but was scarce
> Adjusted in the Tomb
> When One who died for Truth, was lain
> In an adjoining Room—
>
> He questioned softly "Why I failed"?
> "For Beauty", I replied—
> "And I—for Truth—Themself are One—
> We Brethren, are", He said—
>
> And so, as Kinsmen, met a Night—
> We talked between the Rooms—
> Until the Moss had reached our lips—
> And covered up—our names— (No. 449)

The poem's patness of argument, a sentimentality not common in the Dickinson canon, warrants our asking whether the poem means what it seems to mean. Nonetheless, were it not for the last two lines, it might be possible to rest in the poem's assertion of the conventional wisdom that beauty and truth are one. At most, the poem might seem to hint at a slightly troubled and hence troubling contest between meaning-making ideals like beauty and truth and the stultifying processes of the natural world, represented by the moss. But those two lines, with their almost gothic quality, the moss grotesquely crawling up to the protagonists' lips and obliterating not only their names but their capacity to speak their names, suggest that the poem records no ordinary struggle between nature and supernature. For what is at stake here is the very language, the names, which the poem itself constitutes, the names by which the protagonists define their world and for which they have been willing to die. Beauty, truth, and the moss represent two antithetical but significantly related tendencies of the symbol-producing intelligence. Beauty and truth embody the human passion to look beyond nature to the ideal and then to render absolute and specific, in a word, what is immaterial and unknowable; the moss images that desire to transcendentalize the solidly material elements of the physical creation in the same effort to see beyond nature to supernature. In both processes, a concept or word is made to stand as a symbol for a knowable reality, for a universe of interconnected realms, the one earthly, the other divine or supernatural. This is the

symbol as synecdoche or bridge. It affirms the simultaneity of the signifier and the signified. But the symbol thus defined is highly problematical, for it can, and in this poem does, lead the individual into
a situation in which reality, reduced to language, becomes subject to
the instabilities of language, the inability of language to incapsulate
reality.

The poem's plot is simple enough. The "I" of the poem has died for
beauty, her kinsman for truth, and as they meet in death, they revel in
the similarities of their life's undertakings. But dire reservations about
their life-quests hammer away at their serenity even before the awful
moss succeeds in obliterating them completely. Truth's soft questioning, for example, "'Why I failed'?" and his halting, awkward admission, "'And I—for Truth—Themself are One—,'" which is more a
groping for affirmation than a confident declaration of belief, afflict
the poem's characters from the beginning. Furthermore, the poem's
choppy language suggests flashes of annoyance that are accentuated
both by the choice of diction and its deployment on the page. What
may seem, at first glance, joyous ecstasy can, with only a slight altera-
tion in the mechanics of our reading, become an expression of shrill
disappointment. Dying becomes a failure; there is "scarce" hope of
meaningful adjustment to something so vacuous as a "Tomb."

Furthermore, even though beauty and truth work hard to assert
their synonymity with each other and with the cosmic one that they
believe they represent ("Themself are One," says truth, in a peculiarly
jarring combination of singular and plural discourse), they remain ir-
revocably separated in the poem, each a lone and irreconcilable self,
an unyielding "One." Beauty and truth echo one another, but each
speaker has his or her own voice, and the "He" and "I" of the poem
never consummate their relationship. Rather, they remain in different rooms, "adjoining" but never joined, presumably to the end of
time. Beauty and truth may be kinsmen, but they are doomed to be
individual and independent of one another. And what divides them,
what prevents their dramatic reunion in death, is the very grave into
which they so willingly cast themselves, the grave that they believe will
be the means of their redemption but that, as a result of the very same
philosophical, symbolizing tendencies that convert the graveyard

into a theatre of cosmic truth, becomes a barrier or a wall (to recall Dickinson's other poem), a "Room" between themselves and the unity they seek. The effort to harmonize dualisms by means of language, symbols, concretizes them instead.

Part of the problem confronted here is that the attempt to conceptualize and express verbally the inconceivable and inexpressible, forces one back on a terminology that in no way assures the individual that the conclusions reached are the ones that will affirm cosmic unity. For if one can make verbally manifest such intangible abstractions as beauty and truth and cause them to be so much a part of the experiential world that one can die for them, then it is also legitimate to make abstract the substance of the physical world, to press it into the service of some larger metaphysical understanding of the universe. That, after all, is the goal of the Romantic symbolism of nature and the methodology of the idealists from Plato to Mallarmé. But what happens when one attempts to find a symbolic meaning for tombs or moss is that the results tend not to confirm beauty and truth but to deny them. The symbolizing process, thus managed, runs wild, until the very multiplicity of human symbols creates a chaos and fragmentation that are precisely the opposite of what the process initially promises. In fact, as soon as the protagonists decide to waste their life's energies dying for supposed ideals, they set themselves upon the path to failure, for when they convert beauty and truth into quantities expressible in reductively human, i.e., inadequately symbolic, forms, they make them subject to the conditions of mortality. Thus, in the last two lines of the poem, when the moss once and for all buries the poem's idealizing heroes, it does so by silencing their lips and covering over their names, i.e., by obliterating their powers of speech. The protagonists do not succeed in immortalizing beauty and truth, because they have reduced them to the level of language, where they are subject to the disintegrations of verbalization. They do not achieve the perfect unity they seek but instead reduce whatever cosmic cohesion exists to a tightly managed contest between arrogantly hostile and self-righteous elements—the beauty, truth, and moss that carry forward the poem's symbolizing action.

I do not want to suggest that Dickinson does not cherish any ideals

whatsoever, either neoplatonic or Christian. Indeed, Dickinson's poetic mode is finally concerned with establishing a proper context and
meaning for humankind's relationship to cosmic oneness. But in her
view the very nature of idealist perception can lead the mind into an
all-too-easy, havoc-producing infatuation with abstraction. "Ideals,"
Dickinson tells us quite directly in one poem, "are the Fairy Oil / With
which we *help* the Wheel" (italics mine). "But," she goes on to note,
"when the Vital Axle turns / The eye rejects [i.e., must reject] the Oil"
(No. 983). What still more commonly occurs, however, is recorded in
another poem.

> Taking up the fair Ideal,
> Just to cast her down
> When a fracture—we discover—
> Or a splintered Crown—
> Makes the Heavens portable—
> And the Gods—a lie—
> Doubtless—"Adam"—scowled at Eden—
> For *his* perjury!
>
> Cherishing—our poor Ideal—
> Till in purer dress—
> We behold her—glorified—
> Comforts—search—like this—
> Till the broken creatures—
> We adored—for whole—
> Stains—all washed—
> Transfigured—mended—
> Meet us—with a smile— (No. 428)

Ideals may sometimes point beyond this world to another more perfect realm of being, "transfigured" and "mended" beyond their mortal frailty. But the images of this world are "broken creatures," "fracture[d]" and "splintered." They can only feebly record ideal realities.
And yet, mankind either foolishly insists on rejecting these images altogether or, equally foolishly, adores them as "whole." To dismiss
idealism too lightly is, in Dickinson's view, an error. But to fixate on the
ideal, to live entirely within and for the immaterial realm of an ideal
universe, is a problem of equal magnitude, a problem that is central to
Dickinson's redefinition of symbolism. For not only does the immodest

suicidal worship of the ideal also make the "Heavens portable" and "Gods—a lie," burying heaven and God in a transcendentalized and therefore grossly magnified "tomb," but it brings the "Vital Axle" of human life and cosmic rotation to a screeching, grinding halt.

This, I think, is one of the principal subjects of "Before I got my eye put out," which seems to me a virtual model of symbolic reduction. In the poem the attempt to isolate ideal essences from the living whole, and to organize cosmic unity around them, ironically results in a contrary explosion outward into material grossness and multiplicity. The consequence is that the vital processes of sight, feeling, and affection are undermined; unity is destroyed. But "Before I got my eye put out" goes beyond the theoretical concerns of "I had not minded—Walls—" and "I died for Beauty." It also engages the kind of criticism recorded in such poems as "I tend my flowers for thee." For, as in many of the poems discussed earlier, Dickinson is concerned here with the dangerous, reductive conflation that occurs when nature's autonomy is violated and the physical world is made to serve the desire for spiritual knowledge.

> Before I got my eye put out
> I liked as well to see—
> As other Creatures, that have Eyes
> And know no other way—
>
> But were it told to me—Today—
> That I might have the sky
> For mine—I tell you that my Heart
> Would split, for size of me—
>
> The Meadows—mine—
> The Mountains—mine—
> All Forests—Stintless Stars—
> As much of Noon as I could take
> Between my finite eyes—
>
> The Motions of The Dipping Birds—
> The Morning's Amber Road—
> For mine—to look at when I liked—
> The News would strike me dead—
>
> So safer Guess—with just my soul
> Upon the Window pane—

> Where other Creatures put their eyes—
> Incautious—of the Sun— (No. 327)

As in "I died for Beauty" and "I had not minded—Walls—" the I (eye) in "Before I got my eye put out" is forced by its reductive logic to shift its focus inward, to strive toward the nonvision that appears to be a version of the ideal but that is, as Dickinson points out in "I tend my flowers," a blindness not only to nature but to God as well. Stereoscopic human vision, Dickinson's poem suggests, depends upon a proper collaboration of physical and spiritual perception, a joint effort of what Dickinson identifies in the poem as the eye and soul of seeing. Therefore, the persona who opts for spiritual as opposed to physical seeing discovers not only that her blindness is more damaging than she had originally thought it would be, but that the vision that remains in her half-blindness is fragmented and chaotic. She comes to realize, through the course of the poem, that she is reducing the elements of her inherently coherent, because multiple, perception to discrete and disjointed fragments—the "Meadows," "Mountains," "Forests," and "Stars" of the latter portion of the poem.

The speaker's error is to confuse her lower-case, singular "eye" (which by the implied logic of human anatomy must always function in conjunction with another lower-case singular eye) with the capitalized, disproportionately valued "Eyes" of "Creatures" who "know no other way" of seeing. The speaker of the poem rightly rejects the pure sensuality of creature-sight. But in so doing, she also blinds herself to the legitimate merits of properly constituted earthly perception. She puts out her "eye" because she cannot discern the difference between the "eye" that is part and parcel of total physical-spiritual vision and the "Eyes" that are emphatically animalistic.

Although the act of putting out one's eye would seem to connote elements of ritual atonement, the elevating of oneself above the trammels of the flesh, this, as we have been suggesting, is for Dickinson not the case. Although seeing physically, with one's "Eyes," may represent one kind of incomplete response to the fullness of a multifaceted universe, seeing spiritually, with one's "soul / Upon the Window pane," represents another. The poet crystallizes the dilemma of physical versus spiritual seeing in stanzas two, three, and four of the poem. These stanzas are an exquisitely wrought, graphically mimetic model of the competition between physical and spiritual perception. They unabashedly glory in the pictorial delights of the creation, but they leave painfully uncertain which mode of perception, the eyes or the soul, bestows this sensuous-spiritual feast upon the perceiver.

At least two separate, parallel interpretations of these stanzas are possible. In the first, the "But" that initiates the sequence of images suggests a strengthening of the speaker's conviction that insight is superior to eyesight: once, she tells us, I used to appreciate the vision of my animalistic "Eyes"; "but" "Today," "were it told to me . . . That I might have the sky," because "I got my eye put out," how much greater my joy would be than when I saw "As other Creatures, that have Eyes." So eager is the poet to own the sky and everything in it—the Meadows, Mountains, Forests, Stars, even the "Motions of The Dipping Birds," and "The Morning's Amber Road"—that her heart, she tells us, "Would split, for size of me," "The News would strike me dead."

The intimations of heartbreak and death are, of course, metaphors for the poet's joy and astonishment upon discovering the gifts of spiritual seeing. But, as is so often the case in a Dickinson poem, the metaphorical expression carries with it a literal meaning, and it is here that the second meaning of the pivotal "But" comes in. In order to truly "have the sky," Dickinson is saying, one must, in fact, die: one must, in other words, enter the absolute blindness of cosmic nonexistence that, for the individual soul, is death. When the poetic persona says that her heart would split for size of her and that the news would strike her dead, she is implicitly recognizing that the gifts of pure and perfect insight are not to be attained in this life. And if soulsight, that "other way" that human beings must come to know if they are to elevate themselves above the "Creatures," belongs to a realm beyond, then perhaps, the speaker suggests, she has been too hasty in having had her physical eye "put out." The second function of the "But" in line five is to oppose rather than to reinforce the argument that spiritual perception is more important than physical perception: for, were it told to me, the speaker explains, that I might have the sky, and everything in and under it, "Today" and "Between my *finite* eyes" (italics added), *then*, she confesses, my heart would split for size (sighs?) of me, the news would strike me dead, for I would realize that I had already sacrificed the physical vision that would have bestowed upon me these gifts.[4]

The two patterns of meaning set up by the conjunction "But" are related. The realization that soulsight achieves its ends only in death induces the poet's horrified awareness that the loss she has incurred is irreparable in this life. But the solution to the conflict between eyesight and soulsight is not, as one might expect, simply to revert to eyesight. Both eyesight *and* insight, Dickinson wants us to understand, suffer from the same limited particularity of vision, the same lack of stereoscopic depth and three-dimensionality without which the elements of the creation become so many discrete and individuated phenomena. Therefore, the central portion of the poem, with its capitalized and separable meadows, mountains, stars, and so on, represents the vision of both physical and spiritual seeing as each is employed in isolation from the other. "Before I got my eye put out" expresses the sad possibility that the simultaneous employment of eyesight and insight may be unattainable; that we see, in one moment, with our physical vision, in another, through the optics of our spiritual imagination; and that, even if we vibrate between the two modes of seeing, it will be impossible to draw them into an harmonious simultaneity. The narrator, however, like the generality of human beings, ignorant of such potential limitations and uncontrollably desirous of possessing the creation (having it for "Mine") interprets the partial vision of her half-blindness as a whole and absolutely true perception. This, quite simply, is arrogance and greed, and it eventuates in a further impairing of her relationship to cosmic unity. As soon as the narrator articulates to herself the possibility of *having* the sky, either with her eyesight or with her soulsight, the nonspecific vastness of the lower-case sky is shattered and the creation becomes a frenzied multiplicity of place, time, movement, and quality. The desire to make "Mine"—like Adam, to name and therefore endow with symbolic significance the elements of the creation and thereby to possess them—is ultimately

4. For a different reading of these lines, see Ruth Miller, *The Poetry of Emily Dickinson* (Middletown, Conn., 1968), 276–78.

what fractures cosmic stability. Even the poet's heart, we are told, splits. Her affections splinter into so many miserly and avaricious impulses. And she finds herself eternally stranded outside the cosmic creation, with just her "Soul / Upon the Window pane," desperately looking out.

It is important to note here again that nowhere in her criticism of reductive symbolism does Dickinson actually reject symbolism as a literary device. But she records critically the devastating consequences of a mind disposed to treat with the universe as if its discrete components were all neatly consolidated in objects or words. What Dickinson will finally advocate is a symbolism within boundaries, a measured and self-critical symbolism in which the borders between God and nature are firmly drawn. Indeed, Dickinson succeeds in achieving this kind of symbolism even within the poems that criticize reductive symbolic tendencies. But before one can appreciate the manner and means of Dickinson's poetic triumphs over the dangers of inadequate symbolism, it is important to take full stock of the range of perils she believes everywhere threaten the human imagination. For in her view, even poetry, or perhaps especially poetry, can betray the inquirer and the knowledge both. Poetry, Dickinson realizes, can destroy as easily as it can garner and preserve.

If "I died for Beauty" and "Before I got my eye put out" are (among other things) assaults on the mind's propensity toward reductive symbolic thought, "This was a Poet—It is That—" (which immediately precedes "I died for Beauty" both in the Johnson arrangement and in the poet's own packet No. 34) is the vehicle for a brilliantly sensitive statement about how language, so magnificent and powerful in its triumphs, can, if not managed properly, complete the process of reductive fragmentation that idealist thought initiates. "This was a Poet" is in part a poem about words. And it informs us how words, as the agents of thought, can disrupt not only our sense of cosmic wholeness but our sense of personal integrity as well. Like "I died for Beauty" or "Before I got my eye put out," the poem would seem to be exclusively celebratory. It would appear, simply, to extol the skills of the poet who can distil "amazing sense / From ordinary Meanings," and "Attar" from the "familiar species / That perished by the Door," and who is thereby the "Discloser" of an extraordinary "Picture" of reality. It is in just this vein, of course, that George Whicher titles his biography of Dickinson *This Was a Poet*.[5] But, while on the one hand, the poem affirms the power of the poet, it also provides an incisive commentary on the destructive potential of art, and it is Dickinson's awareness of the double valence of art that explains the poem's remarkably distracted quality.

> This was a Poet—It is That
> Distills amazing sense
> From ordinary Meanings—
> And Attar so immense
>
> From the familiar species
> That perished by the Door—
> We wonder it was not Ourselves
> Arrested it—before—
>
> Of Pictures, the Discloser—
> The Poet—it is He—
> Entitles Us—by Contrast—
> To ceaseless Poverty—
>
> Of Portion—so unconscious—
> The Robbing—could not harm—
> Himself—to Him—a Fortune—
> Exterior—to Time— (No. 448)

The traditional interpretation of the poem is familiar to most Dickinson readers. It emerges directly from the poem's major assertions. Explains Thomas Johnson: "It is expected of the poet that he will distill amazing sense from ordinary meanings [and] extract attar from the familiar, which otherwise would perish."[6] But if, on the one hand, the poem seems to celebrate the poet's talents, as Johnson suggests, the odd use of vocabulary in the poem and the strange metaphors these words are made to conjure up (such as poverty, theft, un-

5. George Frisbie Whicher, *This Was a Poet: A Critical Biography of Emily Dickinson* (Ann Arbor, 1957).

6. Thomas Johnson, *Emily Dickinson: An Interpretative Biography* (New York, 1972), 147.

consciousness, and "harm") must be seen as pulling away from the poem's celebratory aspects. In fact, they seem to point to some very troubling elements in the poet's abilities and to posit some startling criticisms of the actual consequences of poetic skills.

The poet is, of course, to be commended for distilling "amazing sense / From ordinary Meanings." But we must also note that (s)he achieves this magical result only through a series of disclosures (the word *disclosure* itself can have negative, traitorous connotations) that are not uncomplicated or inexpensive gifts to the reader. They are, rather, acts of robbery that for some reason or another entitle the rest of us, "by Contrast," to "ceaseless Poverty." Furthermore, the "familiar species" of the ordinary world is seen in the poem to *perish* "by the Door," and though it might be argued that this is the condition of mortal nature, poet or no poet, it is nonetheless the poet who is discovered red-handed, wringing essences from immensities and thereby (in my way of reading the poem) reducing and destroying them.

The poet, in other words, may, in the very attempt to preserve nature, also become a destroyer of the natural order, a burglar who (unintentionally perhaps) succeeds in impoverishing his or her intended beneficiaries. The instrument of the poet's power is precisely the ability to write poems, to make contrasts and to measure out portions, to arrest nature, stop and imprison it and seal it up in the contrasting fragments and meager portions of his poetry. Like Hawthorne's Ayler in "The Birthmark" or the artist in Poe's "The Oval Portrait," Dickinson's poet distils and perfects until only death remains; or, as Dickinson herself puts it in another poem,

> Essential Oils—are wrung—
> The Attar from the Rose
> Be not expressed by Suns—alone—
> It is the gift of Screws—
>
> The General Rose—decay—
> But this—in Lady's Drawer
> Make Summer—When the Lady lie
> In Ceaseless Rosemary— (No. 675)

The wringing of essences from meanings, however grand, is a painful "gift of Screws," a torturing of nature that does, doubtless, give the illusion of endless "Summer" and "Ceaseless Rosemary," but that does so only by destroying one of nature's creatures, the rose, which then lies in a state of perpetual decay.

The problem of the destructive as opposed to constructive potential of art appears frequently in Dickinson's poetry and cannot but influence our attempt to understand her larger aesthetic philosophy. In another poem, for example, Dickinson describes a scene of natural destruction as if it were itself, in fact, a kind of poetry.

> A Visitor in Marl—
> Who influences Flowers—
> Till they are orderly as Busts—
> And Elegant—as Glass—
>
> Who visits in the Night—
> And just before the Sun—
> Concludes his glistening interview—
> Caresses—and is gone—
>
> But whom his fingers touched—
> And where his feet have run—
> And whatsoever Mouth he kissed—
> Is as it had not been— (No. 391)

The analogy between poetry and frost is as much a reflection on art as it is on nature. The "Visitor in Marl" is in effect a poet who creates artistic order, makes the flowers as "orderly as Busts" and as "Elegant—as Glass," by freezing them into a cold lifelessness. And although in this poem the poet's icy, destructive effect on the landscape is interrupted at the crucial moment by the rising sun, the poem concludes with a note distinctly ominous: when Dickinson says that it "is as it had not been," we know that the flowers have been saved from the "Visitor in Marl," but we are nonetheless left with a gnawing suspicion that someday it will be as if "it," i.e., the whole landscape, also "had not been."

Therefore, in "Glowing is her Bonnet" (No. 72), Dickinson entertains the notion that it would be better if nature were not subjected to poetic control. She would prefer it "vanish unrecorded" and be praised not in the numbered feet of verse but by the more authentic appreciation of the world to which it belongs.

Better as the Daisy
From the Summer hill
Vanish unrecorded
Save by tearful rill—

Save by loving sunrise
Looking for her face.
Save by feet unnumbered
Pausing at the place.

"Glowing is her Bonnet" is a light poem that aims at a simple celebration of nature. But it is useful to consider that what stands opposed to nature in this poem is not science or philosophy but art itself.

As Dickinson puts it elsewhere, in an equally playful way, the poet may be a kind of thief, a relative of his similarly humorous burglar-banker father (No. 49), who violates the trust of an adoring and obedient natural world in order to realize his own goals.

I robbed the Woods—
The trusting Woods.
The unsuspecting Trees
Brought out their Burs and mosses
My fantasy to please.
I scanned their trinkets curious—
I grasped—I bore away—
What will the solemn Hemlock—
What will the Oak tree say? (No. 41)

In "I robbed the Woods—" Dickinson maintains a cheerful acceptance of her somewhat less than perfect relationship to nature. But she is not always so willing to laugh away the poet's violation of the natural world. The poet's "Press / Of Imagery," she explains elsewhere, pierces and destroys, with painful results that the poem's language refuses to conceal.

Inconceivably solemn!
Things so gay
Pierce—by the very Press
Of Imagery—

Their far Parades—order on the eye
With a mute Pomp—
A pleading Pageantry—

Flags, are a brave sight—
But no true Eye
Ever went by One—
Steadily—

Music's triumphant—
But the fine Ear
Winces with delight
Are Drums too near— (No. 582)

Like the dreamer of "I tend my flowers for thee," the poet seems almost to kill nature in the effort to poeticize it.

"Arcturus" is his other name—
I'd rather call him "Star."
It's very mean of Science
To go and interfere!

I slew a worm the other day—
A "Savan" passing by
Murmured "Resurgam"—"Centipede"!
"Oh Lord—how frail are we"!

I pull a flower from the woods—
A monster with a glass
Computes the stamens in a breath—
And has her in a "class"!

Whereas I took the Butterfly
Aforetime in my hat—
He sits erect in "Cabinets"—
The Clover bells forgot.

What once was "Heaven"
Is "*Zenith*" now—
Where I proposed to go
When Time's brief masquerade was done
Is mapped and charted too.

What if the poles sh'd frisk about
And stand upon their heads!
I hope I'm ready for "the worst"—
Whatever prank betides!

Perhaps the "Kingdom of Heaven's" changed—
I hope the "Children" there
Won't be "new fashioned" when I come—
And laugh at me—and stare—

> I hope the Father in the skies
> Will lift his little girl—
> Old fashioned—naughty—everything—
> Over the stile of "Pearl." (No. 70)

"Inconceivably solemn" and "Arcturus" present poets in their aspect of destroyers rather than as the creators we normally assume them to be and Dickinson certainly acknowledges them to be in poems like "To pile like Thunder to it's close" (No. 1247), "The Martyr Poets" (No. 544), or "I would not paint—a picture—" (No. 505). In "Arcturus" Dickinson is ostensibly condemning science—the astronomers, biologists, and botanists who label and classify God's creation and thereby interfere with the spontaneity and integrity of the natural universe— for putting flowers in a class or setting butterflies "erect in 'Cabinets.'" But, in fact, the poet is no more respectful of nature's autonomy and vitality than is the scientist she attacks. After all, it is the "I" of the poem who slays the worm. All the scientist does is murmur "Centipede." (In one of her letters to Higginson Dickinson confesses "Today I slew a Mushroom"—L 413). It is the poet who "pulls the flower from the woods," the scientist who "Computes her stamens"; the poet who captures the butterfly, the scientist who displays it in his collection. The poet, like the scientist, errs in holding nature too cheap. In desiring to see nature as a comprehensible symbol of something beyond nature, both poet and scientist succeed only in particularizing, reducing, fragmenting, and even destroying it.

But it is not nature alone that suffers from the poet's improvident intrusion. In "'Arcturus'" the poet acknowledges her own possible disenfranchisement, and she hopes that God will forgive her and thus allow her to enter heaven. She hopes that a loving God will ignore, with paternal wisdom, the poet's naughty invasion of his universe and will therefore consent to "lift his little girl— / Old fashioned— naughty—everything— / Over the stile of 'Pearl.'"

The poet in "This was a Poet" does not promise to fare so well. Although he does not think that his assigning of contrasts and portions can "harm" either his public or "Himself," we learn that it indeed can. For while the poet thinks that he is accruing a divine "Fortune" and thereby securing his immortality, making himself, as it were, "Exterior—to Time," the technical devices of Dickinson's poem—the chopped language and the image heaped uncomfortably upon image (in the last two lines especially)—suggest that what the poet achieves is a total dislocation of self, a divorcing of the self from the self and of the self from the universe and from time, as well. In other words, the poet veritably effects upon himself a distillation and a distortion of his own essences in which the integral self perishes like any other familiar species. "Himself" is divided from "Him" until he has become only a perversely ironic "Fortune," "Exterior—to Time," walled up like Poe's Fortunato in his own conceits or, like the Dickinsonian spider whom we shall meet in a moment, caught in the web of his own fantastic creative multiplicity.

The first line of "This was a Poet—It is That" expresses the problem nicely. There are two grammatical antecedents for the word "That": "Poet" is one and the sentence "This was a Poet" is the other. The opening line of the poem, therefore, seems to be saying that, just as the poet distils amazing sense from ordinary meanings with all of the liabilities which that implies, so the public's statement, its label "This was a Poet," also distils amazing sense from ordinary meanings, with a similar effect. The sentence "This was a Poet" neatly distances the poet from his audience, impersonalizes him, so that he also becomes like a familiar species perishing by the door, the victim of his readers' similarly arresting imaginations. Like the poet, the public controls, delimits, and labels the objects of its perceptions: while in one mood, his readers may elevate the poet into a god ("The Poet—it is He—"), thus letting him have his problematical effect on humanity, nature, and himself; in another frame of mind his audience will degrade him into a "This" or a "That" or a wholly impersonal "it."

The dangerous aspect of poetry as it is here schematized is, then, twofold. Poetry can, if not properly handled, disturb our potentially full and rich interaction with the universe; it can exploit reality as mere subject matter for the interpretative eye and thus render our view of nature fragmented and frozen. But poetry can also be dangerous to the poet who wields this deadly power with careless abandon. The poet who places nature upon the rack is, we discover, as much the tortured as the torturer, for the "fine Ear" must "wince" and "no true

Eye" can behold the "mute Pomp" and "pleading Pageantry" without blinking.

It is not simply that the poet doubts her own artistic capabilities, as she does seem to do in "I would not paint—a picture—."

> I would not paint—a picture—
> I'd rather be the One
> It's bright impossibility
> To dwell—delicious—on—
> . . . .
> I would not talk, like Cornets—
> I'd rather be the One
> Raised softly to the Ceilings—
> And out, and easy on—
> . . . .
> Nor would I be a Poet—
> It's finer—own the Ear—
> Enamored—impotent—content—
> The License to revere. (No. 505)

Nor is the issue that she doubts the power of art in general, although she is certainly capable of such doubts.

> How the old Mountains drip with Sunset
> How the Hemlocks burn—
> How the Dun Brake is draped in Cinder
> By the Wizard Sun—
> . . . .
> These are the Visions flitted Guido—
> Titian—never told—
> Domenichino dropped his pencil—
> Paralyzed, with Gold— (No. 291)

Nor do I even want to suggest that Dickinson is, in "This was a Poet," just arguing for the superiority of nature over art as she does, for example, in this poem:

> The Veins of other Flowers
> The Scarlet Flowers are
> Till Nature leisure has for Terms
> As "Branch," and "Jugular."
>
> We pass, and she abides.
> We conjugate Her Skill

> While She creates and federates
> Without a syllable. (No. 811)

Dickinson, I would like to insist, is pointing to the far more grim possibility that art not only cannot say it all, but that in trying to say it all, in attempting to "conjugate" "Terms," art distorts and perhaps even destroys.

The poet, therefore, must hold herself in check lest she find herself, presumptuous creature that she is, swept off the face of the earth, a victim of the fantastic and flimsy conceits she herself has wrought.

> The Spider holds a Silver Ball
> In unperceived Hands—
> And dancing softly to Himself
> His Yarn of Pearl—unwinds—
>
> He piles from Nought to Nought—
> In unsubstantial Trade—
> Supplants our Tapestries with His—
> In half the period—
>
> An Hour to rear supreme
> His Continents of Light—
> Then dangle from the Housewife's Broom—
> His Boundaries—forgot— (No. 605)

The problem of poetic formulation is, for Dickinson, very much one of boundaries. The artist, she insists, must recognize the proper limits beyond which language cannot and ought not go. It is not that Dickinson is a nature-loving rustic who wants to abandon the whole territory of abstract, literary investigation. Like Emerson before her, Dickinson realizes that idealist philosophy is what frees man from the "despotism of the senses"[7] and puts him in a position to understand the message that nature truly intends to impart. As Dickinson herself puts it,

> Perception of an object costs
> Precise the Object's loss—
> Perception in itself a Gain
> Replying to it's Price—

7. Emerson, *Nature*, in Atkinson (ed.), *Selected Writings*, 27.

> The Object Absolute—is nought—
> Perception sets it fair.

But, unfortunately, perception does not know its own limitations. Like the spider that throws its mock creativity in the face of the only true creator and that actually believes itself more secure for having spun its flimsy web, so the poetic perceiver "then upbraids a Perfectness / That situates so far—" (No. 1071). It is not simply, as one critic has suggested, that the spider is destroyed because it makes itself "vulnerable" to the "disintegrating forces" of the universe when it actualizes its "timeless ideality," or, as other critics have implied, that Dickinson is concerning herself with the inescapable mathematics of perception.[8] Rather, in one of her most significant, most dominant moods, Dickinson wants us to see art as a potential affront to the divine order, a presumptuous attempt to harmonize and synthesize within the meager limitations of human understanding a reality that is clearly superior to the notion of reality bequeathed to humankind and thus beyond the powers of the human imagination. What Dickinson discovers in many of her best poems is a way to poeticize and even to symbolize that does not "arrest" or "pierce" and thereby ultimately "upbraid" all of its achievements. In this way Dickinson endeavors to find a way to set creation "fair." She tries to discover a mechanism of preserving the unconflatable distance between nature and God that protects each in its inviolable integrity and yet that does not prevent the necessary, unifying intercourse between them. How Dickinson symbolizes without simultaneously stultifying, fragmenting, and reducing the universe, how she creates symbols that are humanly meaningful and yet theologically reverent, is, I believe, the key to her poetic technique and the very backbone of her symbolic philosophy.

8. JoAnne De Lavan Williams, "Spiders in the Attic: Suggestions of Synthesis in the Poetry of Emily Dickinson," *Emily Dickinson Bulletin*, XXIX (1976), 23; and Weisbuch, *Emily Dickinson's Poetry*, 161. See also Charles R. Anderson, *Emily Dickinson's Poetry: Stairway of Surprise* (New York, 1960), 90–92.

Chapter Five

When the Soul Selects: Dickinson's Critique of New England Symbolism

*I*N her revision of the symbol usages she considered inadequate or distortive, and specifically in her recognition of the phenomenon of symbolic reduction, Dickinson, it seems to me, was to a large extent reacting to the special history of New England symbolism, to the patterns of perception and diction that she believed characterized both her Puritan ancestors and her Transcendentalist contemporaries. However the Puritans and the Transcendentalists differed, on one central point they fully agreed. The universe, explained latter-day Puritan Jonathan Edwards, is "an ideal one." "Nature," wrote Emerson, is "the symbol of spirit." [1] Furthermore, in the views of both the Pu-

---

1. Quoted by Clarence H. Faust and Thomas H. Johnson (eds.) *Jonathan Edwards: Representative Selections* (New York, 1935), xxvii; and Ralph Waldo Emerson, *Nature*, in Brooks Atkinson (ed.), *Selected Writings of Ralph Waldo Emerson* (New York, 1950), 14. On the relationship between the Puritan and Transcendentalist imaginations, see Perry Miller, "From Edwards to Emerson," in *Errand into the Wilderness* (Cambridge, Mass., 1956); and Sacvan Bercovitch, *The Puritan Origins of the American Self* (New Haven, 1975). See also Octavius Brooks Frothingham, *Transcendentalism in New England: A History* (1876; rpt. New York, 1959), 107–108. Related discussions include: Albert Gelpi,

ritans and the Transcendentalists, certain human beings have been specially equipped, either by the direct intervention of the divine spirit (for the saints) or by the penetration of the oversoul (for the Transcendentalists), to interpret correctly nature's essentially symbolic communications.

This Puritan and Transcendentalist tendency to see the universe and the individual in a relationship of cryptograph and decoder suggested to Dickinson that even the most personal, antitypological forms of symbolic thought, the kinds of symbol usage that might most appeal to a private poet like Dickinson, might be no more capable of escaping the stultifying liabilities of symbolic reduction than sacramental or ideal symbolism. For Dickinson, both groups of American symbolizers were frequently guilty of a symbolic, theosophic hybris that so exaggerated the ability of individual consciousness to interpret cosmic truth and symbolic correspondences and so literalized the accuracy of the individual's perceptions that truth virtually became the exclusive property of the anointed Puritan or Transcendentalist exegete. The vast, subtle ambiguity of cosmic meaning was, by the conflations of that symbolism, hopelessly reduced, detached, and frozen into the particular and limiting symbols of a private or coterie mythology. It is not merely that these Puritan and Transcendentalist tendencies erred in the direction of synecdoche and analogy. The Puritans and Transcendentalists were not simply taken in by nature's "sophistries." Rather, their symbolism, as they commonly defined it, tended to declare itself so absolutely accurate that it became a symbolic reduction monstrously exaggerated. Like many other symbolic systems, it insisted on a conflation of heaven and earth. And that conflation, Dickinson realized, was almost certain to result in an explosion

Emily Dickinson: The Mind of the Poet (New York, 1971), 55–93; Allen Tate, "New England Culture and Emily Dickinson," in Caesar R. Blake and Carlton F. Wells (eds.), *The Recognition of Emily Dickinson: Selected Criticism Since 1890* (Ann Arbor, 1968), 166–67; Hyatt Waggoner, "Emily Dickinson: The Transcendental Self," *Criticism*, VII (1965), 302, and *American Poets, From the Puritans to the Present* (Boston, 1968); John S. Wheatcroft, "Emily Dickinson's Poetry and Jonathan Edwards on the Will," *Bucknell Review*, X (1961), 102, and "Emily Dickinson's White Robes," *Criticism*, V (1963), 135–47; and William Sherwood, *Circumference and Circumstance: Stages in the Mind and Art of Emily Dickinson* (New York, 1968), 138.

into disunity, a mutual excluding of one from the other and of man from a meaningful relationship with either. New England symbolism, Dickinson hinted in her poems, could well strip God of His cosmic power. It could, if not modified, abandon mankind to an isolated, solipsistic existence within an unenlightened, godless, nightmare world of the verbalizing self.

In order to understand Dickinson's attitude toward what she considered the false symbol worship of much Puritan and Transcendentalist thought and the symbolic reduction that accompanied it, it will be useful to review briefly both the leading features of New England's versions of sacramentalism and idealism and the responses of several American writers who intuited their problematical nature. The Puritan faith in cosmic symbolism, especially as that symbolism was found recorded on the scriptural page, was the offspring of a peculiar blend of literary attentiveness and personal self-interest. For a variety of political and theological reasons too complex to explore here, the American Puritans took it upon themselves to apply to biblical exegesis a stunning new literalism. They proclaimed New England the living Israel and identified themselves as the Israelites incarnate—the "visible saints" in Edmund Morgan's phrase. Sacvan Bercovitch has recently described the Puritans' relationship to biblical language as follows: "The Puritan colonies loudly proclaimed their orthodoxy, but when they announced that 'America' was a figural sign, *historia* and *allegoria* entwined, they broke free of the restrictions of exegesis. Instead of subsuming themselves in the *sensus spiritualis*, they enlisted hermeneutics in support of what amounted to a private typology of current affairs."[2] In the Puritans' view, in other words, they and their world were autotypological and antitypological both. They themselves were the symbolic, scriptural center, and that center grew outward of its own divine impulsion. Their words, therefore, had a special power.

2. Edmund Morgan, *Visible Saints: The History of a Puritan Idea* (Ithaca, N.Y., 1963), and Bercovitch, *Puritan Origins*, 112–13. On the problem of Puritan typology, see also Perry Miller, *Roger Williams: His Contribution to the American Tradition* (Indianapolis, 1953), esp. 33ff., and Edmund Morgan, *Roger Williams: The Church and the State* (New York, 1967), 86–94. See also Charles Feidelson, Jr., *Symbolism and American Literature* (Chicago, 1953), 88–89.

Transcendentalism, although it firmly disavowed any close kinship with Puritanism's theological assumptions, did inherit its literalistic faith in a highly private, synecdochic symbolism. For Emerson, nature is not only a "symbol of the spirit," the universe, the "externalization of the soul," it is the creation of the spirit as well: "Nature is not fixed but fluid. Spirit alters, moulds, makes it. . . . Every spirit builds itself a house, and beyond its house a world, and beyond its world a heaven. Know then that the world exists for you"— i.e., exists not only to serve you, but exclusively in your own perceptions. The human spirit would seem literally to create its own world. In this view, the individual's interpretation of the symbols of the material world becomes a commentary on the self, and the validity of that commentary is guaranteed by the fact that the individual is god and exegete both. As Bercovitch suggests, the Transcendentalist "responds to nature insofar as he embodies its spirit in himself, and he symbolizes well insofar as he conforms to nature." Or as Feidelson explains, even more fully:

In his effort to shake off any links with the rational world, [Emerson] projected a world in which only symbols exist. We ourselves, from his standpoint, "are symbols," and we "inhabit symbols." The poetic image is identical not only with the universe it generates but also with the human being through whom it is actualized. . . . Emerson asserts, in effect, the identity of "I mean" and "it means"; he maintains that there is no distinction between the poet's act of "meaning," the poet himself, and the "meaning" of things.

To some extent, Emerson's problem reflects the human problem generally: "Man lives in a symbolic universe," Cassirer tells us. "No longer can man confront reality immediately, he cannot see it, as it were, face to face. . . . Instead of dealing with things themselves, man is in a sense constantly conversing with himself." But in *Nature* Emerson asserts that we can know nature "face to face," that we can see directly and without our own interposed mediation. Thus, the symbols created by Emerson in *Nature* and elsewhere become highly problematic. They are absolute in just the way that Cassirer suggests they cannot be.[3]

The literalism and egocentricity of the Transcendentalist formula-

3. Emerson, *Nature*, in Atkinson (ed.), *Selected Writings*, 3 and 42 and "The Poet," in *ibid.*, 325; Bercovitch, *Puritan Origins*, 59; Feidelson, *Symbolism and American Literature*, 145; and Ernst Cassirer, *An Essay on Man* (New Haven, 1969), 25.

tion (as it is here expressed) and of the Puritan conception it echoes
represented for Dickinson an essential violation of what ought to be
the reverential, tentative quality of the truly religious symbol. As Paul
Tillich suggests, "Religious symbols represent the transcendent but do
not make the transcendent immanent. They do not make God a part
of the empirical world."[4] In large measure, New England symbolism
seemed to Dickinson to try indeed to make the "transcendent immanent." Words, in keeping with the prescriptions of *Nature*, seemed to
have been made into literal signs of natural and theological facts,
when (in Dickinson's view) they could only be signs of fallible human
perception.

Thus, as Dickinson scrutinized the arguments of at least one powerful stream of her Puritan and Transcendentalist predecessors, she
found herself responding, I believe, to a literalness of symbolic interpretation and to a dangerously haughty self-assurance in the individual's ability to comprehend and reproduce the symbolic code. This ar-
rogant literalness, we might note, does not go unnoticed in prior
American intellectual history. Even as early as the Puritan period itself, Roger Williams pointed out the absurdity of literalistic Puritan
hermeneutics.

If . . . Scripture may now literally be applied to nations and cities in a parallel
to Canaan and Jerusalem since the Gospel, and this Psalm 101 be literally applied to cities, towns, and countries in Europe and America—not only such as
essay to join themselves . . . in a corrupt church estate, but such as know no
church estate, nor God nor Christ, yea, every wicked person and evil doer,
must be hanged or stoned, as it was in Israel.

"Only the spiritual Israel," Williams argued, "and seed of God, the
newborn, are . . . one."[5]

Williams's sensitivity to the Puritan heresy and its inevitable results
was revived two centuries later by Nathaniel Hawthorne. In "Young
Goodman Brown," for example, Hawthorne traces through to its re-

4. Paul Tillich, "The Religious Symbol," in Rollo May (ed.), *Symbolism in Religion and
Literature* (New York, 1960), 77.
5. Roger Williams, *The Bloudy Tenent, of Persecution, for Cause of Conscience*, in Miller,
Roger Williams, 150 and 151. Bercovitch discusses Williams in *Puritan Origins*, 109–110.

ductio ad absurdum two Puritan tenets specifically linked to literalistic Puritan exegesis—the doctrines of visible sanctity and spectral evidence. As Michael J. Colacurcio argues, "what Hawthorne suggests is that the 'real' breakdown of faith in Salem Village and its 'enfigured' loss in Goodman Brown are both the result of Puritanism's ecclesiastical positivism, of its definitive attempt to found a church (and beyond it a state) on the premise that visible sanctity can be made to approximate true sanctity." The confident assumption of Puritanism that it could locate and externalize God's community of saints eventuated, according to Hawthorne, in the destruction of the entire Puritan theocracy. Similarly, the displacement by Transcendentalism of visible sainthood from the elect saint to the sanctified everyman produced a comparable confusion between outer signs and inner grace. Writes Colacurcio in another essay:

"Rappaccini's Daughter" seems to depend for its specific conception as directly on the transcendental understanding of faith as "Young Goodman Brown" does on the Puritan problem of spectral evidence. . . . Faith in the literal and symbolic Beatrice is alike a recognition of the Incarnated Word; in both cases the recognition must be spiritual, unmediated by evidence of any other kind.

Colacurcio adds, "Only Emerson's crassly pseudo-spiritualistic, materialistic physicians" (who represent a facile and misdirected Transcendentalism) "would conclude that bad breath is an infallible sign of innate depravity," which is precisely, of course, what Giovanni does conclude.[6] In many of her poems, Dickinson, like Williams and Hawthorne, represents her own responses to the excesses of symbolic literalness that are often expressed by the Puritans and the Transcendentalists. She describes the reductive consequences of the particular symbolic mode of perception that her fellow New Englanders were wont to apply to their interpretations of the cosmos. And she adds to this an awareness of the culpability of language in the heresies of re-

6. Michael J. Colacurcio, "Visible Sanctity and Specter Evidence: The Moral World of Hawthorne's 'Young Goodman Brown,'" *Essex Institute Historical Collections*, CX (1974), 296, and "A Better Mode of Evidence—The Transcendental Problem of Faith and Spirit," *Emerson Society Quarterly*, LIV (1969), 18–19.

ductive symbolism. As Emerson himself had recognized in one of his more skeptical moments, "language overstates" and this is the "intrinsic defect," as he called it, of even the most lofty brands of symbolism.[7]

In the context of the nineteenth-century literary responses to Puritan and Transcendentalist misperceptions of Christian language and symbolism, "The Soul selects" seems to me a self-conscious attempt specifically to indict both Puritan and Transcendentalist modes of interpretation within the same framework of symbolic culpability.

> The Soul selects her own Society—
> Then—shuts the Door—
> To her divine Majority—
> Present no more—
>
> Unmoved—she notes the Chariots—pausing—
> At her low Gate—
> Unmoved—an Emperor be kneeling
> Upon her Mat—
>
> I've known her—from an ample nation—
> Choose One—
> Then—close the Valves of her attention—
> Like Stone—   (No. 303)

The poem has long been a subject of debate among Dickinson critics, some arguing that the poem represents a model of Emersonian self-reliance, others (and this is the more recent position expressed) that the poem typifies the arrogance of an un-Christian self-reliance.[8] The latter view seems to me the correct one, and I think that the earlier view of the poem as being a celebration of the self arose precisely because of the dialectical, essentially philosophical nature of the poem's central argument. For the poem intends to make us see the way in which elements of both Puritanism and Emersonianism share certain

7. Quoted by Feidelson, *Symbolism and American Literature*, 161.
8. See, for example, A. A. Hill, "Poetry and Stylistics," in Seymour Chatman and Samuel R. Levin (eds.), *Essays on the Language of Literature* (Boston, 1967); Simon Tugwell, "Dickinson's 'The Soul Selects Her Own Society,'" *Explicator*, XXVII (1969), item 37; Elizabeth B. Bowman, "Dickinson's 'The Soul Selects Her Own Society,'" *Explicator*, XXIX (1970), item 13; Will C. Jumper, "Dickinson's 'The Soul Selects Her Own Society,'" *Explicator*, XXIX (1970), item 5; and Clark Griffith, *The Long Shadow: Emily Dickinson's Tragic Poetry* (Princeton, 1964), 210–15.

fundamental misperceptions about the self, and how these judgmental errors affect the individual in the most basic areas of his or her social and introspective concerns. The poem, furthermore, casts the crisis of self in a philosophical context. It links psychology, sociology, and theology to a problem in the interpretation and articulation of human perception that is anterior to perhaps all other human interests. The poem is undoubtedly a psychological study of the relationship between the self and the soul, and it traces the effects of a certain egocentric tendency on the relationship between the individual and society and between the individual and God. But the poem does not present this problem in a cultural void. Phrases like "The Soul selects," "her divine Majority," "an ample nation," and "Choose One" are intended to call to mind several of the platform doctrines of Puritan faith—the Calvinist principle of divine, inscrutable selectivity, for example, the covenant of grace, and the analogy between the individual saint and the chosen nation, Israel. The crisis of the relationship between the self and the soul (and between individual and society and between individual and God) has specific origins in America's Puritan past. But it also derives from certain habits of Transcendentalist thought as well. For the poem does not develop its language into a description of a Puritan God. Instead, it recounts the activities of a private, personal, independent soul. The poem, in other words, borrows the trappings of Puritan theology and applies them to phenomena that are in the province of psychology, and specifically to the preoccupations of Emersonian Transcendentalism as they are formulated in such essays as "Self-Reliance" and *Nature*.

The implications of the compounding are important. From the emphatic yoking of family characteristics it is suggested that the Puritan Church, although it claimed to be a communal enterprise whose congregants were at all times subservient to their creator, was essentially egotistical and elitist, and that Transcendentalism, that supposedly democratic faith of all men, was as cruelly cliquish as its Puritan ancestor. In Dickinson's poem, the Transcendentalist soul, in perfect imitation of her Calvinistic father, makes an absolute and passionless judgment to select a "divine" "society" of saints, to choose "One" from among the "ample" nations of the world to be her chosen Israel.

But the poem is more than an attack on the historical phenomenon of Puritan-Transcendentalist snobbery. It is an investigation of the inevitable consequences of a particular dogma that happened to have been shared by Puritans and Transcendentalists. And it is an attempt to demonstrate, graphically as well as thematically, how this dogma, which was dependent upon ill-conceived symbols and types, corrupted our perception of cosmic reality and impaired our relationship to society and the universe. What happens, Dickinson asks in the poem, if we pursue Puritan logic concerning election, visible sanctity, and biblical exegesis to its inescapable implications (as did, for example, Anne Hutchinson, Roger Williams, or Young Goodman Brown)? Might we not discover, she suggests, that we are continually paring down the numbers of the elect until only a "Majority" of "One," every man's own individual soul, exists? In other words, she postulates that, if one believes sainthood to be a visible phenomenon, visible, however, only to the saint in whom the indwelling spirit already resides; and if, furthermore, one grants that there are no objective or universal criteria for the determination of who is or is not a saint· *except* for the externalized and absolutely rendered subjective criteria (the self-created and consequently self-referential symbols) of the saints themselves, then the individual saint may well find himself in a situation in which he can know and accept only himself. American Transcendentalism, in this view, becomes merely the latest manifestation of the antinomian heresy that was implicit in Puritanism itself. Dickinson's identification of Puritan and Transcendentalist doctrines was not meant, as one critic claims, to affirm Transcendentalism as her new "faith," but to condemn those aspects of both American *isms* that involved them in the same spiritual distortions.[9]

For Dickinson, both the Puritans and Transcendentalists could be seen as archly antisocial and self-seeking. Both groups seemed convinced of the infallibility of their judgments, and therefore they dramatized their beliefs—reified them—in their fragmenting sym-

9. On the antinomian impulse in American literature, see Roy Harvey Pearce, *The Continuity of American Poetry* (Princeton, 1961) 124–85. The fact that Dickinson scored passages in the writings of various theologians who treated the problem of solitude and solitariness does not indicate that she accepted their assertions (see Jack L. Capps, *Emily Dickinson's Readings, 1836–1886* [Cambridge, Mass., 1966], 61 ff.).

bols (represented in the poem by the disjointed, capitalized symbols of "Majority," "Chariots," "Emperor," and "One"). The effect of this arrogance was a usurpation of the authority of God and the substituting of a special, literal, ultimately inaccurate interpretation of the universe for its actual and authentic dimensions. According to the logic of the Puritan position as it is presented in the poem, the sainted soul, which in Puritanism was supposed to be the object rather than the agent of election, initiates its own process of selection and rejection. In an antinomian frenzy the soul selects its "own Society"—i.e., not only a society that the soul defines according to its own preferences and priorities, but a society that is itself alone. The soul becomes its own narrowly restricted "Majority" of "One," its own self-sufficient universe, emotionless and unmoved by any and all entreaties from the world outside itself. The "Valves" of its heart and mind, we are told, are closed like "Stone."

Furthermore, the prideful soul dramatized in Dickinson's poem rejects not only the "Chariots" of heaven but the supplications of the "Emperor" himself. Ironically, the fully realized Puritan-Transcendentalist soul, because it images itself in the likeness of its God, excludes God from the society of self. The soul ought to "always stand ajar / That if the Heaven inquire / He will not be obliged to wait" (No. 1055).[10] When the soul fails to "stand ajar," when it bolts the door that would provide it access to heaven (No. 1055), then grace cannot be achieved. The implications of Calvinist and Transcendentalist doctrine, it seems, when carried to their logical extremes, force the soul into a position that is not only antinomian but atheistic as well. In damning the universe the soul, Dickinson implies, damns itself. Spiritual and physical deathliness, therefore, pervade "The Soul selects." The "Mat" upon which the emperor kneels, the "low Gate," and the shutting of the "Door," all image the grave, while the closing of the heart's "Valves" figures death itself. Self-worship is a kind of spiritual death, Dickinson insists. Furthermore, it seems to result, when physical death occurs, in the soul's being totally and absolutely cut off from whatever succor salvation in God might have provided.

10. Clark Griffith, *The Long Shadow*, 212–14.

The logic of the poem is, of course, circular. In a vision of the world founded upon a dour, elitist God, the emulating soul offers and receives no charity. The soul, for example, in the first stanza of the poem, asks explicitly to be left alone: "To her divine Majority— / Present no more—." But the soul's haughty imperative is also a tacit recognition of its own total disenfranchisement, for when the soul shuts the door finally and unequivocally upon the world and God, it is no longer "present" in that world, no longer "present" even to itself. It is as if the soul disintegrates, stubbornly resolving itself into nonexistence. The soul's unconditional assertion of self is also its destruction of self—an idea supported in the poem by the presence of a first-person narrator who is clearly distinct from her soul. The essence of self (the I) and the spirit of self (the soul) are, in "The Soul selects," no longer synonymous or even closely interactive.

Because of the literalistic, reductive inclinations of both Puritan and Transcendentalist symbolizing, material data appear to be spiritual signs. Verbal symbols seem to be hallowed incarnations of the divine or human-divine scheme. But as the form of Dickinson's poem suggests— the capitalizations of the poem's symbolic quantities (the soul, society, door, majority et al.) and the plentiful, disruptive dashes—the symbolic elements of such a vision of the universe are embodiments not of unity but of disintegration and destruction. And the most culpable symbol in the American worship of symbols seemed to Dickinson to be the "Soul" itself.

Dickinson's poem is a carefully conducted investigation into the reductive consequences of a certain kind of symbolic perception that finds its focus, in this poem, in the human soul. Paradoxically, as the soul moves further and further inward toward the exclusive oneness and immateriality represented by the concept of the soul, its cosmic relationships—its relationship to the creation, for example, and its relationship to the self—become impaired and finally collapse. Things outside the soul become more and more individuated and disparate as things inside move closer and closer to unity and nonexistence. In the final moments of the poem, the "Valves" of the poet's feelings and perceptions, as well as the "Valves" of her literal life and the life of the entire cosmic organism, close. She becomes a "Stone"—not an immaterial unity but an inanimate, self-contained, wholly material chunk of what Dickinson calls in another poem "Quartz contentment" ("After great pain, a formal feeling comes—" No. 341). The soul's grotesquely heightened sense of itself, its emphatic and unyielding selfishness, creates a universe of unbridgeable gaps—a Puritan world reduced to extremities, divided between God and man, saint and sinner; a polarized Emersonian universe, totally devoid of Emersonian capacities for self-revision, eternally split into self and other, me and not-me; and a neoplatonic cosmos immobilized in symbols and essences, matter and spirit.

In a system or vision in which every soul is its sainted self-creator, the universe, Dickinson explains, could become nothing more than a chaos of self-sufficient fragments moving in hostile isolation from one another. The soul, like its prototype in a puristic Puritanism or an intransigent Transcendentalism, may not intentionally set out to wreak the cosmic havoc of which it is guilty. But the behavior the soul chooses to adopt, and its linguistic persuasions, may carry with them inescapable consequences that affect not only the world but the soul itself. For, although it is true that the soul consciously controls the selection of its own society, it is not clear, when the door shuts in line 2, whether the soul shuts it or whether it shuts itself: "Then—[pause] shuts the Door." The analogous transitive-intransitive alternatives for the word "Present" in line four have already been noted. Likewise, in stanza three, though the soul does actively choose the "One" that it is to be, it is not so certain whether the soul closes the valves of its attention or whether the valves—acting on some kind of inevitable imperative of their own—close themselves: "Then—close the Valves of her attention." The soul has lost self-control, and even syntax suffers from the disintegrative influences of symbol-wielding arrogance. When the soul chooses to pursue the Adamic course and seek after divinity, it may find itself justly thrust out of Eden and into the fragmented, postlapsarian creation.

For Dickinson, the soul's acute sense of its own regal autonomy determines both its view of the cosmos and the fate of the individual whom such a soul inhabits. The separation of soul from self is examined repeatedly throughout the Dickinson canon. The poet writes in one poem, for example, that "No Rack can torture me . . . Except Thyself may be / Thine Enemy—" (No. 384); and, in another, "Of Consciousness, her awful Mate / The Soul cannot be rid" (No. 894). Dickinson is "afraid to own a Body" and equally "afraid to own a Soul" (No. 1090). The "Soul," she suggests in a poem about "Consciousness," is "condemned to be— / Attended by a single Hound / It's own identity" (No. 822). And as she portrays the relationship of soul and self in another poem:

> The Soul unto itself
> Is an imperial friend—
> Or the most agonizing Spy—
> An Enemy—could send—
>
> Secure against it's own—
> No treason it can fear—
> Itself—it's Sovreign—of itself
> The Soul should stand in Awe— (No. 683)

Psychological torment such as Dickinson describes in these poems, and in others, is a commonplace feature of much familiar Romantic poetry. We need only think of Edgar Allan Poe in the American tradition to see how neatly Dickinson seems to fall within the framework of dark Romanticism. But, for Dickinson, the incentive to describe what she calls the "Funeral" in her brain (No. 280) is no mere striving after introspective verisimilitude. In Dickinson's view, the torture of the mind that afflicts her and her fellow New Englanders results from the peculiarly literalistic way they tended to interpret themselves and their world, their inclination to discover divinity within the fleshliness of self and their desire to find an absolute and material symbol for the immaterial spirit of the divine.

Dickinson's poems on the soul are, therefore, not simply abstract statements about the dualities of mind that have affected all men in all times. Rather, they are specific judgments rendered against American intellectual origins as they are interpreted by Dickinson. I turn again to Sacvan Bercovitch, who explicates the features of this Puritan inner "civil war" as follows: "We can say . . . that [the Puritans] believed 'man's chief concern should be with the welfare of his own soul,' only if

we bear in mind their horror at the 'very name of Own,' their determination 'to *Hate* our *selves* and *ours*,' their opposing views of *soul* and
self." But, as Bercovitch also points out, the Puritans' constant attention to the abnegation of self is as potent a form of "self-involvement"
as any that characterized the Romantics or Transcendentalists, who
were also, we might note, perilously balanced (like Whitman) between
singing the self and celebrating the other.[11] To put it differently, Puritan selflessness can be interpreted as a form of consummate hybris,
and the obsessive devotion to one's immaterial and immortal soul can
be seen as an inverted way of celebrating one's material and very mortal self. Similarly, Transcendentalist universalism could be taken as
being as private and exclusive as any doctrine of the chosen that characterized the Puritan position. When Dickinson's persona, therefore,
says "I'm Nobody," her pun implies, on one level of meaning, that in
having no body but plenty of soul she is indeed a step above the plane
of the ordinary (No. 288). Like "the Drop, that wrestles in the Sea,"
the persona cannot, for all her recognition of cosmic vastness, forget
to argue "me" (No. 284).

The problem is not, for Dickinson, that the self-reliant, independent soul does not represent an attractive option. The different readings of "The Soul selects," as I have already suggested, are undeniably
based on real features of the poem. But Dickinson fully recognized
the dangers of the temptation to absolute self-reliance, and she located their source in the intellectual history of New England.

Dickinson expresses a similar position in "The Soul's Superior in-
stants." Here Dickinson identifies strongly with the soul's lofty and singular position, and yet she also betrays a suspicion that the soul that
has "ascended" beyond the plane of the ordinary and the "Mortal" to
have revealed to it the knowledge of eternity and immortality is vulnerable and somewhat painfully isolated.

> The Soul's Superior instants
> Occur to Her—alone—
> When friend—and Earth's occasion
> Have infinite withdrawn—

11. Bercovitch, *Puritan Origins*, 17 and 20.

> Or She—Herself—ascended
> To too remote a Hight
> For lower Recognition
> Than Her Omnipotent—
>
> This Mortal Abolition
> Is seldom—but as fair
> As Apparition—subject
> To Autocratic Air—
>
> Eternity's disclosure
> To favorites—a few—
> Of the Colossal substance
> Of Immortality. (No. 306)

The soul's solitude, Dickinson fears, may be cold and barren, accentuated by friendlessness and utter isolation: "Her—alone—." And the soul's arrogance is unabidable: "She—*Herself*—ascended / To *too* remote a Hight / For *lower* Recognition" (italics added). The vocabulary is heavy with moral criticism. For what is the nature of this "Superior" or haughty "Mortal Abolition," this regal abolishing of everything human? It is "as fair" "As Apparition," as a ghost or phantom that is not only insubstantial but spectral and ghastly as well.

Dickinson's attitude toward the Calvinist faith of Amherst was, as critics have long realized, highly ambiguous. On the one hand she was disturbed by her own lack of full Christian conviction; on the other, she was repelled by the extremes of religious passion that swept over her friends and relatives. Nonetheless, the keynote of her poetic verdict on Calvinistic Protestantism is, I think, a condemnation of local and historical Puritanism that goes far deeper than an occasional snarl at the church's "Cherubic" "Gentlewomen" (No. 401) or a hurt outcry against a tyrannical deity. Many of Dickinson's poems about the soul suggest that at the heart of her questioning of Calvinist theology is a profound philosophical insight into the ways Puritan definitions can hinder a person's proper relationship to God, to nature, and to other individuals. And the source of the problem, Dickinson suggests, may be the way Puritanism tends to force the individual to look at the self and the soul as absolute chosen quantities and then to project the self and its actions as literal transcripts of divine reality.

Thus, it is an egomaniacal concern with self that, in the following poem, prompts the narrator to attempt to distinguish between soul and self and thereby to destroy the soul.

> I cautious, scanned my little life—
> I winnowed what would fade
> For what w'd last till Heads like mine
> Should be a-dreaming laid.
>
> I put the latter in a Barn—
> The former, blew away.
> I went one winter morning
> And lo—my priceless Hay
>
> Was not upon the "Scaffold"—
> Was not upon the "Beam"—
> And from a thriving Farmer—
> A Cynic, I became.
>
> Whether a Thief did it—
> Whether it was the wind—
> Whether Deity's guiltless—
> My business is, to find!
>
> So I begin to ransack!
> How is it Hearts, with Thee?
> Art thou within the little Barn
> Love provided Thee? (No. 178)

The narrator scans her "little life" because she believes that she can separate the perishable self from the immortal soul and thus preserve the soul. But the effect of her intensive self-examination is to render suspect the initial premise that there is, in fact, an immortal soul to be preserved. Like so many other inadequate modes of synecdochic perception, this Puritan-like self-analysis proceeds along lines of all-consuming analogical hypotheses that not only reduce the soul to hay but then subject it to the hay's ultimate perishability.

Dickinson's Puritan-related poems suggest that Calvinist typology may well force individuals into a view of deity and self that is at odds both with the spirit and the letter of Christianity. Calvinist typology may drive a wedge between the saint and the redeemer, between the soul and the whole of the phenomenal and noumenal universes, both.

And the agency of this destructive power, in Dickinson's view, may well be the literalism and egocentricity that convert the human imagination into an isolated producer of discrete and severed symbols. It is a system that makes man the sole exegete of his own referential symbolism.

It is, of course, Emerson's express purpose, announced in the "Divinity School Address," *Nature*, and other essays, to correct the basic heresies of Puritan faith, to put God back into nature and spirit back into humankind. But if the essential problem with the tendencies of Puritan ideology is not, in Dickinson's view, that it degrades humankind and exaggerates the power of the deity, but, quite the opposite, that through its particular brand of symbolic philosophy it disproportionately magnifies the exegetical authority of the saints and thereby diminishes God, then the affirmation by Emersonian Transcendentalism of a similar kind of symbolism does little to correct the principal problem. As George Whicher has pointed out, one of the functions of Dickinson's poetry is to "test the transcendent ethic." [12] Dickinson does this, in part, by considering one of the Transcendentalists' basic tenets, that it is possible to escape the paradoxes and perilous dilemmas of the symbolic interpretation of God and of nature by relocating all of the elements of experience within a framework of individual consciousness. "Contradiction," Emerson writes, is not the real form of nature: "Nature keeps herself whole and her representation complete in the experience of each mind." [13] In other words, even though Emerson may acknowledge that individuals cannot always know the world, dualistic or otherwise, at the same time he insists that they can know the processes of their own private, independent psyches, and that in the internal world of the mind a whole and entire image of nature is maintained. (Relevant here is Feidelson's definition of American symbolism as discovering a point of departure outside dualism.) Poetry, then, and the symbolic representations of language concern themselves, in the Emersonian view, with nothing more, nothing less,

12. George Frisbie Whicher, *This Was a Poet: A Critical Biography of Emily Dickinson* (Ann Arbor, 1957), 200.
13. Quoted in Feidelson, *Symbolism and American Literature*, 159. Cf. also Emerson, *Nature*, in Atkinson (ed.), *Selected Writings*, 412.

than consciousness itself. This, Dickinson realizes, is the premise on which Emerson, the early, optimistic Emerson, at least, and other Transcendentalists assert that the phenomenal universe in all of its multifaceted variety is an outward projection of the perceiving self. And indeed this very premise has been the starting point of one major critical position in the interpretation of Dickinson's own poems.[14]

But according to Dickinson, the same terms of philosophical idealism that enable the Transcendentalists to turn inward and ignore much of the complexity of external reality may also create within the individual world of self-reflection an identical pattern of emanation, hypostasis, and collapse. This new linguistic or symbolic reality becomes not only a powerful mirror of outside events but, even more, a horrifying culmination of all the tendencies toward dualistic simplification and symbolic reductiveness that initially corrupt our perceptions of the external universe. It does not seem to matter to Dickinson whether you begin with the phenomenal universe and work your way inward to an image of self or if you begin with an image of self and expand outward into a philosophy of cosmic relationships. The abyss-leaping fallacies of synecdochic symbolism and the illusion of the allegedly spiritual authority of sense perception are in no way by-passed by Transcendentalist theory, even though a later, more mature Emerson will rationally insist (in language remarkably similar to that of Martin Foss) that symbols be "fluxional": "the quality of imagination is to flow," Emerson suggests, "not to freeze"—and he will accept, intellectually at least, that "we have no means of correcting these colored and distorting lenses which we are." Nonetheless, the early Emersonianism that set the New England imagination ablaze was not so cautious or restrained, and the consequences for American symbolic consciousness in the middle nineteenth century, so far as Dickinson was concerned, verged on the dangerous.[15]

As I shall try to show in the final chapters of this study, the integrity

14. See for example Inder Nath Kher, *The Landscape of Absence: Emily Dickinson's Poetry* (New Haven, 1974), 94.

15. Emerson, "The Poet," in Atkinson (ed.), *Selected Writings*, 336, and "Experience" in *ibid.*, 359. On Dickinson's criticism of Transcendentalism, see Glauco Cambon, "Emily Dickinson and the Crisis of Self-Reliance," in Myron Smith and Thornton Parsons (eds.), *Transcendentalism and Its Legacy* (Ann Arbor, 1966), 129.

of individual consciousness is for Dickinson, as for the Transcendentalists, a primary component in any quest toward knowledge. It
will not do, therefore, to underestimate the importance of such consciousness for Dickinson's overall symbolic philosophy. But like every
other element in Dickinson's aesthetics, consciousness, too, must be redefined. Dickinson begins this work of redefinition with the Transcendentalist notion that consciousness is as vast and complex as the universe itself: "The Brain—is wider than the Sky— / . . . The Brain is
deeper than the sea— / . . . The Brain is just the weight of God—"
(No. 632), she writes. But it is precisely because of this acceptance of the
vastness of consciousness that consciousness becomes, for Dickinson,
so potentially overwhelming. The fact that "Drama's Vitallest Expression" is "infinite enacted / In the Human Heart" carries with it terrifying corollaries:

> Drama's Vitallest Expression is the Common Day
> That arise and set about Us—
> Other Tragedy
>
> Perish in the Recitation—
> This—the best enact
> When the Audience is scattered
> And the Boxes shut—
>
> "Hamlet" to Himself were Hamlet—
> Had not Shakespeare wrote
> Though the "Romeo" left no Record
> Of his Juliet,
>
> It were infinite enacted
> In the Human Heart—
> Only Theatre recorded
> Owner cannot shut— (No. 741)

Although from one point of view the carefully scripted tragedies of
the human heart, which Dickinson in another poem calls "dying in
Drama," might seem more tame, more controllable than dying in fact,
the fictional reenactment of death within the individual consciousness
is a dying even more painful, more horrific, than the conventionally
proffered definition of death, because so long as consciousness per-
sists, the "dying in Drama" is endless, the "Theatre" is never "shut."

> We dream—it is good we are dreaming—
> It would hurt us—were we awake—
> But since it is playing—kill us,
> And we are playing—shriek—
>
> What harm? Men die—externally—
> It is a truth—of Blood—
> But we—are dying in Drama—
> And Drama—is never dead—
>
> Cautious—We jar each other—
> And either—open the eyes—
> Lest the Phantasm—prove the Mistake—
> And the livid Surprise
>
> Cool us to Shafts of Granite—
> And just an Age—and Name—
> And perhaps a phrase in Egyptian—
> It's prudenter—to dream— (No. 531)

The language of the poem is purposely ambiguous. The poem would seem to be suggesting, simply, that "dreaming," the "dying in Drama," is "prudenter" than the cold "truth" of dying "externally" in "Blood." The dream version of death is presumably a fiction from which we can awaken. It is a "Phantasm" that may frighten us and cause us to jar ourselves into waking consciousness, but it is, after all, only a "Phantasm" in which one's own imagination invents the details and controls their unfolding into dramatic form.

But precisely because the narrator assumes that death can be taken out of external reality and relocated within the dream world of the mind, the dying in drama takes on a literalness and a significance that make it far more terrifying than dying in fact. What Dickinson's poem demonstrates, I believe, is exactly how "dying in Drama" is not "prudenter," how it is not safer or wiser, than dying literally. The third stanza is crucial in this regard, for the vocabulary and syntax make possible an interpretation of the poem that is strikingly alternative to the ostensible one cited above. In this second reading the dreamers wake themselves not lest the dream (one meaning of the word "Phantasm") prove to be a mistake and the dreamers discover they are dead, but lest the conventional concept of death (another meaning of the word "Phantasm") prove to be the mistake and they find that drama is actually what death is—that the "Phantasm" itself (whether it is death incarnate or only a dream of death) will prove to them ("Lest the Phantasm—prove") that it is a "Mistake" to think that playing cannot kill or that a shriek cannot harm. Whether their deaths are literal or merely histrionic, the dreamers are, after all, in some sense dead by the end of the poem, cooled, as it were, to "Shafts of Granite" by their dream.

In other words, when the dreamers jar each other into wakefulness, it is not simply to prove to themselves that they are alive. It is to escape the deathliness not of life but of the dream world itself. The daily cycle of waking and sleeping that the poem describes, is, accordingly, a version of dying even more terrifying than the version represented by the external truth of blood. It affords no respite from death. It promises no resurrection. The poem itself is a model of this seamlessly closed circle in which beginning and end are flawlessly interdependent and continuous: "It's prudenter—to dream—," the poem ends; and it begins, "We dream." The dream world becomes the most grotesque incarnation of the shattering facts of neoplatonic existence, an awesomely literal, because wholly internalized and consciously felt, rendering of an emanation, hypostasis, and epistrophe in which the individual closes his eyes to die and then, horribly, jars himself awake only to sleep and die again, ad infinitum. The consequences of the literalness and continuity of this pattern—the result, in other words, of the translocation of death from the far distant external universe to the vitally present, ever continuous internal universe of self—is to concretize and literalize the experience of dying. The dreamers can no longer hope to be someday delivered to a glorious, everlasting reunion with God. Instead they must metamorphose, while still alive, into their own self-enclosed graves, into the "Shafts of Granite" that recall the "Quartz contentment" and stoniness of another Dickinson poem. Whether death is literal or figurative, whether the dream is a mistake or death incarnate, the dreamers in some sense die: they "jar each other— / And either—open the eyes—" only to be cooled, figuratively, into "Shafts of Granite" by the shock of what they discover, or, literally to die. The "either" in line 10 (while ostensibly referring to either one of the dreamers) implies the unstated "or," the possibility that the dreamers may not open their eyes and that they may literally die of fright.

Dickinson's poem suggests that a Transcendentalist solution to the bewildering finality of death may be no solution at all. The facts of human existence, whether they exist phenomenally in the universe at large or simply within the imagination of the perceiving self, are always and everywhere the same. Furthermore, the tragedies acted out within the human heart are more significant than all others because the "dying in Drama" is an unending scenario, "Drama—is never—dead." In Dickinson's view, then, the problem with a concept of all-supreme, all-dictating consciousness, whether within a Transcendentalist system or some other system, is that it replaces what Emerson rightly identifies as an unsophisticated "labyrinth of the senses" with an equally bewildering and dangerous maze of subjective perceptions. It substitutes a shadow world of fragmentary glimpses for a genuinely informed perception of the world, and it results in a "Vail" of obliterating and reductive symbolic form, a "Maelstrom" of unending illusion and therefore eternal dying that is wholly solipsistic.

> 'Twas like a Maelstrom, with a notch,
> The nearer, every Day,
> Kept narrowing it's boiling Wheel
> Until the Agony
>
> Toyed coolly with the final inch
> Of your delirious Hem—
> And you dropt, lost,
> When something broke—
> And let you from a Dream—
>
> As if a Goblin with a Guage
> Kept measuring the Hours—
> Until you felt your Second
> Weigh, helpless in his Paws—
>
> And not a Sinew—stirred—could help,
> And sense was setting numb—
> When God—remembered—and the Fiend
> Let go, then, Overcome—

As if your Sentence stood—pronounced—
And you were frozen led
From Dungeon's luxury of Doubt
To Gibbets, and the Dead—

And when the Film had stitched your eyes
A Creature gasped "Repreive"!
Which Anguish was the utterest—then—
To perish, or to live? (No. 414)

The position expressed in the poem recalls Emerson's retrenchment in "Experience" from the glib optimism of *Nature*. "Dream delivers us to dream," writes Emerson, "and there is no end to illusion." [16] Existence, as it is defined in the poem, is also a kind of "Dream" from which death, however ghastly it might seem, would somehow free us. But death, it emerges, is not outside the pale of the world of dreams. The "boiling Wheel" that resolutely carries humankind forward toward destruction and the "Goblin with a Guage" that measures out the seconds until the final demise, are part and parcel of both the dream and the antidream that is death. Both are versions of the "Maelstrom, with a notch"—the nightmare vision in which dreams are firmly notched to the reality from which dreams would seem to preserve us.

By the end of the poem, death and dream have changed places. Death becomes a "Film" with which the eyes are stitched in permanent self-reflection and illusion, a "Repreive" not from the agony of life but from the cessation of painful consciousness, from the relief normally associated with death. The maelstrom becomes the awesome reality that recalls the individual from the salvation that is death. The dream and the reality, the maelstrom and death, become interpenetrating currents in the vast ever-churning, ever-narrowing funnel of symbols that the poem describes. In the maelstrom whirl, the individual is forced down through the center of "Dream" and the "luxury of Doubt" into the grim facts of the "Gibbets, and the Dead," which are themselves versions of the same dream, and which offer the same illusion of "Repreive."

But because of the inescapable concentricity of the whirl, the "Re-

16. Emerson, "Experience," in Atkinson (ed.), *Selected Writings*, 345.

preive" is nothing more than a new sentencing, a returning to the flux and flow of the maelstrom contraction and maelstrom expansion, from death to dream to death again. The awakening from dream into life, therefore, as in the poem "We dream," is simultaneously an awakening from dream into death, which is the ultimate dream. Life becomes a process of eternal dying in which the "Anguish" never ceases, for "to perish" and "to live" are one and the same phenomenon. Both occur together within the self-contained, self-referential, self-created universe of the mind, a universe reduced from external cosmos to the internal world of the self.

This kind of universe of self, then, is even more oppressive than the universe of external reality, because the world of the wholly autonomous mind, as Emerson himself acknowledges, offers no escape from its own terrible, translocated implications. The mind may be its own cosmic creator. It may dictate its terms and populate its own, symbolic country. But once the maelstrom reality of circling wheels and cartwheeling goblins is internalized, once it is credited with ultimate reliability, it begins to assume a self-propelling autonomy that usurps the authority of the creating mind and sets into motion a plot in which all the participants in the drama become the tightly tethered puppets of the play's own irreversible momentum. For this reason, "'Twas like a Maelstrom" is written in a fascinating blend of active and passive voice in which the actors' potential control over images and events, even over themselves, immediately collapses into a surrender of authority to some unnamed outside power. Such phrases as "you dropt," "something broke," "God—remembered," and "the Fiend / Let go" are only a few examples of the way in which Dickinson mimetically reproduces the maelstrom whirl in which the actor and the acted upon, the creator and the created, the master and the slave are unified in a pageant of frenzy and chaos that is an unending "Anguish" to all. In Robert Weisbuch's terms, if death is the antitype of which anguish is the type, then the conflation of type and antitype may be a horror in which there is no mediating shorthand, no saving distance between the human and the divine, physiological decay and Christian resurrection.[17]

17. Robert Weisbuch, *Emily Dickinson's Poetry* (Chicago, 1972), 78–107.

In her explorations of Transcendentalist symbolism Dickinson comes to realize that not only does the "Brain" have "Corridors—surpassing / Material Place," but that once the self has locked itself within the corridors of consciousness, the "Body," which is mortal, material, and inescapably linked to the facts of physiological constitution, will not allow the self to escape ("One need not be a Chamber—to be Haunted—" No. 670). And even if the body does not itself conspire in the treacherous assault on isolated consciousness, the mind can provide its own mechanism for molesting its solipsistic egocentricity, as it does in the following poem:

> I know some lonely Houses off the Road
> A Robber'd like the look of—
> Wooden barred,
> And Windows hanging low,
> Inviting to—
> A Portico,
> Where two could creep—
>
> One—hand the Tools—
> The other peep—
> To make sure All's Asleep—
> Old fashioned eyes—
> Not easy to surprise!
>
> How orderly the Kitchen'd look, by night,
> With just a Clock—
> But they could gag the Tick—
> And Mice wont bark—
> And so the Walls—dont tell—
> None—will—
>
> A pair of Spectacles ajar just stir—
> An Almanac's aware—
> Was it the Mat—winked,
> Or a Nervous Star?
> The Moon—slides down the stair,
> To see who's there!
>
> There's plunder—where—
> Tankard, or Spoon—
> Earring—or Stone—
> A Watch—Some Ancient Brooch

> To match the Grandmama—
> Staid sleeping—there—
>
> Day—rattles—too
> Stealth's—slow—
> The Sun has got as far
> As the third Sycamore—
> Screams Chanticleer
> "Who's there"?
>
> And Echoes—Trains away,
> Sneer—"Where"!
> While the old Couple, just astir,
> Fancy the Sunrise—left the door ajar! (No. 289)[18]

The mind, Dickinson suggests, is like a lonely house, set off from daily commerce with the rest of the interactive social world. "Wooden barred" and closed, it is enveloped in the kind of dream-like condition described in "We dream" or " 'Twas like a Maelstrom, with a notch." But the house, the mind, is not as removed from the rest of the universe as it seems. Not only is it vulnerable to the "plunder" of robbers, but the "Windows hanging low," the eyes that are shut in their sleepy dream but that can, at will, open up onto the daylight world, invite this intrusion. Furthermore, those "two" who "creep" and "peep" and wake the mind into an apprehension of "Sunrise" and the two who leave the door "ajar" and force the mind to open out to the world, are the same two. They are the mind itself, the "old Couple" (the two eyes), which inhabits the mind. The windows do not invite the robbers without knowing beforehand that the "Mice wont bark" and the "Walls—dont tell." But the price that the solipsistic, idealist mind may pay for its reentry into the world is high. In this poem it is plundered of its wealth because it can find no way to reconcile its internal gifts with its external commitments. As Dickinson puts it in "One need not be a Chamber," it is "safer" to confront "External" ghosts, literal robbers, than to meet the "Cooler Host" of one's own devising, for the "Assassin" that is the mind itself forces a communion between mind and

18. Virginia Ogden Birdsall, "Emily Dickinson's Intruder in the Soul," *American Literature*, XXXVII (1965), 57. Cf. also Jean McClure Mudge, *Emily Dickinson and the Image of Home* (Amherst, 1975), 6–8.

world that is terrifying in the extreme (No. 670). It is a consummation in which nature (Chanticleer and the moon) must employ violence, perhaps even violation, in order to arouse the "sleeping" "Grand-mama" who is the Sleeping Beauty of our internal reality.

In Dickinson's view the mind offers a precise replication of events outside the mind. But because it also presents a drama that is simultaneously a dream (a Poesque "dream within a dream"), its cycles of horror may never end. They may not permit the lapse into unconsciousness that can be the ultimate escape from reality. As Dickinson once wrote in a letter, "Eternity" is "dreadful" to contemplate because it perpetuates the awful "state of existence" that, in the absence of eternity, death could mercifully alleviate (L 28). And as Clark Griffith has demonstrated, one of the ways Dickinson came to terms with the reality of death was by appreciating just how death provided a respite from life.[19] Dickinson realizes that the soul's pretense to looking at death, fictitiously scanning it and staring at it because it believes that "To know the worst, leaves no dread more—," may force the mind to imprison itself within precisely that reality it wishes to flee. Thinking death into the territory of the mind cannot control it, for the "Looking at Death" and the probing of "Retrieveless things" are themselves intensified versions of "Dying."

The same or similar points are principal concerns in

> 'Tis so appalling—it exhilirates—
> So over Horror, it half Captivates—
> The Soul stares after it, secure—
> To know the worst, leaves no dread more— (No. 281)

and

> I tried to think a lonelier Thing
> Than any I had seen—
> Some Polar Expiation—An Omen in the Bone
> Of Death's tremendous nearness—
>
> I probed Retrieveless things
> My Duplicate—to borrow—
> A Haggard Comfort springs

---

19. Griffith, *The Long Shadow*, 113.

> From the belief that Somewhere—
> Within the Clutch of Thought—
> There dwells one other Creature
> Of Heavenly Love—forgot—
>
> I plucked at our Partition
> As One should pry the Walls—
> Between Himself—and Horror's Twin—
> Within Opposing Cells—
>
> I almost strove to clasp his Hand,
> Such Luxury—it grew—
> That as Myself—could pity Him—
> Perhaps he—pitied me— (No. 532)

The narrators of both of these poems discover that mental solipsism is no antidote for the dangers and tensions of mortality. When the mind, in its own self-circumscribing seclusion, looks out on death, when it "stares after it" or thinks about it, it sees only an endless repetition of the very same cycle of living and dying that the mind had hoped it could evade. Only when one agrees to "let go the Breath" can death be "done" (No. 281). For when one tries to discover "within the clutch of Thought" a "Duplicate" to the self that will neutralize the phenomenon of death, one initiates a collapse into horror in which pity replaces love as the ultimate sentiment of cosmic destiny, and the dying becomes endless.

Dickinson does not in these poems dispute the importance of the inner life. She does, however, suggest that just as one must avoid the dangerous conflating of God with nature if one is to preserve faith, so there must be no mistaking of the mind and of the life within the mind for the created universe and for life as God ordains it. Thus, even as Dickinson affirms that "Each Life Converges to some Centre," she still suggests that "Life's low Venture" cannot by itself accomplish what eternity can and must achieve on its own.

> Each Life Converges to some Centre—
> Expressed—or still—
> Exists in every Human Nature
> A Goal—
>
> Embodied scarcely to itself—it may be—
> Too fair

For Credibility's presumption
To mar—

Adored with caution—as a Brittle Heaven—
To reach
Were hopeless, as the Rainbow's Raiment
To touch—

Yet persevered toward—surer—for the Distance—
How high—
Unto the Saints' slow diligence—
The Sky—

Ungained—it may be—by a Life's low Venture—
But then—
Eternity enable the endeavoring
Again. (No. 680)

The mind can and must pursue its goal, but the sky cannot be gained by
the unassisted self: "As well the Sky / Attempt by Strategy," Dickinson
writes in another poem (No. 359). Although the mind can go through
all the motions of life, death, resurrection, and immortality, the pattern it dramatizes is only a distant parody of these events. Immortality
becomes the prolonging of the consciousness of dying as opposed to
the awaking into an eternality of life-everlasting. (The Dickinsonian
distinction between immortality and eternity will become crucial in
chapter seven.) Therefore, the mind must take careful note of the distance between itself and heaven. It must ever be alert to the dangers
of its desire to put itself at the center not only of its own life but of the
cosmic life as well. As Dickinson puts it in another, related poem:

Growth of Man—like Growth of Nature—
Gravitates within—
Atmosphere, and Sun endorse it—
But it stir—alone—

Each—it's difficult Ideal
Must achieve—Itself—
Through the solitary prowess
Of a Silent Life—

Effort—is the sole condition—
Patience of Itself—
Patience of opposing forces—
And intact Belief—

> Looking on—is the Department
> Of it's Audience—
> But Transaction—is assisted
> By no Countenance— (No. 750)

The "Growth of Man," Dickinson agrees, does gravitate "within." It is, as the early Emerson would have it, wholly autonomous, private, and personal. It achieves "it's difficult Ideal" "Itself," through the "solitary prowess / Of a Silent Life." But even more important, perhaps, the mind achieves its goals through a "Patience of opposing forces / And intact Belief." The mind must accept the "opposing forces" of the external world and of its own opposition to that world. For belief to remain intact these forces cannot be reconciled and thus abated. They must remain in eternal opposition. The "Atmosphere" and "Sun," therefore, may "endorse" the "solitary" life of the mind. They may play "Audience" to the mind's great enactments. But they are wholly separate from the mind, and, by implication, the mind from them. Not to preserve the mind in its inviolable integrity and, vice versa, not to secure the universe from the ravages of the mind, is to lose both universe and self to the fusion that destroys. When things "go to pieces on the Stones / At bottom of my Mind," as they do in another poem, Dickinson tells us that she "blamed the Fate that fractured—*less* / Than I reviled Myself" (No. 747). The mind contains within its own structure the "Stones" that fracture cosmic unity, because it insists on "entertaining Plated Wares / Upon [its] Silver Shelf." The mind, in other words, makes itself vulnerable to the substantial torment of the larger reality precisely because it cannot content itself with granting to the universe the same separate, "solitary" existence that it must similarly afford itself. Both man *and* nature, earth and heaven gravitate separately, "*within.*" It is the confusion between the two, the mind's engulfing of the world, that threatens to destroy them both.

In Dickinson's view, the tendencies of Puritan and Transcendentalist thought clarify the ultimate, faith-destructive liabilities of a desire to see the world in the kind of symbols that conflate inner and outer, God and nature, soul and self. Not only is New England symbolism of this sort reductive, but because it is a *religious* symbolism that seems to insist, perversely, on ignoring fundamental theological structures, it can become the enemy of faith as well. In trying to render the universe as an integrated whole, the constructs confirmed and passed on by the Puritans and Transcendentalists tend to abolish the significant theological distance between man and God. They threaten to collapse the entire universe into an expression of individually saved or enlightened souls. As a result, a new divide is opened. And unlike the divinely ordered, salutary distance between heaven and earth, this man-made abyss is eternally unbridgeable. It is a gulf in which there is no avenue for meaningful intercourse between the deity and His creation. The self is ever isolated in its own literalistic reductive symbolism. It never accedes to resurrection or immortality. It is doomed by its own choice of symbolizing fictions endlessly to dramatize a death that is no longer an agent of Christian promise and that no longer transports humankind to heaven.

Symbolism, Dickinson suggests, must somehow preserve the rational, differentiated structure of the Christian universe. I will now examine some of the means that Dickinson employs for achieving this profoundly religious objective.

Chapter Six

The Assignable Portion: Dickinson's Symbolic Poetics Defined

*M*Y aim in the preceding chapters has been to demonstrate that, in various ways and for a wide variety of reasons, much of Dickinson's poetry is explicitly concerned with exposing the fallacies of various symbolic systems, that at its core Dickinson's poetry, for all its abundant display of symbols, is adamantly critical of many of the strategies we frequently associate with poetic symbolism. It might, therefore, be logical to conclude that the direction that Dickinson's evolving poetics assumes and the course that this study is about to take is toward the defining of an aesthetic of silence, what George Steiner has called a "retreat from the word" and the concomitant belief that "where the word of the poet ceases, a great light begins."[1] Indeed, many of

---

1. George Steiner, *Language and Silence: Essays on Language, Literature, and the Inhuman* (New York, 1967), 39. For critics who interpret Dickinson's poetry as an attempt at reproducing silence, see Donald E. Thackrey, *Emily Dickinson's Approach to Poetry, University of Nebraska Series* (Lincoln, Neb., 1954), 19–22 and Roland Hagenbüchle, "Precision and Indeterminacy in the Poetry of Emily Dickinson," *ESQ: A Journal of the American Renaissance*, XX (1974), 40.

Dickinson's poems, especially her poems about poetry and art, would seem to support just such an interpretation of her work. In one poem, for example, Dickinson tells us explicitly that

> The Definition of Beauty is
> That Definition is none—
> Of Heaven, easing Analysis,
> Since Heaven and He are one. (No. 988)

"Beauty—be not caused—It Is—," she writes elsewhere; "Chase it, and it ceases— / Chase it not, and it abides—" (No. 516). "The Definition of Melody—" she tells us, "is— / That Definition is None" (No. 797).

Words, therefore, may have no role to play in the telling of ultimate cosmic truths.

> "Hope" is the thing with feathers—
> That perches in the soul—
> And sings the tune without the words— .
> And never stops—at all—. . . . (No. 254)

> By intuition, Mightiest Things
> Assert themselves—and not by terms. . . . (No. 420)

> Nature . . . creates and federates
> Without a syllable. . . . (No. 811)

The most important truths of the universe may be too large to be contained within the paradigms of human language.

> We learned the Whole of Love
> The Alphabet—the Words—
> A Chapter—then the mighty Book—
> Then—Revelation closed—

> But in Each Other's eyes
> An Ignorance beheld—
> Diviner than the Childhood's—
> And each to each, a Child—

> Attempted to expound
> What Neither—understood—
> Alas, that Wisdom is so large—
> And Truth—so manifold! (No. 568)

Words may be incapable of conveying the essence of cosmic knowl-edge: "I found the words to every thought / I ever had—but One— / And that—defies me—" (No. 581).

And, yet, as the writer of over 1,700 poems and 1,000 (known) letters, Dickinson is anything but silent. In fact, Dickinson seems abso-lutely to abhor silence, not, perhaps, because she believes in the power of words, but because she is inclined to be even more skeptical of the efficacy of silence. "Silence is all we dread," she begins one poem,

> There's Ransom in a Voice—
> But Silence is Infinity.
> Himself have not a face. (No. 1251)

And even more terrifying to her than silence itself is the attempt to poeticize silence, to make it a part of the linguistic experience.

> There is no Silence in the Earth—so silent
> As that endured
> Which uttered, would discourage Nature
> And haunt the World. (No. 1004)

Silence, in Dickinson's view, may be synonymous with death, and with a ghastly, haunting death at that. Silence may not be ecstatic reunion, in either idealist or Christian terms. It may be utter detachment, in-stead; the lonesome, eternal distance created by a "ransom" or a re-demption that dangles unattainably beyond humankind's reach. How-ever language may distort meaning, it is just possible that silence is simply the absence of meaning, the ultimate cosmic default. There-fore, Dickinson writes that

> Death's Waylaying not the sharpest
> Of the thefts of Time—
> There Marauds a sorer Robber,
> Silence—is his name—
> No Assault, nor any Menace
> Doth betoken him.
> But from Life's consummate Cluster—
> He supplants the Balm. (No. 1296)

Silence, in other words, not only cannot intimate meanings that lie magically beyond human verbalization, but it may destroy existing

meanings, human and cosmic both. As Dickinson suggests in still another poem,

> Great Streets of silence led away
> To Neighborhoods of Pause—
> Here was no Notice—no Dissent
> No Universe—no Laws—
>
> By Clocks, 'twas Morning, and for Night
> The Bells at Distance called—
> But Epoch had no basis here
> For Period exhaled. (No. 1159)

By collapsing all reality into a permanent consistency of "Morning"
and "Night," "silence" in this poem veritably annihilates the "Universe" and all its "Laws" as well. "Silence" of the senses accompanies
the ultimate "Pause" of time, so that when the "Period" at the end of
time and of the poem exhales, i.e., when both time and the structure
of linguistic meaning have died, there is simply nothing left—nor
anything left to say.

Thus, even if Dickinson distrusts words, especially the tendency of
language to employ words as sacramental or idealist symbols, she also
distrusts silence. This Janus-faced critical position, which I believe
characterizes much of Dickinson's work and which may be partly responsible for the vividly rendered hesitancy that permeates her work,
might certainly have left the poet in an impossible dilemma, a damned-
if-you-do, damned-if-you-don't straddling of her literary and philosophical fences. But as Steiner's case for poetic silence itself makes
clear, the "suicidal rhetoric of silence" is only one of the two options
available to the writer "who feels that the condition of language is in
question." The other alternative is to "render his own idiom representative of the general crisis," to make language "convey" through itself
the "precariousness and vulnerability of the communicative act."[2]

Much of Dickinson's poetry is involved in just this kind of mimetic
representation of the crisis of human language, and beyond that, of
the dangers inherent in a symbolic interpretation of language that in-
vests words with their formidable authority. To some degree Dickinson's

2. Steiner, *Language and Silence*, 49.

symbolism can be explained as an attempt to demonstrate the frailty of language. Her symbols, in this view, represent the significant failure of conventional symbolism. The Dickinson who uses symbols to this end is the poet-as-realist, the poet described in chapter one, who likes the "look of Agony" simply because she knows "it's true" (No. 241) and who questions our cosmic knowledge because she knows how faulty our perceptual apparatus really is. Dickinson employs symbols and discusses them because she knows that symbols are a legitimate human concern; we are indeed "animal symbolicum."

But Dickinson's realism transcends the mere acknowledgment that human language and human knowledge are problematical. By placing her poems within a decidedly symbolic framework, Dickinson implies that the verbalization of symbolic consciousness is part and parcel of the poetic act, that without symbols there can be no access to any knowledge whatsoever, even if the knowledge obtained points to the ultimate fallibility of the symbols that communicate it. In other words, Dickinson's symbolism is not just a straw man that she assembles only for the sake of tearing it down again. It is no analogue of what, in one mood, seems to Dickinson a frivolously neoplatonic universe that is created only to be destroyed. Kenneth Burke remarks that "on some occasions . . . we humans might like to exercise our prowess with symbolic systems, just because that's the kind of animal we are."[3] Very much in this vein, Dickinson shows her enjoyment of symbols just as she allows herself to enjoy the dangerous beauty of a world that can as easily kill as it can comfort or the brilliance of a deity who can blind as easily as He can save. Dickinson's symbols, therefore, are a statement about human psychology, an extended insight into man's creative nature. In recognizing the profound psychological and aesthetic necessity for symbols, Dickinson locates what she calls the "assignable" "portion," that part of cosmic experience that is eminently accessible to symbolic representation. By elaborating this kind of symbolism, she demonstrates vital connections between life and language. It is Dickinson's conception of a revised symbolism, carefully set out for us in much of her best poetry, that I will now examine in detail.

3. Kenneth Burke, *Language as Symbolic Action: Essays on Life, Literature, and Method* (Berkeley, 1968), 29.

Like many of the poems we have already discussed, "I heard a Fly buzz—when I died—" is an eloquent and energetic critique of the dangers of apparent symbolic synecdoches and alleged symbolic translucence. Like "These are the days," "This was a Poet," and "I had not minded—Walls—," the poem is pointedly critical of many conventional symbolic assumptions. But in "I heard a Fly buzz" Dickinson does more than simply clarify the dangers of one kind of symbolic seeing. In this poem she explains why, despite her serious reservations about conventional symbolic strategies, she insists on employing the devices of symbolism in her verse; she articulates the essential features of her reformed symbolic language, her concept of a revised symbolism that can acknowledge the imperfections of human perception and then go on to circumscribe those imperfections and incorporate them into a symbolic vision.

> I heard a Fly buzz—when I died—
> The Stillness in the Room
> Was like the Stillness in the Air—
> Between the Heaves of Storm—
>
> The Eyes around—had wrung them dry—
> And Breaths were gathering firm
> For that last Onset—when the King
> Be witnessed—in the Room—
>
> I willed my Keepsakes—Signed away
> What portion of me be
> Assignable—and then it was
> There interposed a Fly—
>
> With Blue—uncertain stumbling Buzz—
> Between the light—and me—
> And then the Windows failed—and then
> I could not see to see— (No. 465)

The poem argues two interrelated theses. The first, which corresponds to the arguments presented in poems like "These are the days" and "I tend my flowers for thee," suggests that to base one's faith in heaven on analogical or sacramental relationships between this world and the next may result in a misperception of both nature and heaven, and that it may also reduce the wholly spiritual heaven to a materialistic kingdom of unmitigated death and decay. The second argument, however, suggests quite a contrary idea. Simply to deny the symbolic correspondences, Dickinson suggests, however flawed and misleading they are, may be to substitute *not* truth for falsehood, but nullity for ambiguity; merely to discard symbolism, in other words, may be to substitute the absence of all meaning and sense for the partial glimmers of understanding afforded by even faulty symbolic seeing.

One way or another, Dickinson's poem about death and a fly is usually and plausibly interpreted along conventional symbolic lines. It is seen as an almost perfect embodiment of the three levels of parallel meaning required by traditional symbolic exegesis, and all three levels (each of them well explicated in recent scholarship) would seem to suggest that the various phenomena associated with death—the biographical details of the deathbed, the psycho-physiological responses of the person who is dying, and the theological or philosophical context in which death occurs—are all facets of a single, multidimensional reality.[4] The poem's symbols, like the symbols in "These are the days," for example, seem to forge a sacramental wholeness out of the apparently disparate elements in which the universe consists. But, curiously enough, the symbolic layers of the poem thus considered do not so much reinforce each other as they contradict one another. Each of the symbol's multiple meanings in some sense invalidates each of its other meanings. The fly, for example, can be interpreted as both a literal, physical housefly, existing in the concrete reality of the external world, and as a metaphor for the death of consciousness, a death that would, for all intents and purposes, obliterate the existence of the literal, physical world. One set of significations has the effect of re-

4. Among the many excellent discussions of this poem see Charles Feidelson, Jr., *Symbolism and American Literature* (Chicago, 1953), 90; Caroline Hogue, "Dickinson's 'I heard a Fly Buzz when I Died,'" *Explicator*, XX (1961), item 26; George Frisbie Whicher, *This Was a Poet: A Critical Biography of Emily Dickinson* (Ann Arbor, 1957), 298; Thomas W. Ford, *Heaven Beguiles the Tired: Death in the Poetry of Emily Dickinson* (University, Ala., 1966), 113; Ronald Beck, "Dickinson's 'I Heard a Fly Buzz,'" *Explicator*, XXVI (1968), item 26; Will C. Jumper, "Footnote to 'Dickinson's I Heard a Fly Buzz': One More Swat," *Poet and Critic*, VI (1971), 33; and Robert Weisbuch, *Emily Dickinson's Poetry* (Chicago, 1972), 99ff.

pudiating the other. Similarly, the windows that fail are intended to signify, simultaneously, the external windows of the house, the windows that are the eyes, and the window that is the soul, and yet, the total eclipse of the outer world essentially denies the existence of eyes and soul both; and if the eyes and soul cannot see (another version of the death of consciousness), then it is as if the literal windows do not exist. The combined effect of this set of potentially self-isolating and mutually annihilating symbols is, I believe, to create, not a unity of cosmic experience, but as the symbol's many meanings begin to split apart and cancel each other, a nullity instead.

The poem's conclusion becomes the fitting end to what I would see as the continuous symbol-discarding process of the poem, for it is precisely when the "Fly" interposes itself "Between the light" and the speaker that the windows fail, "and then," the narrator tells us, "I could not see to see—." In these concluding lines the speaker brings together the discrete currents of the poem's symbolizing activities. She asserts the apparent interpenetration of all realms of existence as most symbolic systems insist that we must. She does this, however, not by rhapsodizing on the perfect harmony of the multifaceted, interpenetrating universe, but by depicting the collapse of all perception and of all faith—of all presumed symbolic correspondences—in death. As the fly, which is the principal symbol in the poem, positions itself between the speaker and the light—the light of nature, of eyesight and insight, and of divine revelation—all of the "Windows" "then" fail, and "then," the poetic persona tells us, she can no longer "see to see." As consciousness fades, the world fades, and vice versa; as the world and consciousness ebb out, the promise of Christian immortality (represented by the "King") also disappears. Because of the intrusive symbol, the fly, the speaker can no longer see physically or spiritually, nor can she see any reason to see, physically or spiritually. Every element in the cosmic design seems to fail in its task of confirming and supporting every other element. The symbolic structure, of the universe and of the poem, collapses. A void swallows up consciousness and the poem both, and the poem ends "I could not see to see—," with those infamous Dickinsonian dashes at the end.

The concluding lines of the poem transform what appears to be a poem of symbolic parallelisms into a renunciation of symbolic perception, a statement about the "fraud" that may well "cheat" the Christian symbolist of the revelation of the "King." The fly emerges as the dark agent of this renunciation, not only because of what it denotes symbolically but because of the very fact that the narrator has determined to interpret it along conventional symbolic lines. A symbol, the poem is suggesting, depends for its existence upon conscious perception; it has no independent existence. When, therefore, death comes and consciousness fails, the symbols of consciousness also fail. Thus the fly comes to represent death and decay on all levels. Physical death, according to the logic of the poem, equals intellectual death, which in turn equals spiritual death. But the fly is forced to represent this consummately destructive equation only because the speaker of the poem aids and abets in endowing it with symbolic meaning. Just as the speaker in "These are the days" is willing to accept birds and sophistic skies and autumnal seeds as authentic verifications of the fact that scripture, like nature, is ambiguous, so the persona in "I heard a Fly buzz" allows herself to believe that the "King" may well be symbolized by a petty, disgusting housefly with all that that portends for her faith. It is the individual's perceiving consciousness, in other words, that enables birds, flies, flowers, and whatever to usurp the place of the deity because the individual is willing to grant them divine signifying status. Thus, human beings allow their mortal optics to focus on what is trivial and decidedly material at the very moment when we feel they ought to be elevating their sites to a higher plane.

One of the major aims of "I heard a Fly buzz" is, I think, to describe the process whereby a set of certain symbolic assumptions can destroy Christian faith. The fly frames the poem: "I heard a Fly buzz," the speaker begins, and she ends: "then it was / There interposed a Fly—." But the persona does not actually *see* the fly; that is, the fly does not enter symbolically into her conscious perceptions until a number of significant events have already occurred. The first of these is the speaker's decision in stanza one to pursue a course of analogical reasoning: "The Stillness in the Room," she tells us, "Was like the Stillness in the Air— / Between the Heaves of Storm—." The speaker of the poem assumes that the universe is dualistic and that sacramental or ideal correspondences can be found to relate its various components. The stillness in the room, the narrator hypothesizes, is like the stillness outside before a storm; and if one analogical extension is possible, why not another? The stillness in the death room or in the room of the speaker's mind becomes, in the poem, like the stillness that precedes apocalypse, that other celestial storm presumed to have parallels in the natural world.

As the narrator images the world in analogically based symbols, the universe becomes a bifurcated entity in which two literally material realms are counterpoised on either side of a moment of stillness, death. And if all earthly phenomena, such as heaves and storms, have their heavenly counterparts, what, the speaker thinks to herself, might that grotesque little fly represent in the cosmic design? The tendency toward materially solid, analogical perception bestows upon the fly the only kind of meaning consonant with the fly's physical nature. Because he is an agent of decay, the fly metamorphoses into a cosmic vulture and finally into a Miltonic Satan, a Beelzebub, the guardian of a grossly material, reduced and inverted mirror-heaven that attempts, and, for this persona, succeeds, in supplanting the truly spiritual heaven of God. In fact, the moment that the speaker lets her faith in heaven depend upon concrete symbols, she has already yielded to the devil's temptation.

But the fly's destructiveness issues from a second cause as well, from another tendency of thought that is quite the opposite of the first, and it is in Dickinson's recognition of this second aspect of the problem that she lays the groundwork for her process of revision. "I willed my Keepsakes," the speaker explains, "Signed away / What portion of me be / Assignable—*and then it was* / There interposed a Fly—" (italics added). The fly's interposition between the speaker and the "light" directly follows the speaker's willing away of her keepsakes, her final gesture (in harmony with drying her eyes and suppressing her sobs) of earthly renunciation. The symbolic assumptions of Christianity, the poem seems to be suggesting, can require that the individual engage in two contradictory, mutually exclusive activities: one is the highly suspect process of an automatic sacramental symbolism, which grants flies, birds, and flowers their significances in the first place; the other, declaring the very opposite of such symbolic faith, is the last-hour renunciation of all keepsakes, signs, and symbols that robs symbols of their meanings. When the narrator wills away her keepsakes, when she signs away those evidences of her earthly existence that seem to *keep* her in life ("What portion of me be / Assignable" reads as synonymous with "What portion of me be"), she simultaneously, even if inadvertently, divests herself of that same set of symbols by which she and her company are able, albeit remotely and unevenly, to envision and affirm the existence of heaven.

Analogies between earth and heaven, we begin to realize, depend for their validity upon images that are transferable from one realm of existence to another. But if images are not transferable, if stillness is simply that and not a hiatus between two analogically related halves of existence, then the symbolism that would bridge the cosmic dualism or posit a nondualistic condition cannot be expected to transmit true knowledge or yield genuine faith. On the other hand, to abandon the symbol, to say, simply, "I could not see to see—," forfeits the possibility of knowledge (and ultimately of faith) altogether. The fly, then, interposes itself between the speaker and the light in two antithetical and yet interdependent ways. As a symbol that is the material embodiment of unmitigated death and decay, the fly, like the birds in "These are the days" or the flowers in "I tend my flowers," robs the speaker of her faith. And as an image of the renunciation of symbolic correlations, as a symbol of the death of symbolic consciousness, the fly deprives the speaker of all sense, all perception. "I could not see to see—" the poem ends. Human beings cannot, Dickinson implies, spend a lifetime conceptualizing the world in symbols and then, at the final moment, reject symbolic perception and somehow, magically, transcend.

In "I heard a Fly buzz—" Dickinson dramatizes what is for her the most serious paradox in the crisis of human perception and knowledge: that when individuals contemplate seriously the implications of conventional symbolism, especially for faith, they are forced to disparage and distrust its devices; and yet, despite this, they are compelled by the structure of the human imagination, and by the exigencies of life in a multifaceted universe, to employ some kind of symbol as the only means available for envisioning and comprehending the universe that faith affirms. As I have already noted in chapter one, for a philosopher like Cassirer there is essentially no universe apart from the symbolic one that we perceive or create, and the implications of this fact, as Kenneth Burke develops them, suggest that human language, which is itself symbolic, does not merely define concepts but independently realizes events: "language" and thought, he asserts, are "basically modes of action rather than . . . means of conveying information." Because we see through "terministic screens," "the nature of our terms affects the nature of our observations [and] *many of the 'observations' are but implications of the particular terminology, in terms of which the observations are made.*"[5] Human consciousness, in other words, is locked into one form of symbolic universe or another. Human beings, by nature, perceive symbolically. Their universe is not only inevitably but literally symbolic. These are the kinds of convictions with which Dickinson is operating—poetically. Therefore, despite the fact that, for her, phenomenally speaking, the universe is not a cohesive whole but a collection of incommensurate components and although the cosmic fragmentation into quantitative substance is, in her view, inescapably painful and problematic, she also acknowledges that without the differentiated elements of earthly phenomena and without our correlative language of symbols, there can be no knowlege at all.

Dickinson does not deny, of course, that there may well be components of human nature that are more in touch with divine reality than any fragment of its mortal intelligence. But just as the universe itself communicates with us in disparate moments of sense information, so those components of self, she stresses, whatever they are, have no way of being verbalized except through symbols. They can be comprehended, in other words, only through our "terministic screens" and

5. Burke, *Language as Symbolic Action*, 46.

articulated only through the strategies of language. This is one of the things we come to understand in the following poem:

> The first Day's Night had come—
> And grateful that a thing
> So terrible—had been endured—
> I told my Soul to sing—
>
> She said her Strings were snapt—
> Her Bow—to Atoms blown—
> And so to mend her—gave me work
> Until another Morn—
>
> And then—a Day as huge
> As Yesterdays in pairs,
> Unrolled it's horror in my face—
> Until it blocked my eyes—
>
> My Brain—begun to laugh—
> I mumbled—like a fool—
> And tho' 'tis Years ago—that Day—
> My Brain keeps giggling—still.
>
> And Something's odd—within—
> That person that I was—
> And this One—do not feel the same—
> Could it be Madness—this? (No. 410)

Once the vital "Strings" of phenomenal being have "snapt" in death and the poet's creative "Bow" is "to Atoms blown," there is, simply, no way at all to think or perceive or articulate. Knowledge may be right at hand, within absolute reach for the first time, but as language is reduced to an insane, hysterical mumbling and as consciousness is eclipsed either in madness or in death, the soul loses its capacity to "sing." It is robbed of the ability to understand what it has discovered and to communicate it.

Without consciousness, in other words, there is no link between the phenomenal and the transcendent. A soul, therefore, that is no longer tethered to conscious life cannot be imagined to experience reunion or rebirth but is seen as lonely and abandoned, suspended between two departing realms of experience.

Departed—to the Judgment—
A Mighty Afternoon—
Great Clouds—like Ushers—leaning—
Creation—looking on—

The Flesh—Surrendered—Cancelled—
The Bodiless—begun—
Two Worlds—like Audiences—disperse—
And leave the Soul—alone— (No. 524)

With the "Flesh—Surrendered—Cancelled—," there is no way of transferring knowledge from the one sphere to the other. For, as Dickinson puts it elsewhere,

Heaven is so far of the Mind
That were the Mind dissolved—
The Site—of it—by Architect
Could not again be proved— (No. 370)

Human nature is so constituted that "Heaven" cannot exist for us without our capacity to perceive it.

When, therefore, the narrators of "I heard a Fly buzz" and "The First Day's Night," and other Dickinsonian narrators as well (consider, for example, the speaker in "Just lost, when I was saved—" No. 160) lose rational consciousness, they lose that part of themselves that is capable of anchoring them to the concrete, knowable reality of earth. But the mind is also "Capacity" and "idea," and as a king of immortality unto itself, as an image of divine vastness and infinite fairness, it projects humankind forward into the kingdom of God, a kingdom that is not only a place but a concept of time.

This Consciousness that is aware
Of Neighbors and the Sun
Will be the one aware of Death
And that itself alone

Is traversing the interval
Experience between
And most profound experiment
Appointed unto Men— (No. 822)

I defer, for the moment, discussion of Dickinson's conception of consciousness as a temporal and temporalizing phenomenon, even though the relationship between time and timelessness, like the relationship between place and placelessness, is central to Dickinson's most significant poetic achievements. In fact, it is the relationship between spatial and temporal axes that finally describes the heart of the Dickinsonian universe. But what must be grasped first is that, for Dickinson, symbolism, whatever its assumptions and whatever its strategies, must be formulated in terms of all-pervading consciousness. Without consciousness, Dickinson asserts, there can be no knowledge, and even more importantly, there can be no way of knowing: "And then the Windows failed—and then / I could not see to see—."

The language of consciousness, Dickinson believes, is definitely symbols: a "sheen must have a Disk / To be a sun—," she writes in one of her poems (No. 1550); and in another,

> The thought beneath so slight a film—
> Is more distinctly seen—
> As laces just reveal the surge—
> Of Mists—the Appenine— (No. 210)

In many of her poems Dickinson seems to demonstrate the converse of Jung's proposition that "no content can be conscious unless it is represented to a subject."[6] Unless an object or idea is susceptible to symbolic representation, she believes, it is meaningless, or worse, maddening.

Is, then, Dickinson simply a sacramental or idealist symbolist for whom symbols either bridge otherwise unbridgeable distances or conflate disparate terms in a symbolic construct in which dualisms do not exist? The purpose of this study is not to deny that Dickinson uses symbols. Nor do I wish to claim that she uses symbols simply to undermine them. Nonetheless, Dickinson, I believe, is neither a sacramental symbolist nor an ideal one; her symbols neither bridge nor transcend. For Dickinson's criticism of such conventional symbolism is a prominent, unmistakable feature of her verse—thematically and structurally. Her exploration of the problems and powers of symbolism, like her probing of language as observed in chapter one, forces us to

6. C. G. Jung, "Aion," in Violet S. deLaszlo (ed.), *Psyche and Symbol: A Selection from the Writings of C. G. Jung* (Garden City, N.Y., 1958), 2.

reassess in a wholly fresh way just how it is we know anything at all; it compels us to reconsider how, once knowing, we express this knowledge.

Dickinson's critique of symbolic perception, coupled with her constant use of symbols and her direct expressions of symbolic affirmation, initiates a process of symbol revision that is fully articulated, fully demonstrated in her best, most comprehensive poems. At the crux of Dickinson's symbolic poetics is a definition of consciousness that enables it to be symbolic on the one hand and yet to recognize the dangers of symbolic seeing on the other. Dickinson qualifies symbolism in such a way as to take it out of the realm of a despotic fixation and fully integrate it within a firmly theistic vision.

For Dickinson consciousness is not an unmixed blessing. Transcendentally exaggerated, it can effect its own kind of eclipse. It can become so enamored of its symbolizing powers that, in an effort to escape the implications of external reality, it can imprison the self, inescapably and eternally, within a version of that reality translocated from without to within. But for Dickinson there is another kind of consciousness. This consciousness is a species that does not sever the vital strings that keep it safely linked to the phenomenal creation. It is a consciousness that does not disavow its primary existence as a feature of physiology and nature. But it is a consciousness that also recognizes its affinity with God and with the powers of divine creativity.

The role this consciousness must play in the perception and creation of the universe seems to be the principal concern of one of Dickinson's shortest but most philosophical poems. This easily trivialized poem is, I believe, extraordinarily useful in comprehending the outlines of Dickinson's symbolic poetics. The system of cosmic organization that it so simply details is basic to the larger projections of Dickinsonian symbolism. Dickinson writes,

> To make a prairie it takes a clover and one bee,
> One clover, and a bee,
> And revery.
> The revery alone will do,
> If bees are few. (No. 1755)

The physical universe, as it is here hypothetically represented, issues from the active interpenetration of three primary elements: the nuclear fragment or seed, we may say, of material substance (the clover); the catalyst or inseminator of the physical world (the bee); and the imaginative consciousness that is capable of perceiving the products of the union (revery). "To make a prairie," the poem begins, with the simplicity and self-assurance of an elementary science textbook, "it takes a clover and one bee." But immediately the author's confidence in her formula begins to falter. As in so many of her more elaborate statements on the same set of existents, the cosmic tendency toward stasis and polarization, the fragmentation characteristic of physical substance and symbol both, begins to assert itself: "One clover, and a bee," she repeats, reversing the terms of the equation and testing the results. But the sum of the parts, whether one formulates them as "a clover and one bee" or "One clover, and a bee" simply do not add up to a "prairie." To name something, to isolate it and pronounce its identity, is not to give it extensible meaning. It is certainly not to enable it to "enter into the equation of which it is a part," to quote again from Foss's strictures on symbolic reductiveness. Like the universe in "I had not minded—Walls" or in "I died for Beauty," the universe in this poem emerges as a collection of self-contained and unrelated fragments that defy meaningful intercourse with one another. The splintered lines of the poem embody a static immobility, a balance and an equality of fragments that is so absolute and unrelenting as to be a total barrier to dynamic perception. (Although we do not have a holograph copy of this poem, we can speculate that Dickinson's own version contained plentiful capitalizations and dashes.) In the deadening language of an allegedly mathematical equation, "One clover, and a bee" equals "a clover and one bee," nothing more. It is, to note another implied metaphor, as if the clover and the bee are engaged in an act of ritual courting in which the two partners coyly and amorously confront one another but in which neither one is willing to yield itself to the other and to consummate the union. Both the clover and the bee, in fact, contend for superiority (note the interchanging of the definite and indefinite articles, "a" and "one") but neither succeeds in subduing the other and the two together do not succeed in merging into a single harmonious unity. The implied neoplatonic-Christian plot does not circle back into oneness but opens up into a cycle of endless frustration.

In the end, revery, the conscious mind, quickens the sterile suspension and dissolves the jealous competition. "To make a prairie," the poem suggests, requires the clover and the bee *and* some way of bringing them together. Revery is the catalyst that excites natural process, the "fairy oil" that keeps the universe in creative motion. It is the agent of symbolic seeing that not only gives nature meaning, but without which nature can have no life, no substance. Although the bee, as its name implies, is also an agent of being, and revery and the bee are, therefore, in some senses, versions of one another, natural being (the existence of the natural world) is of no consequence without human consciousness (a human being) to perceive it.

All of this could seem to be simply mystical or Transcendentalist except for the fact that Dickinson's poem, despite its stress on human consciousness, is very quick to assert that "revery alone will do" *only*, and this is the important point, "If bees are few," and not, we infer, if clovers are few. As Dickinson writes elsewhere,

> A little Madness in the Spring
> Is wholesome even for the King,
> But God be with the Clown—
> Who ponders this tremendous scene—
> This whole Experiment of Green—
> As if it were his own! (No. 1333)

Though a slight, good-humored indulgence in one's proprietary inclinations may be "wholesome," "even for the King," to contemplate seriously one's ownership of nature is more than a "little Madness." The "clover," the indisputably material essence of the created universe, prevents the egomaniacal expansion of reductive consciousness. As Dickinson puts it in another of her poems about clovers and be[e]ing,

> A single Clover Plank
> Was all that saved a Bee

A Bee I personally knew
From sinking in the sky—

Twixt Firmament above
And Firmament below
The Billows of Circumference
Were sweeping him away—

The idly swaying Plank
Responsible to nought
A sudden Freight of Wind assumed
And Bumble Bee was not—

This harrowing event
Transpiring in the Grass
Did not so much as wring from him
A wandering "Alas"— (No. 1343)

The "Clover" fastens the "Bee" (being) to reality, positions it at the center between heaves of "Firmament" and "Billows of Circumference." The "bank," Dickinson writes in one of her letters, is "the safest place for Finless mind" (L 319); the bee belongs in the physical creation of "Clover" and "Grass." The "Bee" and the "Clover" may not in themselves be sufficient to withstand the pressures of the "Freight of Wind" that threatens to carry them into aetherial oblivion. Furthermore, it may take the poet to say "Alas." She alone, it seems, can put the natural drama in its full context of meaning. But it is the "single Clover Plank" that saves the bee, not the poet. Without the clover (and the bee) there can be no drama, no nature for the poet to contemplate.

The philosophical system that informs the symbolic logic of "To make a prairie," and many other of Dickinson's poems as well, is perhaps most usefully thought of as material-idealism, the coexistence of reality's constituent phases in total equality of status and in absolute separateness. In Dickinson's view, the antithetical qualities that define reality as we can know it—the transcendent and the earthly, mind and matter, idea and incarnation, revery and bee—are not each mirrors of the other. They do not imply that the universe is a diadic sweep of two analogous heaves. Nor is one set of referents ever to be subverted in the cause of the other. Neither is to be abandoned in the effort to shake loose the shackles of material corruption in order to transcend.

Rather, each term in the cosmic equation is made an independent equal of all the other terms. Each remains valid and valuable in and of itself. Thus, if one puts the Dickinsonian formulae of "To make a prairie" through their mathematical paces, one discovers that, since the clover = the bee and the bee = revery, the bee = the clover = revery, and all of the terms, individually and additively, equal the prairie. Each term has its necessary and legitimate role to play in the cosmic equation, and therefore each term must unhesitatingly be preserved. Revery, simply, cannot operate without the clover, which links imagination to concrete phenomena. Dickinson's symbolism is determined and specified by the fact that the clover remains a clover throughout the poem, and it is precisely because it remains a clover, because it does not metamorphose into a reflection of something else that is not a clover, that it preserves the function of revery, of the symbolic human imagination.[7]

This kind of symbolism is, I think, the compound form that Dickinson employs in a great many of her poems, even in those poems that were examined earlier in this study for their antisymbolic arguments. Dickinson destroys one kind of conventional symbolism not because she wants to eclipse perception or assert mystical silence, but because she wants to prepare the way for the kind of symbolism I have now begun to describe.

In the following poem Dickinson presents in virtually discursive terms her rationale for the underlying symbolic revision that, I believe, she employs again and again to brilliant effect.

> By my Window have I for Scenery
> Just a Sea—with a Stem—
> If the Bird and the Farmer—deem it a "Pine"—
> The Opinion will do—for them—
>
> It has no Port, nor a "Line"—but the Jays—
> That split their route to the Sky—

7. For a related point, see B. J. Rogers, "The Truth Told Slant: Emily Dickinson's Poetic Mode," *Texas Studies in Literature and Language*, XIV (1972), 330. George Whicher also makes a relevant comment, *This Was a Poet*, 292, as does Paul Tillich in "The Religious Symbol," in Rollo May (ed.), *Symbolism in Religion and Literature* (New York, 1960), 77.

> Or a Squirrel, whose giddy Peninsula
> May be easier reached—this way—
>
> For Inlands—the Earth is the under side—
> And the upper side—is the Sun—
> And it's Commerce—if Commerce it have—
> Of Spice—I infer from the Odors borne—
>
> Of it's Voice—to affirm—when the Wind is within—
> Can the Dumb—define the Divine?
> The Definition of Melody—is—
> That Definition is none—
>
> It—suggests to our Faith—
> They—suggest to our Sight—
> When the latter—is put away
> I shall meet with Conviction I somewhere met
> That Immortality—
>
> Was the Pine at my Window a "Fellow
> Of the Royal" Infinity?
> Apprehensions—are God's introductions—
> To be hallowed—accordingly— (No. 797)

Like many other of her poems, "By my Window" expresses the poet's highly skeptical attitude toward conventional symbolic machinery. The "Sea—with a Stem," the narrator realizes, may or may not be a symbol of cosmic relationships. Or it may or may not be a "Pine," as the birds and the farmers insist. In either case, it is a matter of "Opinion" or arbitrary inference, of what Dickinson, we recall, elsewhere labels seeing "Provincially." In the final analysis, Dickinson tells us, what counts so far as cosmic belief is concerned is "Faith" and not "Sight." And she therefore explains, "The Definition of Melody—is— / That Definition is none—." Immortality, it seems, must be met with "Conviction" and nothing else.

But by the end of the poem the speaker is voicing an attitude toward cosmic symbolism that is very different from that which the first five stanzas would lead us to believe she will espouse. "Apprehensions," she decides, are after all "God's introductions— / To be hallowed—accordingly—." In other words, while for five stanzas of the poem the speaker tries to prove how inadequate and tentative our symbolic perception really is (she knows, for example, that the symbol she has chosen is deficient in some of its parts—"It has no Port, nor a 'Line'"—and that it is uncertain in others—"if Commerce it have"—), by stanza six she is willing to entertain directly the question that she has just demonstrated is totally untenable: "Was the Pine at my Window a 'Fellow / Of the Royal' Infinity?"

The question, as it is finally put, is neither rhetorical nor supercilious. What allows the narrator to ask it is that by stanza six she has already accepted the inviolability of the universe's fundamentally material-idealist organization, a fact that she was not willing to accept at the beginning of the poem. What was definitely, in her view, a "Sea— with a Stem—" in stanza one is now just as definitely a pine after all. The designation *pine*, she realizes, is not simply a matter of opinion, the word *pine* in attributive quotation marks. It is the literal fact of the matter, the word *pine* without quotation marks. Ironically, by acknowledging the tree for what it is and by abandoning her suggestively symbolic position, and by then and only then asking the question whether or not the pine symbolizes immortality, Dickinson is able to check the wildly errant rovings of her conventionally symbolizing imagination. And, by having come through the process of simultaneously symbolizing and criticizing her symbolizing, she becomes aware that the essence of true cosmic symbolism is to arouse in the perceiver the very attitudes of apprehension that are expressed throughout the poem and that cause her to question the foundations of her symbolic belief in the first place. Her final query converts a false symbolism into a true one. "Apprehensions," then, are not symbols in the ordinary sense of the word. They are, however, symbols nonetheless, symbols that point to the very deficiencies of ordinary symbolic perception and that prove how incommensurate immortality and nature really are. The poet preserves immortality, in other words, by pointing out that it is a realm of reality that is in no way continuous with the phenomena of jays and pines and farmers. Immortality, therefore, is in no way qualified or restricted or reduced by the implications of mortal existence. "Apprehensions," Dickinson explains, are "introductions" to the fearsome ambiguousness of cosmic meaning. For this reason, they must "be hallowed—accordingly—." The pine must be hallowed both for what it is—a tree—and for what it is not, a symbol of an interfused, analogously whole universe. As it is hallowed for those two things, it initiates a process of symbolic contemplation that ultimately demonstrates to the narrator of the poem not how disparities can be rendered whole, but how mortality and immortality must be maintained as discontinuous and incommensurate spheres. It demonstrates that just as sight informs us of the mortal realm, so faith, the faith of scriptures and of Christian belief, informs us of eternity; it shows us that the symbol must not conflate but segregate.

Like Anne Bradstreet before her, Dickinson realizes that to avoid the temptations of nature's "delectable" seduction it is not enough, simply, to draw analogies between heaven and earth that seem to cause heaven to shine by comparison. Rather, one must recall the utter difference that distinguishes between heaven and earth and between man, who is a creature of God's grace, and nature, which is only the most degraded and imperfect reach of the divine creation. Thus, Bradstreet's own analogizing, sacramentalizing habit of mind forces her at first to conclude that humankind, compared with nature, is not immortal after all.

> When I behold the heavens as in their prime,
> And then the earth (though old) stil clad in green,
> The stones and trees, insensible of time,
> Nor age nor wrinkle on their front are seen;
> If winter come, and greeness then do fade,
> A Spring returns, and they more youthfull made;
> But Man grows old, lies down, remains where once he's laid.
>
> By birth more noble than those creatures all,
> Yet seems by nature and by custome curs'd,
> No sooner born, but grief and care makes fall
> That state obliterate he had at first:
> Nor youth, nor strength, nor wisdom spring again
> Nor habitations long their names retain,
> But in oblivion to the final day remain.

Only faith and its discrimination between the law of grace and the law of nature can recall her from the despair her error induces.

> Shall I then praise the heavens, the trees, the earth
> Because their beauty and their strength last longer?

> Shall I wish there, or never to had birth,
> Because they're bigger, & their bodyes stronger?
> Nay, they shall darken, perish, fade and dye,
> And when unmade, so ever shall they lye,
> But man was made for endless immortality.

The poem's conclusion is crucial to Bradstreet's own revision of sacramental symbolism, and it is useful for understanding Dickinson's as well, especially as it is embodied in a poem like "I died for Beauty." Bradstreet's poem ends:

> O Time the fatal wrack of mortal things,
> That draws oblivions curtains over kings;
> Their sumptuous monuments, men know them not,
> Their names without a Record are forgot,
> Their parts, their ports, their pomp's all laid in th' dust
> Nor wit nor gold, nor buildings scape times rust;
> But he whose name is grav'd in the white stone
> Shall last and shine when all of these are gone.[8]

For the narrator of "By my Window," the pine is neither a failed symbol—a symbol that ought to have been a "Sea—with a Stem—" but that simply is not—nor an antisymbol, a symbol that images the failure of symbolic perception. Because Dickinson's speaker, like Bradstreet's before her, comes to hallow nature in just measure, her symbol is able to communicate to her (and to the poem's readers) a message of real moment. The protagonist of "By my Window" grows toward an awareness of how she can evade the perils of failed symbols or antisymbolism, and, by the end of the poem, she achieves a genuine answer to her initial question. "Apprehensions," she affirms, are indeed "God's introductions— / To be hallowed—accordingly—."

Unfortunately, not all of Dickinson's narrators are quite as successful as the narrator of "By my Window." As we have already seen, the speaker of "I heard a Fly buzz" may arrive not at knowledge but at a totally annihilating eclipse. This may also be the fate of the narrator

8. All quotations from Bradstreet's *Contemplations* are from Perry Miller and Thomas H. Johnson (eds.), *The Puritans: A Source Book of Their Writings* (2 vols.; New York, 1963), II, 564–70. In "Dickinson's 'Summer had Two Beginnings,'" Lawrence Walz, I think, falls directly into the trap of false correspondences Bradstreet is describing—*Explicator*, XXXIII (1974), item 16.

of "I died for Beauty." Similarly, the personae of "I had not minded—Walls—" and "Before I got my eye put out" may, by the end of their narrations, be blinded by their experiences, while in "These are the days" and "A Bird came down the Walk," the speakers seem not finally to succeed in strengthening their faith but in losing it entirely. Yet, in each of these poems, the poet (Dickinson) does achieve a resolution of the basic symbolic tensions that cause the poems' protagonists so much pain. Although all of these poems can be read on one level or another as diatribes against a symbolic interpretation of the universe that is either sacramental or idealist, unific or synecdochic, each one of them also contains elements that point beyond skepticism and the destruction of meaning (which are themselves varieties of meaning) toward a comprehensive, integrated view of cosmic relationships. And this view, at some moment in the perceptual process, does require symbolic notations.

Dickinson's poems are often organized in two discrete symbolic stages (which are equivalent to the multiple voice phenomenon many other critics have already noted).[9] In stage one Dickinson dismantles the symbolic apparatus that so encumbers cosmic vision that we cannot see to see. But then, in stage two, Dickinson in varying degrees reclaims for human knowledge those symbolic devices that, if rightly understood and properly managed, can convey an accurate portrait of cosmic reality. Controlling the misperceiving symbolist within the poems is at least the shadow of the poet who does create the groundwork of a genuine cosmic symbolism.

Thus, in "I heard a Fly buzz," it is not the poet of the poem who accepts the analogical premises of the "Heaves of Storm" philosophy and who is therefore carried at the end to perceptual eclipse. Rather, it is the narrator who errs in her symbolic reasoning. For the poet and for the reader the fly can communicate an authentic vision, and it succeeds in communicating this vision symbolically: like all symbols, the fly brings the noumenal and the phenomenal into some kind of relationship. But the fly is no ordinary symbol, for what it is made to sym-

9. On Dickinson's ironic other voice, see Clark Griffith, *The Long Shadow: Emily Dickinson's Tragic Poetry* (Princeton, 1964), *passim*; also Sharon Cameron, *Lyric Time: Dickinson and the Limits of Genre* (Baltimore, 1979), 57ff.

bolize about the earthly and the transcendent is not the analogical closeness or synecdoche that joins the two, but the total disparity that keeps them separate. Despite its symbolic meaning, the fly never stops being a perfectly literal, asymbolic housefly. It is never allowed, imagistically or symbolically, to escape the ordained boundaries of its irreversible materiality, and those boundaries are what prevent its horrifying merger with the divine and its destruction of faith. By preserving the fly's two meanings uncompounded, the poet enables it to be a natural object and a supernatural signifier both. And that, in turn, allows the fly to furnish an accurate representation of cosmic reality, a reality that is itself discontinuous and not compound. In being made to emphasize the difference between itself and God, the fly is able to confirm for us the existence of the "King," the same king whose existence is eclipsed by the same fly when its symbolic meaning is misinterpreted by the narrator of the poem.

According to Dickinson the symbol that attempts (or that is employed in an attempt) to intimate divine realities through static, analogical equations, the symbol that tries (or that is forced), in vain, to fuse things that are created disparate, is doomed to failure. But the symbol that points to the contrast between the laws of nature and the laws of God, the symbol that represents the members of cosmic interrelatedness in their proper discreteness and inviolability, can effectively put us in touch with divine truth. It is the divinely ordained gulf between the material and the immaterial that affirms salvation, resurrection, and reunion. And it is the symbolizing of this gulf that puts them beyond the restrictions and reductions of the physical universe and our creaturely perceptions.

Thus, in "I died for Beauty," the end of the poem does finally move toward the assertion of a profoundly beautiful, truthful unity that, though beyond the grasp of the poem's narrator, is not undiscoverable for us. We, the readers, have been made to see the possibility of a genuine relationship between beauty / truth and the moss. The poet has clarified for us the process whereby that relationship is apprehended and made manifest. As we said earlier, the conventional symbolism of beauty and truth in the opening lines of the poem, their incorporation by the narrator and her kinsman into the daily processes of physical existence, makes these cosmic ideals vulnerable to the finality of physical death. When Dickinson's persona tells us, therefore, that "the Moss had reached our lips— / And covered up—our names—," we understand, in terms of the poem's critique of conventional symbolism, that the material creation has obliterated both the symbolic universe and the spiritual one.

And yet we sense that the poem's hushed and reverent conclusion does contain a muted promise as well as a declarative warning. We feel that the final lines of the poem are, in and of themselves, an assertion of beauty and truth in which all of the disruptive words ("lips") whose existence bespeaks the failure of beauty and truth and all of the destructive symbols ("names") that incorporate the immortal spirit into a perishable reality have been made to disappear. How, according to Dickinsonian logic, can the moss simultaneously destroy beauty and truth and also preserve them? How can we as readers discern the difference in the moss's two antithetical functions? Dickinson is not, I think, dealing in this poem with ineffable paradoxes. Nor is she allowing one strand of argumentation neatly to cancel the other: the poem does not, in one critical terminology, self-consume.[10] Rather, Dickinson's poem describes a process in which a series of meticulously delineated steps issues in a suggestion of the poet's hoped-for result. Dickinson devotes her energies early in the poem to demonstrating how painfully isolating and destructive the symbolic turn of mind can be in order that, by the time we arrive at the poem's conclusion, we have available to us two alternative ways of understanding the moss's final action. If we align ourselves with the poem's protagonists and share their symbolic premises, then the symbolic moss is for us as well as for them an agent of consummate destruction. But if we have correctly heeded the message of the poem's critical argument—either before our arrival at its concluding lines, or, having read the poem in toto, before we return to these last two lines a second time—and if we have come to recognize the great divide that separates spirit and

10. Cf. Stanley E. Fish, *Self-Consuming Artifacts: The Experience of Seventeenth-Century Literature* (Berkeley, 1972).

nature and that makes ordinary symbolism an anathema to the divinely constituted universe, then the moss can well be interpreted as more than a false symbol that inadvertently destroys beauty and truth. It can be apprehended as a symbol of the relationship between transient nature and the lofty ideals that, in being in no way contingent upon nature's perishability, are thus affirmed by that perishability.

The moss, then, is a symbol complex; it is constituted by a symmetry of material and ideal referents. Its silencing of lips and its burying of words, therefore, do not destroy beauty and truth. But neither do they lead directly to their emergence, even though one strand of the poem's logic would seem to suggest that the cessation of symbolic consciousness is synonymous with the attainment of divine reality. In other words, the moss does not confirm ordinary symbolic consciousness, but neither does it result in the perceptual failure that, while capturing one element of beauty's and truth's real character, also eclipses consciousness or drives it insane. Because the moss is a symbol, it preserves symbolic consciousness. But, like the pine and the fly, and unlike beauty and truth as they are conceptualized earlier in the poem, it is a symbol that directly prevents cosmic conflation. It protects the sacred integrity both of nature and of God, and in protecting the inviolability of each, it provides the basis for a new understanding of beauty and truth in newly defined symbolic terms.

In order to insure that, as Bradstreet put it, "he whose name is grav'd in the white stone" of eternal salvation "shall last and shine," the individual must be able to maintain his own distance from the implications of a wholly naturalistic universe. In "I died for Beauty" we are made to perceive the gap dividing heaven from earth, nature from mankind. It is this gap that secures and dramatizes God's promise that we shall rise again. In the final analysis beauty and truth emerge not in defiance of the moss but because of it. The moss proves to us that beauty and truth cannot be quantifiable categories of human experience that we can incorporate at will into our physical reality. Beauty and truth dwell where physical reality is not, in the eventual silencing of lips and the disappearance of names that is penultimately achieved for us in our reversing or undoing of symbolic conflations. The universe, in Dickinson's view, must be symbolized if it is to be comprehended. But it must be symbolized "accordingly"—according to our fullest faith in the theologically protective distance between God and His creation.

By a similar set of assumptions, the "Walls" in "I had not minded—Walls—" are likewise true and meaningful symbols. Like the pine, the fly, and the moss, they insist upon their own materiality. Thus they insure that heaven will be kept distant from earth, idealism distinct from materialism. In being a barrier between the two incommensurate reaches of the divine universe, the walls that Dickinson describes stand in opposition to the awful disintegration of idea into matter. They oppose the equally horrifying expansion of matter into idea. In other words, they prevent the conflation of one cosmic constituent with the other that initially causes the universe of law to dissolve into nothingness and then to proliferate into a blinding profusion of cobwebs and veils—walls infinitely multiplied and obstructive. Were the universe "one Rock" or one homogeneous substance, then there would be no need for walls. But precisely because it is composed of two unrelated substances, it is necessary to divide between them, to prevent the collapse that is the baffling intermingling and splintering of one inviolate realm within another. The orderly walls of dichotomy protect us from the maze of divisive walls, the enveloping, suffocating cobwebs and veils of eternal division. Human eyes, as Dickinson shows us in "Before I got my eye put out," are not synchronized, not truly stereoscopic in effect, because the eye of sight and the eye of faith see independently of one another, one on either side of the wall that separates the mortal from the immortal, humankind from God. One needs both the walls and the plural number of eyes in order to see accurately, in order, in fact, to see at all.

I could continue to reopen earlier discussions of many other poems in order to demonstrate how their criticisms of symbolism can ultimately and justifiably be redacted into suggestions for a revised symbolism of the variety I have been describing. But let me conclude this part of my discussion by reviewing only two further examples: "These are the days when Birds come back" and "A Bird came down the Walk." These poems, like the ones discussed above, also employ their symbolic critiques in order to evolve a new mode of symbolic perception. Once the implications of the antisacramentalism of the poems have been made clear, once it is understood that the speakers of the poems have been deprived of anything more holy than a "Communion in the Haze" or have even been deserted by their Christ, it becomes apparent that both poems do provide a realistic and true theological perception. The first poem ends,

> Oh Sacrament of summer days,
> Oh Last Communion in the Haze—
> Permit a child to join.
>
> Thy sacred emblems to partake—
> Thy consecrated bread to take
> And thine immortal wine! [11]

And the second concludes,

> And he unrolled his feathers
> And rowed him softer home—
>
> Than Oars divide the Ocean,
> Too silver for a seam—
> Or Butterflies, off Banks of Noon
> Leap, plashless as they swim.

The principle that informs the symbolic achievements of these poems suggests the same two-stage evolution that provides the symbolic structure for "I heard a Fly buzz," "I died for Beauty," and "I had not minded—Walls—." "The Sacrament of summer days" and the "Last Communion in the Haze" do in the end represent a sacred and consecrated set of emblems, but not at all because they image that other communion experience on which they cast serious doubt. The symbols of summer and autumn, when rightly understood, are sacred because they project difference, not similarity. They fix nature in a realm that is clearly not subject to the laws of divine grace. And the "Haze" that they perpetuate and that can deceive those who do not see rightly, allows us finally to distinguish between true religious faith, which must see through the haze, and the lowly mortal intelligence

11. I refer the reader, again, to Charles R. Anderson's excellent discussion of "These are the days": *Emily Dickinson's Poetry: Stairway of Surprise* (New York, 1960), 145–49.

that tries absurdly, through logic, to make the haze coincidental with faith.

In the last lines of "These are the days," the lines that are most directly theological and that declare the poet's faith, we hear in effect two different voices, both intoning the same words but each conveying a different meaning.[12] The first voice becomes, we realize, an object of poetic or philosophical dispute. It is the voice of the rejected symbol apostate. The second voice, however, resonates with the depth of symbolic awareness derived from the first voice. It carries us back to the kernel of communion meaning before the words were reduced by symbolic pretentiousness, symbolic sloppiness. The effect, all-in-all, is not stereophonic, but superphonic. One voice, the second, emerges strong and prevails. The communion of which this voice speaks is genuine; its invocation of sacred emblems is blessed by true theological awareness.

In a somewhat different but related way, the bird's flight from the clutches of his symbolizing Christian antagonist in "A Bird came down" gives way to an image of rare and seamless beauty that suggests that, just as the living deity in "'Arcturus' is his other name" will, the speaker hopes, lift his "naughty" girl "Over the stile of 'Pearl,'" so He will prove here His infinite capacity for love by bringing home to its *proper* home even the decidedly unsaintly, unredeemed bird. The many symbols of the poem—the bird, the beetle, and the angle-worm—cannot dramatize a parallel between God and nature. They can, however, put the poet in mind of the kind of relationship that does characterize the God-nature universe, a relationship in which frail nature, and human beings, too, must be passive recipients of the divine will.[13]

Most significant about Dickinson's use of symbols in these poems, and in many other poems as well, is that in the final moments the poems do achieve a meaning that seems very close to and is yet absolutely different from the goals of a sacramental or ideal symbolism.

12. Cf. Cameron, *Lyric Time*, 57ff.
13. For a different view, see Douglas A. Noverr's "Emily Dickinson and the Art of Despair," *Emily Dickinson Bulletin*, XXIII (1973), 161–67.

Dickinson arrives at her moment of truth not through the synecdoches and analogical assertions of conventional symbolic logic, nor through the total opposite, the abnegation of symbolism and the simple assertion of silence. Rather, by treading a carefully delineated middle ground between the worship of symbols and their total rejection, Dickinson is able to create a species of symbolism that confirms the existence of heaven by fixing images of heaven and earth firmly in the mind and then by disallowing the correspondences that would collapse and compound those images.

By affirming the absolute, substantial existence of nature within the context of faith, Dickinson preserves the sacred distance that separates heaven from earth and protects heaven's holiness. Thus, the fragmentation everywhere evident in some of the poems first looked at in this study and everywhere mixed with Dickinson's appreciation of natural beauty is not viewed as an external cosmic affliction. The "Great Globules" of "Scarlet Rain" in "The name—of it—is 'Autumn'—" and the "Authorized Arrays" of the "Crews—of solid Blood" in "Whole Gulfs—of Red" do metamorphose in the final lines of the first poem to an eddying, "like a Rose—away— / Upon Vermillion Wheels," and in the second "promptly" as in a "Drama" to bowing and disappearing. Or in "She sweeps with many-colored Brooms," by the end of the poem and the end of the day as well the plying of the "spotted Brooms" ceases and the "Brooms fade softly into stars," while the "Sun," which in another poem must rise "A Ribbon at a time," setting the world into frantic motion, is finally met at evening by a power that puts everything to quiet rest once more: "A Dominie in Gray— / Put gently up the evening Bars— / And led the flock away—" (No. 318). In all of these poems natural disorder is temporary. It is intended to dramatize for humankind the lack of perfection and wholeness in nature as compared with the perfection and oneness in God. In fact, nature's beauty derives from its energy and chaotic appearance. It is our compensation for life in this world, and it must not be confused with any other kind of reality. Eventually divine unity will supervene. It will repair the frayed ends of beauty. It will consolidate truth out of illusion. In the very end the whole of cosmic chaos will disappear. As Dickinson puts it in "The Mountains stood in Haze,"

> So soft upon the Scene
> The Act of evening fell
> We felt how neighborly a Thing
> Was the Invisible. (No. 1278)

A curtain does fall on the cosmic drama. But the stage manager is not nature, the manifest. It is God, the "Invisible."

Dickinson's happy endings and her assertions of transcendent faith in no way deny the dangers of the "terministic screens" through which we are compelled to see the universe. But for Dickinson poetry is a series of well-defined intellectual acts wherein the tendencies of imagination, firmly and irremovably implanted within the mind, are fully acknowledged and credited and then are purified and reformed until they are made truly capable of expressing cosmic meaning. "To pile like Thunder to it's close / Then crumble grand away / While Everything created hid / This," Dickinson explains, "would be Poetry" (No. 1247). Poetry identifies and exposes the bits and pieces of the creation. It even disseminates a few of its own. And as Dickinson puts it in another poem,

> Crumbling is not an instant's Act
> A fundamental pause
> Delapidation's processes
> Are organized Decays.
>
> 'Tis first a Cobweb on the Soul
> A Cuticle of Dust
> A Borer in the Axis
> An Elemental Rust—
>
> Ruin is formal—Devils work
> Consecutive and slow—
> Fail in an instant, no man did
> Slipping—is Crashe's law. (No. 997)

Poetry demonstrates "Delapidation's processes," the "organized," almost elemental "Decays" of language. But then poetry gives meaning to the fragments, illuminates the conflicts. Dickinson's poetry, I believe, attempts to describe the epistemology whereby the cosmos dramatizes its meanings. "True Poems flee," Dickinson tells us (No. 1472). What remains after the carefully delineated procedures of her symbolism have been completed is the knowledge that appears to be circumferential or slant but that is, in fact, a precisely defined, exactly discriminated model of our symbolic perception of the universe. Dickinson's symbols are not in and of themselves meanings; they do not mirror cosmic correspondences; they are not transparencies or synecdoches. They do, however, point us unmistakably to cosmic processes, and they establish relationships in a universe that is characterized by segregation and division and not by homogeneity.

Chapter Seven

The Mind's Journey to Immortality: The Symbol Reconstructed Through Time

*B*ECAUSE the symbol can be made to demonstrate its own recognizable invalidity as a signifier, because it can be made to symbolize a dynamic equation of interrelationships as opposed to a static equivalency of synonyms, Dickinson feels entitled to use symbols of a carefully specified sort. Having faced squarely one immense limitation of human language—the fact that the transcendent and natural universes are separate, autonomous realms, and that the symbols of language, therefore, have no real or necessary connection to the ideas they represent—and, at the same time, having acknowledged the imperative of consciousness to stabilize or corporealize the abstract in the concrete, Dickinson finds herself finally able to proceed to her special kind of symbolic order, an order that recognizes the incommensurability of the component parts of the universe.[1]

1. For a different but related point, see Roland Hagenbüchle, "Precision and Indeterminacy in the Poetry of Emily Dickinson," *ESQ: A Journal of the American Renaissance*, XX (1974), 39–41; and Inder Nath Kher, *The Landscape of Absence: Emily Dickinson's Poetry* (New Haven, 1974), 9. See also Charles R. Anderson, *Emily Dickinson's Poetry: Stairway of Surprise* (New York, 1960), 47–62.

But Dickinson realizes that even her compound symbolism is not
sufficient to convey the most significant dimensions of the ultimate
subject of her inquiry, the realm of deity. For our concepts of heaven
and of God, she feels, are not related most fundamentally to our notions of place and placelessness, but rather to our understanding of
time and timelessness. Beyond Dickinson's symbolism of cosmic in-
equalities there is a related symbolic form that not only signifies the
spatial dimensions of the divine universe but that propels the mind on
a journey in which it explores the relationships of time as well as of
substance. This is the journey in which the mind arrives at a perception of God and immortality and then comes back again to report what
it has seen. In this journey, Dickinson believes, the life of language
reaches all the way into the life of eternity. It is the journey that I now
want to map out.

In *Lyric Time: Dickinson and the Limits of Genre*, Sharon Cameron has
dealt extensively with the relationship between time and timelessness
in Dickinson's poems, and she has concluded that for Dickinson the
very form of the lyric poem and the peculiarities of Dickinson's verse
style constitute the poet's qualified solution to the limitations imposed
on human consciousness by temporality. The lyric, argues Cameron,
arrests time, at least momentarily. It releases the mind for an instant
of unbounded timelessness.[2] But Dickinson's poems more often than
not dramatize the speaker's failure to achieve timeless transcendence.
Her symbols of time do not stop time any more than her other symbols decompose matter and transmit immediate transcendence. On
the contrary, Dickinson's poems often emphasize time—both by prolonging the interval of the poem through its broken, halting stutter,
and by accentuating temporal concepts within the poem's images and
thematic concerns. For in Dickinson's view, just as the mind needs
some kind of image by which to preserve its visual consciousness, so it
needs temporal units in order to prolong the interval of that consciousness, to enable the mind to resist the ever-impinging forces

2. Sharon Cameron, *Lyric Time: Dickinson and the Limits of Genre* (Baltimore, 1979),
195–96.

of perceptual eclipse that overtake it in a poem like "I heard a Fly buzz—." The mind, Dickinson insists, cannot subdue matter without first engaging matter on its own terms. Similarly, it cannot expand into a state of immortality without first grounding itself concretely in notations of some kind of time. Therefore, time, *as time*, is an important element for Dickinson in the process that eventually leads out of time into eternity. For this reason, the measures of time, like the keepsakes of life, must be preserved. This is not to say that time is not also the enemy. Time stands between human life and life everlasting. It divides eternity into the minutes and hours of our human travail. In fact, the consciousness that time preserves is itself a problematical commodity—at moments gloriously in touch with divine reality, at other moments precisely that element of self that stands between the individual and God. But to transcend time and consciousness, the individual, according to Dickinson, will have to work through time, if only to discard it in the end.

The ambivalence Dickinson feels about time and timelessness and about consciousness and its loss is everywhere evident in her poetry. Before examining this aspect of Dickinson's concern, however, let me quote from Ernst Cassirer's exposition of the time dimension in symbolic form, since Cassirer's discussion may provide insights into the procedures and solutions with which Dickinson responds to the time-timelessness dilemma. Although in the following passage Cassirer is referring to the mythifier rather than the symbolist, his discussion of time and the symbol suggests, first, how the human mind depends upon concepts of time for its most fundamental responses to the universe, and second, how the religious imagination forces us to wrest the universe from the grasp of temporalizing restrictions. Cassirer explains that the mythifier's real comprehension of cosmic facts

does not begin when the intuition of the universe and its parts and forces is merely formed into definite images, into the figures of demons and gods; it begins only when a genesis, a becoming, a life in time, is attributed to these figures. Only where the divine explicates its existence and nature in time, where the human consciousness takes the step forward from the figure of the gods to the history, the narrative, of the gods—only then have we to do with "myths" in the restricted, specific meaning of the word.

But, then, Cassirer continues, there comes a moment in the evolution of human consciousness when humanity finds it necessary to dispense with the boundaries of time. A true theism or monotheism, in Cassirer's view, develops out of the conviction that time is illusory, that it is simply the

medium through which the idea of a lawful order governing and permeating the universe is apprehended. . . . The fundamental revelation of the divine does not occur in the form of time which nature discloses in the transformation and periodic recurrence of its forms [for this] form of change can provide no image of God's imperishable being.

Time, in other words, initially defines the boundaries of the experiential world and gives them apprehensible form. But then, precisely because it defines "religious" and "biological" boundaries and thus seems to limit and restrict them forever, time must be stripped of its autonomous existence. It must be made subservient to the timeless deity whose purposes are omnipresent and whose existence is eternal.[3]

For Dickinson, the process of temporalizing and detemporalizing the universe (as described by Cassirer) presents the same problems inherent in the symbolizing and subsequent desymbolizing of it. Consciousness, which depends on time and the symbol, is eclipsed the very moment that the conceptions of immortality and immateriality are broached. For this reason the meaning of eternity may never really be secured by the human mind. The concept of eternity may remain no more than an incomprehensible obverse.

Thus Dickinson suggests that

> Forever—is composed of Nows—
> 'Tis not a different time—
> Except for Infiniteness—
> And Latitude of Home—(No. 624)

Eternity, this poem insists, can be "experienced Here." "Forever" can be inferred from the "Nows" of mortal existence (No. 624, l. 5). Time, in other words, would seem to be what makes eternity manageable and comprehensible in human terms.

3. Ernst Cassirer, *The Philosophy of Symbolic Forms*, trans. Ralph Manheim (3 vols.; New Haven, 1953–57) III, 104–105 and 109.

If you were coming in the Fall,
I'd brush the Summer by
With half a smile, and half a spurn,
As Housewives do, a Fly.

If I could see you in a year,
I'd wind the months in balls—
And put them each in separate Drawers,
For fear the numbers fuse—

If only Centuries, delayed,
I'd count them on my Hand,
Subtracting, till my fingers dropped
Into Van Dieman's Land.

If certain, when this life was out—
That your's and mine, should be—
I'd toss it yonder, like a Rind,
And take Eternity—

But, now, uncertain of the length
Of this, that is between,
It goads me, like the Goblin Bee—
That will not state—it's sting. (No. 511)

The speaker's conditional promise to "wind the months in balls" or count the centuries on her hand is not, in this poem, an eloquent way of saying that so long as she believes in resurrection no time is too long. It is an articulation of the belief that the concept or experience of time becomes treacherous when it begins to lose its manageable particularity. Only when human beings cease to be conscious of time is time dangerous. Therefore, the poet tells us, she will keep time units "each in separate Drawers, / For fear the numbers fuse." She is afraid that if she does not keep time in strict accounting it will become an infinitely continuous interval. It will become unbearably painful and oppressive like the "Goblin Bee" (a phantom of being rather than being itself) "that will not state" or give calculable definition to "it's sting." The very fact that eternity is so long and therefore incomprehensible to the human mind paradoxically necessitates that the mind divide time into workable units and deal with it in fragments. The individual must fracture time in order to endure it even if not to conquer it. If it were simply a matter of waiting from summer to fall, Dickinson explains, then she could "brush the Summer by . . . As Housewives do, a Fly." If it were simply a question of a lifetime, then she could "toss it yonder, like a Rind." But precisely because the relationship between time and eternity is unknown, because the gap between the two dimensions extends over more centuries than human beings have fingers, the poem must record precisely each and every moment. Only because

> The Months have ends—the Years—a knot—
> No Power can untie
> To Stretch a little further
> A Skein of Misery—(No. 423)

is time bearable. Only because time implies termini or ends are we assured that the "Skein" of human "Misery" will not stretch endlessly on.

And yet Dickinson also realizes that time cannot really be considered a friend, for time, as Cassirer points out, delimits deity and ties it to the perishability of mortal life. Time is a veritable prison sentence, a term, that holds the individual captive between eternity and immortality, caught in the maelstrom whirl between the midnight of primordial unity and the midnight of reunion with God—"Behind Me—dips Eternity— / Before Me—Immortality— / Myself—the Term between—":

> 'Tis Miracle before Me—then—
> 'Tis miracle behind—between—
> A Crescent in the Sea—
> With Midnight to the North of Her—
> And Midnight to the South of Her—
> And Maelstrom—in the Sky— (No. 721; cf. poem No. 624)[4]

Nor is consciousness itself, which time is meant to preserve, an uncomplicated gift. Although it would sometimes seem that in Dickinson's lexicon immortality and consciousness are synonymous, interchangeable terms, she is ever aware of the ways in which human consciousness is not immortal. For her, in fact, mortal consciousness seems to be most fully defined by its temporal limitation. True, Dickinson does on

---

4. On the power of time to imprison, see Clark Griffith, *The Long Shadow: Emily Dickinson's Tragic Poetry* (Princeton, 1964), 88; and Anderson, *Stairway of Surprise*, 130.

one occasion claim that immortality is "costumeless consciousness" (No. 1454). And she elsewhere plays with the notion that

> There is a Zone whose even Years
> No Solstice interrupt—
> Whose Sun constructs perpetual Noon
> Whose perfect Seasons wait—
>
> Whose Summer set in Summer, till
> The Centuries of June
> And Centuries of August cease
> And Consciousness—is Noon. (No. 1056)

But the rationalistic, theological Dickinson inclines toward the view that human "Consciousness" is finite and that it communicates its instructions through the rational, countable limits of time. In attempting to traverse the interval between this world and the next, consciousness does not succeed in bringing the soul to heaven. Rather, it manages to impose on heaven all of the corrupt materialistic conditions of earth.

> This Consciousness that is aware
> Of Neighbors and the Sun
> Will be the one aware of Death
> And that itself alone
>
> Is traversing the interval
> Experience between
> And most profound experiment
> Appointed unto Men—
>
> How adequate unto itself
> It's properties shall be
> Itself unto itself and none
> Shall make discovery.
>
> Adventure most unto itself
> The Soul condemned to be—
> Attended by a single Hound
> It's own identity (No. 822)

Consciousness is not preserved without cost. By the end of the poem it is a "Hound" that condemns the "Soul" to retain its earthly "identity" at the expense of true reunion with God. As Dickinson puts it in another poem, "Consciousness" is the Soul's "awful Mate" from which "The Soul cannot be rid" (No. 894). Or, as she writes in still another poem,

> A single Screw of Flesh
> Is all that pins the Soul
> That stands for Deity, to Mine,
> Upon my side the Vail—
>
> Once witnessed of the Gauze—
> It's name is put away
> As far from mine, as if no plight
> Had printed yesterday,
>
> In tender—solemn Alphabet,
> My eyes just turned to see,
> When it was smuggled by my sight
> Into Eternity—
>
> More Hands—to hold—These are but Two—
> One more new-mailed Nerve
> Just granted, for the Peril's sake—
> Some striding—Giant—Love—
>
> So greater than the Gods can show,
> They slink before the Clay,
> That not for all their Heaven can boast
> Will let it's Keepsake—go (No. 263)

Dickinson is understandably reluctant to let her "Keepsake" go. And yet the "Keepsake" is a painful, destructive "Screw" that "pins the Soul" to the "Flesh" and thus disenables its ascent to God. The "single Screw of Flesh," like the "single Hound," suggests that the eternality of consciousness, the preservation of the "Alphabet" of phenomenal reality (cf. No. 568), cannot be made synonymous with immortality. It is instead a power that may actually usurp or subvert immortality, or at least our understanding of it. It is a jail "term" that imprisons humankind within the realm of the mortal and the momentary. Temporal consciousness may be a central agency of our conceptualization of eternity. But it is a power that often forgets its ultimate powerlessness. It can ignore the fact that it is earthly and that immortality is divine. It believes literally that "forever is composed of nows."[5] How Dickinson solves the dilemma of a temporal consciousness that must persist into eternity and yet simultaneously step aside to admire the supervention of immortality constitutes one of her greatest achievements as a poet.

In "I felt a Funeral, in my Brain" Dickinson remorselessly tackles the paradox of a rational, temporal consciousness that is the only instrument for knowledge of the life beyond death, but that is clearly in and of itself not capable of moving beyond the world of earthly images and earthly time, the world to which it properly belongs.

> I felt a Funeral, in my Brain,
> And Mourners to and fro
> Kept treading—treading—till it seemed
> That Sense was breaking through—
>
> And when they all were seated,
> A Service, like a Drum—
> Kept beating—beating—till I thought
> My Mind was going numb—
>
> And then I heard them lift a Box
> And creak across my Soul
> With those same Boots of Lead, again,
> Then Space—began to toll,
>
> As all the Heavens were a Bell,
> And Being, but an Ear,
> And I, and Silence, some strange Race
> Wrecked, solitary, here—
>
> And then a Plank in Reason, broke,
> And I dropped down, and down—
> And hit a World, at every plunge,
> And Finished knowing—then— (No. 280)

At first glance the poem would seem to be a fairly straightforward deathbed narrative, much like "I heard a Fly buzz," in which the narrator reports the events and sensations of her own death. The "Mourn-

5. See Kher, *Landscape of Absence*, 226.

ers" "treading" "to and fro," the "Service" "beating" "like a Drum,"
the lifting of the "Box," and the tolling of the church "Bell" represent
an external, objective event, a funeral service. But, by employing implicit analogies between external and internal events, the story enacted in the poem also comes to represent the process of the speaker's
dying. It images the moment of her transition from life through
death to, presumably, the life beyond. The treading, beating, creak-
ing, and tolling are not just sounds and sensations of the outside
world. They are subjectively perceived internal phenomena as well,
the throbbing and beating of the speaker's dying heart, the eclipsing
of her conscious mind.

Thus, the universe in the poem seems to emerge as a duality of
analogical structures poised on either side of an all-perceiving consciousness. This consciousness, we observe, first attempts to record
parallels between the mortal and divine. Then it tries to infer knowledge about those events for which it does not have direct empirical
evidence by analyzing those events it has witnessed and experienced.
The speaker formulates this "Heaves of Storm" proposition in stanza
four: the "Heavens," she tells us, are to "Being" as "Bell" is to "Ear."
Heaven, in other words, articulates meanings that humankind must
listen to and try to comprehend. Appropriately enough for the ostensibly Christian overtones of the poem, the two parallel realms reach a
point of near conflation in the image of the church bells. The tolling
of the bells becomes a combination of earthly sensations (both Christian and physiological) and divine event.

But the difficulty with the parallelisms, analogies, and symbolisms of
the first four stanzas of the poem is that they do not, in fact, heighten
our knowledge of immortality. The supposed interconnections between the emissions and receptions of sound and meaning give way to
an earthly deafness. The speaker finds herself in "Silence," not re-
united with God in heavenly immortality but, rather, "Wrecked" and
"solitary," "here" on earth. Human consciousness, which interprets
the various elements of the ongoing symbolic enactment, and immortality, which is what the speaker hopes to achieve through consciousness, emerge as two noncommunicating realms. And the poem sug-

gests that there can be no easy, no justifiable assertion of logical access from one to the other. As in "I heard a Fly buzz," the speaker's analogical perception of reality results in a total loss of consciousness—an eclipsing of phenomenal and spiritual reality both. The result seems to be that one simply "cannot see to see" or that one cannot hear to hear. Immortality remains beyond the pale of consciousness, both as something to be symbolized and as something to be achieved. Apparently a belief in immortality that depends upon the images of the conscious mind must, like consciousness itself, be limited and mortal.

But "I felt a Funeral, in my Brain" does not conclude in the total silence that threatens to overtake the speaker in stanza five and that does in fact obliterate narrative consciousness in "I heard a Fly buzz." By the end of stanza six the speaker does make her way to some kind of fully credited knowledge. "I . . . Finished knowing—then—," she finally declares. What happens to release the speaker from the silence and stasis of the fifth stanza is quite simply that a "Plank in Reason" breaks. The funeral in the brain does not refer simply to the speaker's contemplation of her literal, physiological funeral, which, of course, includes her brain and which prompts her to embark on her course of errant reasonings in the first place. The funeral is also the burial of her imprisoning, rationalistic consciousness. The contemplation of this second funeral, the realization that in death the analogizing reason that limits humanity to earthly perceptions also dies, is actually capable of termination, enables the speaker to change the direction of her thinking. It allows her to set out on a wholly different journey, one that can redeem consciousness and lead her toward a well-founded vision of the divine.

The indefinite, suspended word "then," which concludes the poem, might seem to be only a variation of the dread word "Silence." It might appear to be no more than a device for avoiding the precise articulation of what does happen "then" or of what, indeed, *then* is. The whole last statement, in fact, might seem to imply that in death the individual is finally finished with knowledge altogether. But the word and the sentence that end the poem are meant, I believe, to furnish us with meaningful alternatives to silence and obliterated consciousness. They are intended to pry the poem loose from the deadly track on which it has been traveling and to point it in an entirely new direction. This new direction not only leads to knowledge but it demonstrates how knowledge can and must be attained. In Dickinson's view, the universe is not primarily a spatial entity, incidentally acting out its destiny in perpetually running time. Nor, conversely, is it a temporal phenomenon fixing its events in space. It is not, in other words, a movement in time from place to placelessness, nor is it a transition from *now* to *then*, which occurs against the backdrop of *here* and *there*. Rather, the universe, Dickinson insists, is a multidimensional complex that is defined by the skewed relationship between place (and implied placelessness) and eternity (with its concrete notations in time). Thus, in Dickinson's view, symbolism can err in conceiving the universe as basically a series of parallel layers of meaning. Dualistic or synecdochic symbols may synthesize only two terms in what would appear to be an analogically structured proposition. Such symbols represent a logical attempt to connect *here* and *there*. They suggest a rational relationship between *now* and *then*. But logic and reason, in Dickinson's view, are tendencies of thought that must ultimately be transcended. Therefore, it is only when the "Plank in Reason" breaks and the psyche enters a whole new realm of symbolic relationships that she can finish "knowing—then." The narrator expects that the momentum of her symbolic logic, as expressed in the opening stanzas of the poem, will propel her forward into heaven. But this is not the case. Suddenly she discovers that she is dropping "down, and down," hurtling headlong through the bottom of her false analogies, bisecting reason.

Life and death, the poem is suggesting, may not be evenly spaced points on an ascending continuum of being. And just as we cannot, through death, climb the gradations that lead from a phenomenal *here* to an implicit, immaterial *there*, so through conventional symbolic representation we cannot expect to imagine ourselves already *there* by traveling the highways of an infinite set of loci and moments. *There* is just not the relevant term. *Then*, we discover, is. As Dickinson puts it,

> And *then* a Plank in Reason, broke,
> And I dropped down, and down—

And hit a World, at every plunge,
And Finished knowing—*then*—[italics added]

Human beings, Dickinson is telling us, must journey from *here*, which is a spatial concept, to *then*, which is the negation of a temporal one. They must begin on one pole of an axis of being and somehow (Dickinson will show us how) wind up on the opposite pole of a wholly different axis. To some extent the speaker is "Finished" with "knowing," at least according to any ordinary sense of the word *knowledge*. But this does not signal the cessation of her consciousness. The mind finishes its earthly existence "knowing" not about *here* and its analogue, *there*, but "knowing" about *then*, a concept to which it has had no access until "then." Consciousness is preserved, because the processes of intellection that seem to be abnegated when the mind realizes that it cannot cross the abyss separating the mortal from the divine are now being employed to do precisely what they have been created to do: to bring the poet to the brink of the gulf and to point the direction that the soul or faith must now follow alone. This process puts immortality beyond the reach of mortal demise. It so redefines the terms of knowing that consciousness does not cease but moves into a wholly new configuration of responses, a configuration of which we mortals have only the most intermittent awareness. Dickinson expresses the same point in another poem.

I saw no Way—The Heavens were stitched—
I felt the Columns close—
The Earth reversed her Hemispheres—
I touched the Universe—

And back it slid—and I alone—
A Speck upon a Ball—
Went out upon Circumference—
Beyond the Dip of Bell— (No. 378)

For Dickinson immortality is not located within the other reach of analogous heaves of storm or on the far side of the pendulum swing whereby the bell's tongue tries to communicate between this world and the next. Rather, it is to be found in the center of the abyss that divides place from timelessness. It occupies the space that separates the terms of earthly description from the significations of heavenly reality. In other words, immortality exists at the fulcrum moment where the imaginary heaves and bells achieve temporary stasis *not* before they resume their analogy-making activity, but before they abandon such efforts at symbolic duplication altogether. When the "Heavens" are "stitched" and the "Columns" are closed, then earth does not project heaven. Instead, it reverses direction altogether, leaving the poet "Beyond the Dip of Bell—." In literal fact, immortality is an aspect of eternity. And eternity, Dickinson explains, has no conceivable counterparts in the temporal universe. Imaginatively, however, in our limited mortal perceptions of reality, immortality is apprehended when we allow our thoughts to veer sharply away from the ordinary course of human logic, which posits heaves and bells in the first place. It is imagined when we permit ourselves to travel in direct opposition to the usual track of our everyday reason. Then and only then, Dickinson assures us, can we make our way through the maze of collapsing intersections that are bred by analogy and the synecdochic, translucent symbol, to arrive, not at a concept of a new place or even at the imaginative disappearance of that place, but at a sphere that is not even to be conceptualized in relation to geography or its absence, a sphere that is wholly defined in relation to the absence of time. As Dickinson writes of the "Cleaving" in the "Mind" that, in "I felt a Funeral," releases "Sense,"

> I felt a Cleaving in my Mind—
> As if my Brain had split—
> I tried to match it—Seam by Seam—
> But could not make them fit.
>
> The thought behind, I strove to join
> Unto the thought before—
> But Sequence ravelled out of Sound
> Like Balls—upon a Floor (No. 937)

Once true meaning has been reached, the supposedly analogical halves of the brain can no longer be made to fit together, "Seam by Seam." The knowledge that is contained between the halves is not, the narrator discovers, a synthesis or a compromise between two separate parts. Instead, it is the first stage or instancing in a "Sequence" that has no relationship to the experiential world—the world of "Sound"—with which the speaker is familiar.

What brings the poet to the brink, what sets the cleaver to cutting through the distorting parallelisms and dualisms, is not, however, some mystical intuition or bizarre insanity or leap of faith that is essentially antisymbolic. Rather, the impetus for the speaker's journey to immortality is contained in the very pressure of her symbolizing imagination. The "treading" of the "Mourners" and the "beating" of the "Drum" can, if falsely understood, image a distorted vision of heaven. But, if properly conceived, they can cause the imprisoning "Plank in Reason" to break and "Sense" to break through. Reason itself must be made to become discontinuous. It must be forced to resemble the disconnected halves of the universe. The "knowing" that it can thereby achieve will, like immortality itself, occupy the atemporal space between. Therefore, what the speaker sees as she falls through the vacuous center of her own mind, as she broaches her own component of the expanded consciousness that is immortality, is not unity itself but the myriad worlds of analogy and symbol without which unity has no conceivable form or meaning. Objectified analogy is the material on which the mind must operate. It is what the mind must dismantle, split apart, if the speaker is to proceed toward full knowledge. Therefore, although we must be careful that the symbolizing imagination not be allowed to become synonymous or synchronous with the many symbols and analogies it confronts, nonetheless we must acknowledge that the mind cannot function without symbols. Symbols provide an image through which the mind can cut, and in so doing, break out of its own stultifying grooves of rational disposition. Only when the "Plank in Reason" breaks can the mind embark on its imaginative journey to God.

For Dickinson the conceptual journey from *here* to *then* removes us from the flat and reductive, two-dimensional graph of a geographically and temporally defined universe. It delivers us from false symbols and directs us to a genuine perception of the multidimensionality of the divine universe. This journey to immortality is the subject of two of Dickinson's finest poems: "There came a Day at Summer's full" and "Because I could not stop for Death—." According to Dickinson, we begin this journey firmly locked within the rigidly circumscribed inquiries of the mortal imagination. We set out from within an area where time and place are hopelessly fused in the trappings of conventional reason and of traditional symbolic configuration. We begin where mobility is limited to the unenlightening, degrading shuttle that carries the mind "to and fro" between *here* and *there*, *now* and *then*, following the restrictive tracks of parallelism and analogy. But the journey to immortality can arrive at its destination. If the mind is properly instructed in understanding its symbols, and if it can learn how to transform false symbols into true ones, it can provide an exit from the narrow and self-defeating grooves of its own limiting reason. Consciousness can expand the boundaries of its own room. It can cause them to approach the limitlessness that is eternity and thus to approximate in its own symbolic terms the multiaxial complexity of the universe. To use a Dickinsonian metaphor, consciousness can pry loose the screws that pin the soul to the flesh without wholly snapping the strings that enable the soul to sing.

In "There came a Day at Summer's full" and "Because I could not stop for Death," Dickinson is concerned with much the same kinds of problems that trouble her in such poems as "I heard a Fly buzz" and "I died for Beauty." Her solution, as in the poems we investigated earlier, is a symbolism that keeps an annihilating fusion at bay and that affirms the distance between heaven and earth. But in these poems Dickinson's major emphasis is not on heaven as a place. It is, rather, on heaven as a dimension of timelessness, as eternity. And the procedure she follows in them is similar to the procedure of "I felt a Funeral, in my Brain." By a sharp swerve away from the ordinary terms of rational discourse that usually stipulate the venue of human being, the narrators in these poems are able to conserve all of the concretizing validity of their symbolic apprehensions while simultaneously breaking through the rational constraint that would prevent the soul's arrival in the nonanalogically structured entity known as eternity. In other words, immortality is successfully imagined in these poems without violating either the demands of symbolic consciousness or the facts of cosmic disparateness. It is conceptualized at the moment when the narrator is able to think herself, through the use of symbols, to the space between object and meaning, into the atemporal interval that separates nature and God and that is for humankind a version of immortality.

"There came a Day at Summer's full" asks directly, what is resurrection? in what does immortality consist? And the poem answers that resurrection and immortality are neither the total suspension of the natural order as we know it nor simply its analogical continuation ad infinitum. They are neither the extinction of consciousness nor its eternal prolongation. Rather, resurrection and immortality constitute a wholly unique realm of existence that is totally discontinuous with mortality and yet is reached through it.

> There came a Day at Summer's full,
> Entirely for me—
> I thought that such were for the Saints,
> Where Resurrections—be—
>
> The Sun, as common, went abroad,
> The flowers, accustomed, blew,
> As if no soul the solstice passed
> That maketh all things new—
>
> The time was scarce profaned, by speech—
> The symbol of a word
> Was needless, as at Sacrament,
> The Wardrobe—of our Lord—
>
> Each was to each The Sealed Church,
> Permitted to commune this—time—
> Lest we too awkward show
> At Supper of the Lamb.
>
> The Hours slid fast—as Hours will,
> Clutched tight, by greedy hands—
> So faces on two Decks, look back,
> Bound to opposing lands—
>
> And so when all the time had leaked,
> Without external sound
> Each bound the Other's Crucifix—
> We gave no other Bond—

Sufficient troth, that we shall rise—
Deposed—at length, the Grave—
To that new Marriage,
Justified—through Calvaries of Love— (No. 322)[6]

Like "These are the days when Birds come back—," which we examined earlier, this poem begins by testing the validity of a sacramental interpretation of nature. And, like the other poem, it concludes
that whatever the speaker of the poem prefers to think (in line 3),
nature is not the incarnation of Christian events that she thinks it is.
The solstice in this poem is a purely seasonal demarcation in a cycle
that distinguishes between one half of a temporal year and another.
Therefore, the "Sun," we are told, "as common, went abroad, / The
flowers, accustomed, blew, / As if no soul the solstice passed / That
maketh all things new." The sun and the flowers are oblivious to the
apparent Christian meaning of this seemingly pivotal event in the natural calendar. The sun, furthermore, which has presumably stopped in
its course, thereby suggesting that it may be an image of immortality,[7]
defies the very concept of solstice in that it continues to mark off the
measures of chronological time. Similarly, the flowers, which have
seen all this before and are therefore "accustomed" to it, continue to
blow their petals, ultimately, we know, into death and into the generation of another yearly cycle. The poem raises the awful doubt explicitly: it is, the speaker says, "as if" the "solstice" has passed "no soul,"
"as if" the summer solstice has nothing whatsoever to do with spiritual renewal or even with the poor Christian soul who imagines that
she is being given either a preview of divine eternity or a naturalistic
substitute for it.

The problem inherent in the speaker's apprehension of the summer solstice is that, like most sacramental symbolism, it distorts nature
into a synecdoche of transcendent meaning. When, therefore, she discovers the frailty of the natural symbol—the fact that the solstice is no

6. For two different, representative discussions of this poem, see Caroline Hogue,
"There Came a Day at Summer's Full," in Charles Chud Walcutt and J. Edwin Whitesell
(eds.), *The Explicator Cyclopedia* (Chicago, 1966); and William Howard, "There Came a
Day at Summer's Full," in *ibid.*

7. *Webster's International* cites as an obsolete definition of solstice, "a stopping or
standing still of the sun."

solstice after all—she is put in danger of missing the legitimate comforts that a wholly theological belief in immortality could have provided. Theological belief, we are reminded, properly belongs to the voluntary realm of faith and not of compelling, demonstrable proof. Only the crucifix can provide the "troth" of resurrection. The speaker of the poem recognizes this. She knows that the "symbol of a word / Was needless." Yet she cannot help but indulge her verbalizing predisposition to convert nature into a symbolic transcript. She assumes that the solstice is a preparatory experience in an analogically structured universe, that it permits us "to commune—this—time— / Lest we too awkward show / At Supper of the Lamb." But the fact is that the solstice does not image immortality.

The result of the speaker's focusing on time as if it were not time at all but rather an intimation of timelessness is that she begins to magnify its importance disproportionately. Time, rather than eternity, becomes the holy object of her desire, and she covets it with a ferocity that is in direct opposition to the mood in which she ought to be regarding it. "The time was scarce profaned, by speech," she writes; "Each was to each The Sealed Church, / Permitted to commune *this— time—*" (italics added). Because of her analogical premises, time and timelessness begin to seem veritably synonymous and interchangeable. Communion and the sacrament, therefore, become more important than actual resurrection. The speaker, whose emotions are in any case heightened by the physical passion aroused in her by her mortal as opposed to her divine lover, clutches greedily at time (stanza five). She attempts to arrest time rather than allow it to move on to the timeless, Christian eternity of which it is only, presumably, the faintest intimation. Because of the speaker's conventionally symbolic mode of apprehending time, the "Day at Summer's full" becomes for her a literal and totally solipsistic embodiment of eternity. It becomes a "full" resurrection, "Entirely for me," as she puts it. No wonder, then, that she is reluctant to allow nature to give way to supernature, or for time to dissolve into eternity. As far as she can see, heaven and immortality are attainable in this life, without the supervention of death.

But for Dickinson time and the images of time (or of the negation of time) cannot by themselves be the measures of eternity. The solstice-as-eternity is only an illusion. It is the instant masquerading as the eternal. Therefore, by falsely assuming that "forever" can be composed of "nows," the speaker of this poem comes perilously close to imprisoning her mind eternally within an untranscendental, material world of her own imaginative distortions. Her view of a summer's day "Entirely" for her threatens to collapse heaven into earth and to confine it there, forever unredeemed and unredeeming. In this poem, then, as in "These are the days" and "I heard a Fly buzz," Dickinson is pointing to the danger of using one frame of reference, which is worldly, to adduce another, which is divine. She is warning against the dangers of formulating one's vision of heaven in a symbolic language that can conflate the natural and the divine and then eclipse one or both of them and destroy faith.

Fortunately, however, for the misguided lovers of the poem, the divine universe has its own resources for resisting humankind's effort to conflate and confound it, in this case to confuse time with timelessness and to prevent the flow of natural time into eternal supernature. For time itself will not let the lovers rest long in their delusion that the "Day at Summer's full" is literally or even figuratively a moment of resurrection. Time has its own "greedy hands"—its temporal clock hands—with which to oppose the "greedy hands" of the lovers who would attempt to violate time's inevitable passage and hold onto it. "The Hours slid[e] fast—as Hours will," we are told. Time prevails in the tug of war between the lovers and the clock. Time passes, and the lovers discover that the "Day at Summer's full" is not resurrection or even a type of it. The solstice is not immortality or its natural incarnation. And the lovers are not, in their mortal estate, "Each . . . to each The Sealed Church / Permitted to commune this—time—." Furthermore, as the hours of temporal reality slide by, as indeed they must, one of the lovers dies: "So faces on two Decks, look back, / Bound to opposing lands." Death completes the speaker's realization that the solstice is not a symbol of divine eternity. Not only does the symbol lead to a false relationship with time, but, she begins to understand, the attempt to combine divine reality with natural reality results in a gap between the human and the godly that her symbol cannot bridge.

Yet at the moment that Dickinson is describing this ultimate defeat of the old solstice symbol, she is also creating, in the very language of her poem, a new symbol. This symbol can, she believes, accurately represent divine realities. Furthermore, it is capable of restoring the promises of faith that the more conventional symbol has destroyed. Thus, the poem's verbal units—the unattached "hands," the faceless "faces," the unchartered "ships"—create a language of absolute, uncharacterized force in which the terms themselves possess magnitude and direction. It is a language, we may say, of vectors, a living language that specifies interactions and interrelationships but that does not denominate or depend upon essences. Therefore, just as the poem's "hands" are both temporal and human, so the numerically and topographically unspecified "faces on two Decks" refer not only to the two human faces of the lovers separated in death but to the faces of the clock on one ship and of any number of human beings on the other. Clock-defined time and the human beings who function within the atemporal universe of God must eventually part company. And when "all the time" of temporality has "leaked" out, humanity is able to sail off into a genuine immortality.

The image of the multiply defined faces, glancing at each other as they move off in their diametrically opposed directions, replaces the image of the sun as the symbol of cosmic deployment and process. At first glance the new symbol might seem to be no more than a variation on the earlier symbol. Analogous faces tied ("Bound") to different but parallel realms of reality stare at each other mirror-fashion, thus apparently dividing the universe into a familiar bifurcated duality in which the one half, associated with life and time, complements the other half, connected with death and with the timelessness that death implies. Like solstice, heaves, and bell, the faces seem to posit a moment of quiescence between the opposed realms (a moment, perhaps, of stillness or silence) that becomes the basis for the symbol through which we effect the harmonious consolidation of dissonant halves.

But, unlike its more conventional relatives, the symbol created by the "faces on two Decks . . . Bound to opposing lands" is not two-dimensional and flat. It rises out of stasis and enters into a dynamic interaction of tensions—"Bound" now meaning *headed for* rather than *tied to*. This new force-field of tensions conveys more than the extensible space of the universe. By the end of the poem, it is able to communicate to the lovers and to us the nature of the crucifixial tension that defines the universe and that we ourselves must embrace. Only in this way can we realize our faith symbolically and yet secure it against the skepticism and doubt that conventional symbolism inevitably raises. In one of its planes of representation, the symbol of the "faces on two Decks" does recapitulate the image of the solstice sun and does, therefore, depict a universe divided on one axis between place and placelessness and on the other axis between time and timelessness. But in another equally articulated plane, the plane that is ushered in by the cessation of time in stanza six, the image of the "faces on two Decks" bisects the other vectors of opposition in the poem. It thereby symbolizes the tension between the geographical, temporal system of symbolic notations (which the "faces" also represent) and the trans-spatial, transtemporal absence of symbols that is literally reflective of cosmic realities when time has "leaked" and clock faces and human faces have departed from one another in opposite directions. In other words, the symbol of the "faces on two Decks . . . Bound to opposing lands" contains within its own structure a mechanism of self-contradiction and self-correction. It refutes the very terms of space and time by which it describes cosmic reality. In this way it provides a cosmic vector that is manifest at direct right angles to the plane of intersections that the poem *seems* to be describing. By abolishing our usual notations of time, it puts the symbol out of reach of the ordinary, static reductiveness of conventional symbolism.

For Dickinson the universe is irrefutably determined in all of its dimensions by the existence of "opposing" tensions—of one human hand tugging against another, of one clock hand pulling away from its mate, of antithetical sets of clock-and-human-hands similarly vying with one another, of ships sailing off in different directions both within the same time scheme and in different time schemes, of compass points signaling bipolar direction and of navigational charts sketching the universe as a series of distributive longitudes and latitudes. These sets of self-contained and other-directed oppositions, which everywhere score life in the universe, do not point to a magnetic attraction among parts. They suggest absolute repulsion. They do not intimate unity and harmony at the center of things. Rather, they dramatize how intrinsically opposed to one another the elements of reality have been created. The divine universe, therefore, cannot be symbolized as a fecund rotundity of a summer solstice sun promising eternal unity and peace. Somehow the symbol, to be a true symbol, will have to incorporate within its own mechanisms an awareness of the cosmic tension that exists both in time and place and between time-and-place and timelessness-and-placelessness. It will have to signify the tension that is in turn opposed and finally dissolved by a definition of reality that is not dependent upon or determined by the terminologies, or the negations of the terminologies, of time and place. Therefore, the lovers of the poem receive their "troth" in an image of self-contained opposition moving out of one transfixed time scheme into a wholly antithetical plane of being; they "shall rise— / Deposed— at length, the Grave—." They will understand cosmic reality, therefore, only when they stop trying to escape its real tensions by pretending that the round, untense "Day at Summer's full" is indeed a type of resurrection or that the summer solstice can offer them communion, in "this—time" or in any other. They will achieve their vision of grace when they choose to embrace those very same crucifixial tensions that they would have liked to have symbolized out of existence in their image of the sun. Thus Dickinson writes, "Each bound the Other's Crucifix— / We gave no other Bond." The solstice symbol has been replaced by another symbol, the quintessential Christian symbol that turns out to be a symbol of crucifixion and resurrection, both. The lovers, like all the saints, are "bound" on a journey that is determined by the concrete facts of Christian reality. But they are able to join their journey to a vision of what that journey means when they voluntarily decide to bind themselves to the crucifixial pain that is implicit in the Christian scheme. In true Puritan fashion they work to achieve a self-consciousness that for all intents and purposes is the only activity left to the government of human beings in a Calvinistic universe.

When the lovers bind each other's crucifix, they are, in effect, reenacting the original act of crucifixion that itself was responsible for determining the events of resurrection and immortality in the first place. They are evoking an event that in itself was not symbolic but was a literal linking of time and place to eternity. To be sure, this resurrection defied the laws of nature, thus effecting the covenant of grace and redeeming the creation. It laid the groundwork for the sacramental symbolism Malcolm Ross describes. But resurrection also contradicted our normatively human notions of symbolic reality and synecdochic conflation. For when Christ is risen, when he who might have been the most fully evolved model for a symbol of the divine ever granted us—literally the divine incarnate—is resurrected into heaven, he leaves totally behind his earthly trappings. Christ does not remain eternally compound. He does not live forever, either on earth or in heaven, as a synthesis of the mortal and the divine. Rather, when he enters (or reenters) eternity, he escapes not only the limitations of earthly mortality but the impure conditions of material-spiritual conflation to which his status as "Son," as divine representative, had reduced him.[8] Sacramentalism, it seems, is only one stage in the divine process. Through his crucifixion Christ is restored to unadulterated deity.

By the end of the poem the lovers are able to bring to the image of the cross this newly attained, more fully theological consciousness of its ultimate, reformed symbolic meaning. Thus they lift themselves out of a two-dimensional conceptualization of the cross and of cosmic relationships. They escape the intersecting material-spiritual axes, whether those axes are meant to represent the intersections of time and place on earth and by implication the parallel intersections of timelessness and placelessness in heaven, or whether they are conceived of as literally diagramming the intersections of two bipolar continuums, the one of time and timelessness, the other of place and placelessness. They are able to "rise" or leak into a new dimension that in "I felt a Funeral, in my Brain" represents a total deviation from the plane of the ordinary and the familiar, an escape from the grooves and analogisms that reduce the crucifix and the universe to symbolic objects of a simplistic variety. We note that the lovers' last religious act involves two crosses, not one: each binds the other's crucifix, not simply his or her own.

8. As I suggested in chap. three, Dickinson would seem to be an antitrinitarian. Cf., esp., poem No. 357, "God is a distant—stately Lover—."

Dickinson's poem builds to its climactic affirmation of faith not by resolving the presumably superficial antagonisms of seemingly uncomplicated crucifixial tensions (as the speaker tries to do early in the poem in the symbol of the sun), but by fully exploiting the oppositional strain of one crucifix resisting another. The confusion between the hands and the faces of the clocks and the lovers, for example, suggests that there is no single, clearly defined, two-dimensional relationship between time and timelessness that can easily be resolved by following the path of analogy so that we can get out on the other side of two precisely balanced "Heaves of Storm." Rather, the tension between temporality and atemporality is a multiaxial phenomenon. It is an opposition that occurs both in purely mechanical and scientific terms (in clocks) and in strictly human, biological terms (in people). Finally, it is a conflict that leads to a confrontation between these two different frameworks in an additional tension in which clocks struggle against lovers, suns wrestle with souls, and suns and sons enjoy no felicitous pun-encoded relationship to one another. These different sets of crosses themselves form a new kind of multidimensional cross. At the center of the intersection between time and eternity, life and immortality, is the moment of resurrection that is not simply an extension of one realm into another or the direct renunciation of one realm as it is crossed over and canceled by the other. Instead, there is a plummeting "down, and down" or a sliding or leaking or a rising in which one leaves the cross of the phenomenal universe and enters into the kingdom of God.

This new plane of existence is not achieved through the mystical transports of the soul. It is not reached by symbol rejection. Rather, it is acquired through the rational acceptance and redefinition of the old time relationships and their symbols. Therefore, to gain access to what salvation means in human terms, the lovers must first subject themselves to the immobilizing power of the intersecting analogies that despite their ultimate reductiveness do articulate one fundamental aspect of cosmic reality. They must begin their journey to knowledge by pinning themselves to the symbol of the interfused planes of the time-eternity, place-placelessness continuums that everywhere crucify human life and keep it securely locked within the restrictive

temporal materiality of the physical universe, the world of deceptive
solstice imagery. Thus, the solstice, which is necessarily the subject of
our investigation from the beginning of our acquaintance with the
poem and which in phenomenal fact stimulates our inquiry into immortality, is an important element in a valid symbolic process even
though its role is not what the speaker initially "thought" it would be.
The speaker's error occurs when she interprets the summer's fullness
as a symbol of resurrection. For the "solstice," if looked at properly, is
primarily a symbol of motion and oppositional tension, not of stasis
and reconciliation. The solstice is not the cessation of time. It is not
eternity. Therefore, when the speaker of the poem tells us that it is "As
if no soul the solstice passed / That maketh all things new," thus cata-
pulting herself into her troubled quest for clarification, the syntax of
her lines is, in typical Dickinsonian fashion, so tortuously convoluted
that it allows for several antithetical interpretations that collectively,
oppositionally, point the direction to a new, more genuine interpretation of solstice. Is it the soul, we ask in these early lines, that passes the
solstice? Or is it the solstice that passes the soul? And, in either case, is
it the soul or the solstice "That maketh all things new"? In other
words, is solstice the standing still of the literal sun, and by implication
of Christ the son and the whole phenomenal creation in immortality?
Or is the solstice the standing still of the human soul? Is it the infinite
duration of consciousness through eternity? The two meanings of
solstice are in direct, unresolved opposition to one another.

In these lines Dickinson is pondering whether immortality occurs in
the world out there or in the self-contained universe of the mind. And
she concludes that it occurs in the moment of genuine stasis that is
neither a *forever* composed of *nows* nor a *now* infinitely protracted. It
occurs in the period of transition from now to forever, when one rises,
deposed, into a new dimension. The "Day at Summer's full / Entirely
for me—" becomes the symbol of a process whereby the *here* and *now*
of the temporal universe are made to define a plane of existence that
is precisely the plane that must be resisted by faith. It guarantees the
premises of faith because it tells us what it is we leave behind. It
images the ways in which immortality is not a physiological phenome-

non, reduced and restricted by the implications of physiology. Discovering immortality, the poem claims, is a wholly spiritual event. It occurs when the terms of our perception are redeemed in death, when we are "Justified" and therefore made capable of "knowing— then."

Dickinson's achievement in "There came a Day" is, at one and the same time, to question the whole concept of temporal stasis (which may all too easily be equated with immortality) and to affirm it. She is able to reassure us that immortality is indeed a fact of existence. And she actually resurrects an image of immortality, the solstice. By the end of the poem the solstice has been made to convey the complexity of her subject. It exposes and embraces legitimate cosmic tensions, and thus it constitutes an intellectually and emotionally valid symbol of resurrection and immortality. Furthermore, it is a symbol that derives from the phenomenal world to which human consciousness, which must perceive and measure it, most naturally belongs. In its entirety the poem reconstructs our ordinary symbolic consciousness. It makes us receptive to a new and wholly usable symbol of cosmic realities.

In "Because I could not stop for Death—" Dickinson again grapples with the perplexing tension between time and timelessness. As in "There came a Day," she argues that the condition of immortality is achieved only when the mind disengages itself from the frame of human temporality. And here too she insists that the mind depends upon its own frail devices in order to grasp the new dimension that is divine timelessness.

> Because I could not stop for Death—
> He kindly stopped for me—
> The Carriage held but just Ourselves—
> And Immortality.
>
> We slowly drove—He knew no haste
> And I had put away
> My labor and my leisure too,
> For His Civility—
>
> We passed the School, where Children strove
> At Recess—in the Ring—

> We passed the Fields of Gazing Grain—
> We passed the Setting Sun—
>
> Or rather—He passed Us—
> The Dews drew quivering and chill—
> For only Gossamer, my Gown—
> My Tippet—only Tulle—
>
> We paused before a House that seemed
> A Swelling of the Ground—
> The Roof was scarcely visible—
> The Cornice—in the Ground—
>
> Since then—'tis Centuries—and yet
> Feels shorter than the Day
> I first surmised the Horses Heads
> Were toward Eternity— (No. 712)[9]

The key to the meaning of the poem lies in the paradox with which it begins and which is exploited later in the poem in the details of the carriage ride to eternity. "Because I could not stop for Death," the speaker explains, "He kindly stopped for me—." For the speaker to "stop," i.e., to die, would mean, of course, that she would lose consciousness. Like the narrator in "I heard a Fly buzz," or the speaker in the early lines of "I felt a Funeral" and "I saw no Way—," she would no longer be capable of seeing or hearing. She would certainly not be capable of reporting the facts of immortality, if indeed such facts existed. But it is death that stops in this poem, and when death stops being death, then immortality follows: "The Carriage held but just Ourselves— / And Immortality."

And yet "Immortality," as it is presented in the poem, is not just something toward which human beings journey in death. It is not just the third component in the inevitable process of living and dying. Rather, it is also a component of consciousness itself, somehow co-extensive not only with death but with life as well: the speaker, death, and immortality all occupy the same carriage at the same time. Therefore, the scenes the speaker sees along her journey are facets of life's

9. For differing interpretations of this famous poem, see Allen Tate, "Emily Dickinson," in Richard B. Sewall (ed.), *Emily Dickinson: A Collection of Critical Essays* (Englewood Cliffs, N.J., 1963), 21–23; Robert Weisbuch, *Emily Dickinson's Poetry* (Chicago, 1972), 214–44; and Griffith, *The Long Shadow*, 127–34.

processional as well as death's. They are moments occurring both within the framework of the temporal universe *and* in the suspension of the terms of that universe in eternity.

At first glance the scenes the narrator describes would seem to have nothing whatsoever to do with immortality: the "School, where Children strove / At Recess—in the Ring," the "Fields of Gazing Grain," the "Setting Sun"—these are moments in the ongoing temporal processes of life: youth, maturity, and death. But when the speaker reaches the ultimate boundary of phenomenal existence—the "Setting Sun" and its counterpart, the "House" that is the grave—she and her companions do not have to pass out of time to enter eternity. Rather, they are suddenly halted in their tracks, where they themselves become the static center around which the rest of the material universe revolves: "We passed the Setting Sun— / Or rather—*He passed Us*—" (italics added).[10]

Is Dickinson, then, saying that immortality is indeed synonymous with consciousness, and that immortal consciousness equals eternity? She certainly seems to be denying that immortality is a linear journey from here to there or from now to then. In fact, immortality does not seem to be any kind of journey at all. It seems, rather, one eternally protracted pause or surmise, a condition of uninterrupted orientation "toward Eternity." And yet immortality is not to be equated with the meaningless and mindlessly repeating circles traced out by children striving in a ring at recess or by stalks of grain facelessly gazing on one another or by the sun mechanically setting to rise again. Immortality journeys past these circles in the poem. It leaves their endlessly repeating orbits behind in the temporal universe to which they belong, while it continues on to eternity. Nor is immortality eternity. Immortality is only one of three passengers who ride the carriage that is supposed to arrive in eternity.

What is "Immortality," then? What kind of journey do we make through life to death and through death to life everlasting? Even more important, how is that journey to be described? Dickinson's answer is not, I think, expressed in the word *circumference*, to which so

10. See Weisbuch, *Emily Dickinson's Poetry*, 114.

many of her critics recur. It cannot be contained in what Anderson calls the "motion of encompassing."[11] For what the poem as a whole symbolizes, what immortality means for Dickinson, is not the self-contained, pointlessly rotating motion of a temporal circle, or even of temporal circles within atemporal ones, but rather the pause at the unfluctuating center of another circle that is not, in Dickinson's terms, coincidental with the circle of life or with any of the circles that contain or are contained by it. This circle has its center on the circumference of life and its own circumference is conceived of as being, in Dickinson's geometrics, at right angles to life. This is the circle that is rotating "toward Eternity," the circle in which units of time, like "Centuries" and a "Day," lose their meaning because this circle no longer circumscribes or is circumscribed by a temporal universe.

The poem is Dickinson's attempt to overcome the implications of what we might call an "uncertainty principle." The universe, she tells us, exists as two mutually exclusive sets of time systems. Both of them are directly related to one another, and they are interdependent. Only one of them, however, can be known at any one instant. Time and eternity, therefore, are imaged in the poem as two tangential wheels. Each cycles permanently in place. And yet each, because of its proximity to the other, achieves for the other the illusion of movement, of an authentic passage through time. Thus, when time consciousness predominates, as it does in life, eternity seems to be the cessation of time. Time is the journey; eternity the static center. But when eternity is arrived at, then time, by reference to eternity, becomes static. The children, the grain, and the sun seem to rotate in fixed, futile circles, going nowhere, while eternity then acquires velocity and becomes an eternally moving carriage ride. One can know directly, immediately, either stasis or motion, not both. And, yet, since neither time nor eternity has absolute meaning for us and both are defined only in relation to each other, it is possible, if one properly preserves the separateness of the two realms, to learn about the other phenomenon relativistically. Immortality is not consciousness infinitely expanded. It is not the circle of life continuing ad in-

11. Anderson, *Stairway of Surprise*, 55; also Albert Gelpi, *Emily Dickinson: The Mind of the Poet* (New York, 1971), 94–127.

finitum or merging or running into the circle of eternity. Nor is immortality the eclipsing of consciousness, the imagined collapse of the circle of life into the center of the circle of eternity. Rather, immortality is the moment of quiescence between the two rotating wheels of time and eternity. It is the point of transition from the circumferential experience of the one wheel into the axial center of the other. And it occurs when the individual passes the "Sun," or "rather," the "Sun" passes individual mortals. Dickinson puts it this way in another poem:

> Two Lengths has every Day—
> It's absolute extent
> And Area superior
> By Hope or Horror lent—
>
> Eternity will be
> Velocity or Pause
> At Fundamental Signals
> From Fundamental Laws.
>
> To die is not to go—
> On Doom's consummate Chart
> No Territory new is staked—
> Remain thou as thou art (No. 1295)

Eternity can be reached in one of two ways. Either it will be obtained by the "Velocity" of a carriage ride that will take the individual through time or out of time to timelessness. Or it will be discovered in the eternality of "Pause" in which the individual remains changeless and conscious as the universe journeys onward to death. In either case, eternity will occur "At Fundamental Signals / From Fundamental Laws." It will be a product of the laws of the universe and of the laws of consciousness: "Remain thou as thou art," the poem advises. "No Territory new is staked" because the "Laws" that govern the universe and the self are synonymous and constant. They everywhere point "toward Eternity."

"I felt a Funeral, in my Brain," "There came a Day at Summer's full," and "Because I could not stop for Death" take Dickinson's special kind of symbolism to its highest levels of achievement. These poems do not content themselves with a cosmic portraiture that is simply emotionally reliable and intellectually valid. Instead, they strive for a mimesis

so total that it can reenact a temporal as well as a geographic unfolding of cosmic processes and laws. They attempt not only to script a
cosmic drama but to set that drama into production. The "Funeral,"
the "Day at Summer's full," and the carriage ride are material-idealist
symbols in action. They are words that, in Dickinson's terminology,
"live." They demonstrate the deficiencies of conventional symbolism
and by so doing they suggest what death, burial, and resurrection
might really mean. They tell us how immortality can be realized, fic-
tively within the mind, and literally within the universe. They redeem
the symbols that can redeem human consciousness.

Dickinson's critique of ordinary symbolic activity is in the final analysis a means for freeing the mind from the conflationary tendencies
that destroy faith. It prepares the ground of consciousness so that a
new kind of symbolism, a symbolism created from the connatural separateness of the material and the ideal, can take root. It is this remarkable kind of symbolism, I believe, that we find in various stages of
flourishing development in the Dickinson canon. It is a symbolism so
poised and fragile that, like so many of the flowers of Dickinson's
verse, its full blooms begin to wilt the moment we pluck them with our
indelicate critical hands. And yet it is a symbolism so hardy, so vital,
that the species itself survives in spite of our assaults upon it. And precisely because it survives, because it continues to bring forth new glo-
ries to each generation of Dickinson readers, it displays the "troth"
that can link immortality to life.

Index